E-Learning: Technology, Training and Teaching

E-Learning: Technology, Training and Teaching

Edited by **Albert Traver**

LANRYE
INTERNATIONAL

New Jersey

Published by Clanrye International,
55 Van Reypen Street,
Jersey City, NJ 07306, USA
www.clanryeinternational.com

E-Learning: Technology, Training and Teaching
Edited by Albert Traver

International Standard Book Number: 978-1-63240-168-7 (Hardback)

Printed in the United States of America.

Contents

Preface

Adaptive E-learning is advisable for students with unique profiles, specific interests, and from various areas of knowledge, so that profiles may be able to contemplate particular aims of the students, altogether with various preferences, knowledge level, learning style, rendering psychological profile, etc. Self-directed learning also needs to be taken into consideration. Self-directed learning, unlike adaptive E-learning, is linked with autonomy in learning; it is a reasonable link for readiness for E-learning, where students direct their own classes as per their own requirements. This book informs us about the On-Job Training and Interactive Teaching for E-learning, talking about the inspirations to be contemplated for E-learning. It also engages with the problems faced in E-learning in fields like engineering, medical education and biological studies; different approaches to E-learning; as well as the implementations of E-learning environments.

This book is a comprehensive compilation of works of different researchers from varied parts of the world. It includes valuable experiences of the researchers with the sole objective of providing the readers (learners) with a proper knowledge of the concerned field. This book will be beneficial in evoking inspiration and enhancing the knowledge of the interested readers.

In the end, I would like to extend my heartiest thanks to the authors who worked with great determination on their chapters. I also appreciate the publisher's support in the course of the book. I would also like to deeply acknowledge my family who stood by me as a source of inspiration during the project.

Editor

Part 1

Motivations for the Online Learning

Courseware Adaptation to Learning Styles and Knowledge Level

Boyan Bontchev and Dessislava Vassileva
Department of Software Engineering, Sofia University, Sofia
Bulgaria

1. Introduction

According to initial design of adaptive e-learning, content of an adaptive course should be suitable for students with different profiles (Brusilovsky, 1996). These profiles may contain information about goals, preferences, knowledge level, learning style, rendering psychological profile, and more. Typically, the learning content is developed for some groups of students that have similar values of one or several parameters of the student's profile. For more groups of students an adaptive course is designed, the more personalized it is.

Adaptive Hypermedia Systems (AHS) use models and techniques for adaptive content delivery. They are widely used for technology enhanced learning together with applications for adaptive e-learning, intelligent tutoring, adaptable multimedia delivery and adaptive computer games. AHS are entirely oriented to individual learner profiles. In the context of e-learning area, AHS deliver hypertext and hypermedia content which is in line with particular set of parameters of individual learner profile or group of learners (Dagger et al, 2005). Adaptive content delivery must be executed in accordance with a pedagogical strategy. Thus, in order to assure high quality of an adaptive course it has to embody sufficient number of teaching strategies. Such strategies are supposed to be appropriate for different types of students diversified according learning style, level of knowledge, shown performance, preferences and specific goals, learning history or learners needs, etc. (Bontchev, Vassileva, 2009). Strategies are realized by techniques for achieving adaptation such as adaptive navigation, adaptive content selection and link annotations (Conlan, 2003). Another less frequently used method for the realization of adaptive content delivery is by using automatically generated curriculums for each student according to his/her profile or through definition of education storyboards, applying appropriate instruction strategies and methods. Except adaptation techniques, AHS must choose parameters of the student profile which are to be used for controlling adaptation process and to be consistent with the applied teaching strategies. Some researchers emphasize the content adaptation to current learner skills and level of knowledge (Karagiannidis and Sampson, 2002), while others include as well other parameters such as learning history, learners' needs, learning styles of given style family, goals and preferences (Velsen, 2008).

The present chapter is focused on courseware adaptation to both learning styles and learner's performance as two very important metrics of the learner model. Within the scope of ADOPTA (ADaptive technOlogy-enhanced Platform for eduTAinment) project, there was developed a software platform for adaptive content delivery based on a conceptual model supporting adaptivity to learning styles and learners performance, i.e. shown knowledge level (Bontchev and Vassileva, 2011). After presenting an overview of the conceptual model and platform architecture, the chapter discusses approaches for construction of course storyboards adaptive to learning styles and knowledge level of individual learners. It provides a description of a methodology for adaptive course storyboard design and management and, next, shows how this methodology may be used for practical development of an adaptive course in XML technologies. Finally, the chapter considers some practical results collected during pilot experiments with the platform using the adaptive course within a field trial with bachelor students in Software Engineering at Sofia University, Bulgaria. The results concern assessment of efficiency of adaptivity and are summarized from survey conducted after finishing the adaptive course.

2. Background

The main issues treated by modern research in the field of traditional and adaptive e-learning, may be summarized as follows:

- creation and reuse of learning objects (Collis and Strijker, 2004) thanks to metadata that provides information about a learning resource (Friesen, 2005);
- support of content adaptation to different learning styles (Vassileva and Bontchev, 2011);
- development of adaptive learning courses, which use various pedagogical approaches to different students with different learning style, level of knowledge and preferences (Vassileva, 2010).

2.1 Learning objects and metadata

Learning objects (LOs) represent a popular paradigm for creating teaching materials. Instead organizing teaching into lessons and courses that meet predetermined objectives, LOs paradigm provides educational content divided into smaller independent units that can be used both separately and combined statically or dynamically with others.

Generally, the term LO may be used in different meanings, shapes and with different granularity. IEEE Learning Technology Standards Committee (LTSC) defines learning object as any object, digital or not, which can be used for education or training (IEEE LTSC, 2004). LOs have several main properties as follows:

- modularity - LOs may be used both separately and together with other aggregate;
- interoperability - in order LOs to be portable between different environments and platforms, they are packaged according to the Sharable Content Object Reference Model (SCORM) standard (Rey-López et al, 2002);
- reusability - facilitates authors of content, who can use learning objects in different contexts and for different purposes;
- accessibility - LO should be accessed anywhere, anytime and can be used in different networks. For this purpose, each LO should be annotated with appropriate metadata.

Metadata provide specific information about a resource such as description of its context, characteristics, common usage and features. Metadata can describe an object regardless of its level of aggregation such as a collection of resources, a resource or component of a larger object. The purpose of using of metadata is to improve and facilitate retrieval of information. Furthermore, they can support interoperability, integration of an object and its identification.

There are three main types of metadata (NISO, 2004):

- *narrative* or *descriptive metadata* that describe resources in such a way that they can be more easily detection and identification. They include items such as title, creator or author, publishers, language;
- *structural metadata* that define in what way and how complex objects are placed together, such as how learning objects are included in a page;
- *administrative metadata that provide information* for assisting resource management. For example, where, when, in what format and size a file is created.

The most popular and used metadata standards practically used in the field of e-learning are two - Dublin Core (DCMI, 2009) and IEEE Learning Object Metadata (LOM) (IEEE LTSC, 2004).

2.2 Approaches for creating adaptive courses

While developing adaptive course, there are two main points which must be taken into account. The first of them is the choice of appropriate teaching strategies that will be realized within in the course. The second one is the selection of a method for constructing an adaptive course. The choice of pedagogical strategies is based on the objectives set out in the course such as to make it suitable for learners with different levels of knowledge of students, different way of adoption of information, different ways of understanding, different goals, preferences, etc. (Paramythis and Loidl-Reisinger, 2003). Approaches to construct adaptive courses can be basically divided into three groups (Vassileva, 2010), which are based on:

- *a network of concepts* – concepts are linked to connections reflecting the rules under which the learner can move from one concept to another. In the simplest case this is the sequence in which they should be visited by students (Weber et al, 2001). There are two chief disadvantages of this approach: first at all, it is difficult to add more than one rule to a relationship. The second drawback is that a representation in the form of network of the learning process hampers its monitoring;
- *creation of several traditional courses* - learning content in each is different from others and it is appropriate for a group of learners. The disadvantage of this method is that if you add a new group or condition for adaptation you will need to create a new course or revise the contents of all courses;
- other way to create adaptive *course is by setting rules for transition from one concept or page to another one* (Grimón, 2009). These rules can be implemented in two main ways – either they can be programmed in the course itself or, otherwise, to be described in a particular format that is understandable to the system delivering adaptive content. The first approach requires programming skills by the author and intensive labour. The second one allows more freedom of the author and the ability to add transition rules and criteria for selecting the most appropriate content.

2.3 Impact of learning styles

Learning styles are determined by emotional, psychological, physical and sociologically dependant characteristics of an individual. They define ways of extracting, learning and generalization of knowledge and competences by learner and, thus, are very important when trying to improving the performance of given learner (Lindsay, 1999).

Various families of learning styles have been developed during last decades. There may be encountered four basic types of approaches for identifying different learning styles (Sadler-Smith, 1997):

- learning styles presenting personal cognitive characteristics about dependence or independence in given area;
- styles dealing with specific learning preferences;
- approaches combining elements of cognitive and personal learning preferences;
- styles determined by ways of processing information - based on the cyclical model of (Kolb, 1984) for converger, diverger, accommodator, and assimilator styles and, as well, on the Honey and Mumford model (Honey and Mumford, 1992).

The Honey and Mumford's model is based on the theory of Kolb according to which learning process has two bipolar dimensions - perception (y axis in fig. 1) and processing of information (x axis). Thus, four styles can be formed by this two-dimensional coordinate system, where one of them is often dominant to the other styles. The model includes the following four predefined learning styles: *activist* (fond of new ideas and experiments and looking for challenges of practical tasks rather than listening to lessons), *reflector* (preferring to observe subjects from different perspectives and to reflect about their characters), *theorist* (opposite to activist, looking for formalization, concepts and logical theories) and *pragmatist* (opposite to reflector, prefers to apply theoretical ideas into practice). Fig. 1 represents graphically relations between learning styles of Kolb (in internal circle) and Honey and Mumford found in (Munoz-Seca and Silva Santiago, 2003). The activist matches Kolb's styles of accommodator and diverger and feeds from concrete experience, while the theorist corresponds to converger and assimilator and benefits from abstract conceptualization. The

Fig. 1. Learning styles of Kolb versus styles of Honey and Mumford

pragmatist corresponds to accommodator and converger and looks for active experimentation, while the reflector is stacked to diverger and assimilators and prefers reflective observation.

The learning styles of Honey and Mumford are widely used within pedagogical strategies for adaptive learning. Therefore, the learning stylistic character is polymorphic as far as it is represented by levels of affiliation to several learning styles. These levels are determined by a specific style test performed before starting adaptive learning.

2.4 Existing adaptive e-learning platforms

In recent years, the field of adaptive e-learning systems marks significant progress with the emergence of many new applications, realizing and reflecting new trends in this area, and improvement of old ones. Some adaptive e-learning platforms enabling to define different teaching strategies in one course are as follows:

- InterBook (Brusilovsky et al, 1996) – its aim is to deliver to learners educational content in form of adaptive electronic textbooks. This electronic textbooks consist of specially annotated HTML pages and the InterBook provides tools for their creation and presentation. In InterBook learning content is organized into a network of concepts. Each HTML page of an electronic textbook is associated with a set of concepts. For each concept, InterBook stores individual level of knowledge of the learners and based on it dynamically generates links between pages. In this way adaptation is only to knowledge of learners;
- NetCoach (Weber et al, 2001) – similarly to above system knowledge of each course are organized in a network of concepts. Links between them are two types. The first type shows what additional concepts are needed to acquire a certain term. The second type indicates that a concept is assumed to be acquired by a student if he/she has already learned several other. The NetCoach implements adaptation to learner knowledge and goals, but it does not support adaptation to learning styles;
- PERSO (Chorfi and Jemni, 2004) – it is an adaptive e-learning system based on processing and natural language recognition. It uses sophisticated techniques to understand the information entered by students and their requirements and on this bases the system constructs a curriculum. PERSO does not support standards for learning content and course packaging and adaptation to learning styles;
- AHA! (De Bra et al, 2006) - educational content is stored in fragments, pages and concepts. Pages are represented as XML files. The pages contain information about different concepts and their relationships. Moreover, pages are composed of fragments, for each of which are defined conditions. These conditions specify whether a fragment will be visible to a learner. In this system, as in InterBook adaptation is implemented again only to knowledge of students.

Main drawbacks of considered systems are basically two - lack of effective support of adaptation to learning styles and lack of a convenient graphical interface with which a course instructor can monitor how the course will proceed for different learners (most systems provide a scheme of relationships between concepts and learning objects, however, it makes not clear how to conduct the training process).

ADOPTA platform covers the shortcomings mentioned above (Bontchev and Vassileva, 2009). It provides several tools with rich, comfortable and effective interface for creating adaptive courses and it supports learning styles of all kinds (the ADOPTA system is not oriented to a specific family of learning styles). ADOPTA is consistent with a specific conceptual adaptability model of AHS (Vassileva and Bontchev, 2009) called triangular model. The next part of the chapter is devoted to description of this model and of software architecture of the ADOPTA platform.

3. Overview of the ADOPTA conceptual model and platform

The ADOPTA platform supports adaptive e-learning content delivery according to contemporary requirements of AHS such as interoperability based on exchange of educational materials and activities, reusability of LOs and, most important, construction of e-learning courses with adaptation to user learning styles and user knowledge level (Velsen, 2008). The software architecture of the platform is oriented to the ADOPTA conceptual model of adaptive hypermedia, so next sub-sections briefly presents this model.

3.1 Principal conceptual model

The ADOPTA platform is compliant to a special triangular conceptual model of AHS conceived as an extension of the AHAM reference model (De Bra et al, 1999). The AHS triangular model is described in details in (Vassileva et al, 2009) and uses a metadata-driven design approach separating narrative course storyboard from educational content and adaptation control engine (ACE). Fig. 2 represents a mind map of this triangular model which refines the AHAM reference model by dividing in three the separate models describing learner, domain, and adaptation. It follows a brief description of both structure and semantic of these sub-models.

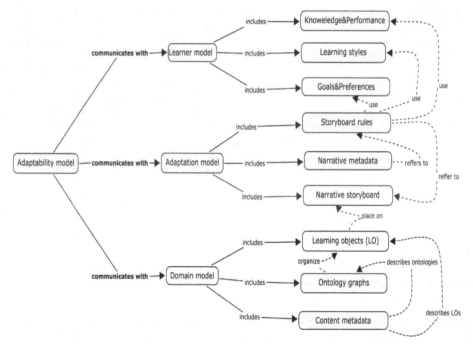

Fig. 2. Mind map representation of the ADOPTA model (Bontchev et al, 2009)

3.1.1 Learner model

The chief specifics of the learner model conclude in separation of a sub-model of goals and preferences from another sub-model of shown knowledge and performance, as the first sub-model is appropriate to be used for personalization while the second one is suitable for adaptive content selection. The model of learning style (such as activist, reflector, pragmatist and theorist) is detached as another sub-model as far as it determines the adaptive navigation throughout the narrative storyboard. Learning character is polymorphic and includes affiliation to several learning styles which is set before starting adaptive e-learning by dedicated pre-tests. On other side, learner's knowledge level may be assessed many times during adaptive learning process in order to adapt content through adaptive content selection.

3.1.2 Domain model

The domain model is composed of domain ontology, multimedia learning content granulized in LOs according to the SCORM standard, LO's metadata as defined by IEEE LOM (Learning Object Metadata) and, as well, ontology metadata. The ontology represents semantic references such as of type IS_A (i.e., a term is of subtype of another term) and of type HAS_A (a term has a relationship with another term or concept) between terms of given knowledge domain and is built during content composition process by content author. It is used for browsing, filtering and searching of LOs when the instructor disposes appropriate LOs onto course pages of a storyboard graph of the course in order to be delivered to the learner adaptively according his/her learning style and knowledge level.

LOs are annotated by LOM metadata with three main purposes:

- instructors use LOM annotations in order to dispose LOs onto pages of given path within the storyboard appropriate for a learning character with specific polymorphic style. As well, they take into account LO's complexity level and may dispose onto one page several LOs about a concepts and having different levels of complexity;
- the adaptation control engine selects for the page going to be delivered to the learner LO with appropriate complexity according his/her result shown at last intermediate assessment;
- export/import facilities assure interoperability with other e-learning systems thanks to LOM annotations of LOs been exported/imported.

3.1.3 Adaptation model

The adaptation model (AM) is responsible for the design of adaptive e-learning courses. In each of these courses is included a set of pedagogical strategies and each of them is suitable for students with a learning character. Adaptive courses contain learning objects with different complexity and the instructor of the course determines what level of student knowledge is appropriate to visit the relevant content. Furthermore, AM defines rules for selecting the most appropriate teaching strategy for a student accordance with his/her learner model. AM consists of three sub-models - narrative storyboard, storyboard rules and narrative metadata. The narrative storyboard sub-model includes a description of a storyboard graph for each course. Storyboard graphs are represented in form of directed graph, which has two types of nodes - control points (CP) and narrative pages. Narrative pages consist of a list of LOs but CPs include questions assessing students' knowledge. Between two CPs the course instructor can define paths named work paths (WP) that consist of interconnected narrative pages. Each WP refers to a pedagogical strategy and it has a weight which indicates the suitability for a learning character. The storyboard rules sub-model includes the logic of choice for passing through a narrative graph and for determining which LOs are visible to a learner. The narrative metadata sub-model contains metadata for storyboard rules such as annotations of links between narrative pages, thresholds in CPs, which determine level of assessment performance for continuing to next CP or for returning back to the previous CP.

3.1.4 Adaptation control engine

The adaptation control engine (ACE) communicates with each of the three main models (learner model, domain model, and adaptation model) in order to generate and deliver the most appropriate learning content to the learner. The main task of the ACE is to select the most suitable WP of the narrative storyboard graph for a learner as taking into consideration his/her learning styles and shown by him/her knowledge and performance. For a learner the best WP is calculated using the following formula:

$$\max_{(k)} \left\{ \frac{\sum_i W_{WPk}(c_i) * Wc_i(l)}{\|W_{WPk}(c)\| * \|Wc(l)\|} \right\} \tag{1}$$

where – k is number of WPs from the current CP to the next; c_i is one of learning styles; $W_{WPk}(c_i)$ is the weight of the k-th path WP_k for c_i and $W_{Ci}(l)$ is level in which a learner l belongs to the learning style c_i and this value is determined by test at the beginning of each course (Vassileva, 2010).

Other basic functions of the ACE are following:

- selecting the appropriate LOs in narrative pages;
- selecting the appropriate test questions in CPs;
- calculating test results of answers;
- updating weights of WPs based on these results.

The formula for updating the weight of WP, after solving test in CP $k+1$, is following:

$$W_{WPk}(c_i) = W'_{WPk}(c_i) + \frac{W''_{WPk}(c_i) + (R - P) * Wc_i(l)}{N} \tag{2}$$

where – $W_{WPk}(c_i)$ is the new weight of WP_k for c_i; WP_k is k-th WP from CP k to CP $k+1$; c_i is one of learning styles; $W'_{WPk}(c_i)$ is initial value of weight for path WP_k for c_i; $W''_{WPk}(c_i)$ is the difference from the value of current weight and initially set weight WP_k for c_i; R is test result of a learner l for CP $k+1$; P is adjustment parameter with default value equal to the threshold defined for CP $k+1$. The goal of P is to restrict the increase of the value of $W_{WPk}(c_i)$ in case of unsatisfactory test results; $W_{Ci}(l)$ is level in which a learner belongs to the learning style c_i; N is the number of students passed until the moment through the path WP_k. Thus, it will avoid the incorrect situation, where weights of the WPs which have passed more students through are higher (Vassileva, 2010).

Thus, for a particular user, the best path is calculated and stored for the learner as current work path. When learner asks for the next page, adaptive engine may hide objects with specific complexity level that are not important for this user. As many users may pass through this path, ACE has to remember user tracks. The learner may abandon the work path determined by ACE (by clicking on a link leading to another page outside of the path), the ACE continues tracking traversed pages and provides return back to the calculated path by adding the link "Return to the WP" to each page. In the end of the path, the learner reaches the next control page, where ACE generates a test including some of the questions linked within the ontology to LOs delivered to the learner by showing pages of the storyboard graph. As far as these delivered LOs are with complexity level suitable for the individual learner, the questions related to these LOs will be appropriate to this learner, as well.

As well, ACE stores some statistics of learner feedbacks to determine which pages are useful for which kind of users. This gives the adaptation engine ability to learn from their skills and perform better estimations for paths for further learners.

3.2 Platform architecture

As an adaptive e-learning platform, ADOPTA includes an authoring tool, an instructor tool, an adaptation control engine and a set of administration tools, all communicating through a common data repository. Fig. 3 represents the principal architecture of the ADOPTA platform. The work process of mastering and delivery of adaptive courseware defines five working roles:

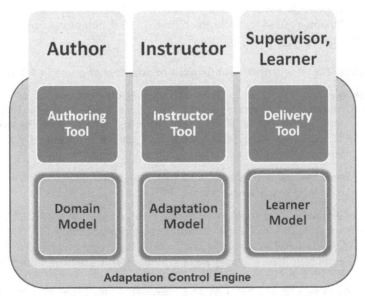

Fig. 3. Principal architecture of the ADOPTA platform

- Author – responsible for design of annotated LOs organized within ontology, by means of the authoring tool;
- Instructor – uses the instructor tool to design a course as a narrative storyboard for courseware delivery with adaptation to learning styles and knowledge, respectively by defining work paths disposing LOs onto pages appropriate for style and knowledge level; as well, the instructor should define paths weights, link annotations and assessment grade thresholds in control pages, as explained in the next chapter;
- Supervisor – responsible for tuning and controlling the adaptation engine, e.g. starting and stopping adaptation behaviour for a given student group, tracking progress of every learner, etc.;
- Learner – solves test for determining his/her learning character (polymorphic learning style) and, next, follows the chosen course by receiving adaptive content from the delivery tool and solving assessment tests at control points
- Administrator (not shown in fig. 3) – controls all the users by means of administrative tools.

As presented in the figure, the tools for authoring learning contents, adaptive instructional design and adaptive content delivery are based respectively on the models describing domain, adaptation and learner, as explained before. The adaptation control engine uses all these three models in order to perform a successful control over the adaptation process.

4. Field trial

An adaptive e-learning platform should be evaluated regarding its functional and quality properties, within a field trial under practical working conditions. In order to evaluate experimentally the ADOPTA platform described in the previous section, the field trial involved design of an adaptive course and its delivery to four-year students of the bachelor program in Software engineering at Sofia University, Bulgaria. The present section explains in detail the methodology used for creation of the field trial and, next, some issues about the design and delivery of the adaptive course.

4.1 Methodology for design and management of adaptive courses in ADOPTA

ADOPTA uses a special methodology for creating e-learning courseware allowing various instructional strategies for adaptive design using non-linear course storyboards. The methodology strongly depends on the strict separation and independence between the three main sub-models within the conceptual model and on the mechanisms used for course delivery with adaptation to learning style and student knowledge level.

Fig. 4 depicts basic methodology steps to be followed when designing adaptive courses. Several key issues should be discussed here:

- Creation of annotated LOs is supposed to be executed by using the ADOPTA authoring tool, however, any other authoring environment compliant to the SCORM (Rey-López, 2002) and IEEE LOM (Learning Object Metadata) standards (IEEE LTSC, 2004). ADOPTA authoring tool allows interoperability with other systems by means of facilities for export and import of LOs. Organization and annotation of LOs is of key importance because it facilitates their usage while designing and maintaining the storyboard graph of an adaptive course. For example, LOs annotations about their appropriateness for specific polymorphic learning character (comprising of a combination of learning styles) and given complexity level are to be used for creating a storyboard graph providing adaptivity toward learning styles and knowledge level. While IEEE LOM is used for annotating LOs by setting and inheriting appropriate metadata from types to sub-types within the ontology, the ontology itself is to be annotating using OMV (Ontology Metadata Vocabulary) (Hartmann et al, 2005);

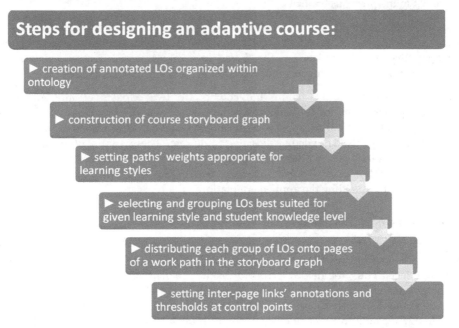

Steps for designing an adaptive course:

► creation of annotated LOs organized within ontology

► construction of course storyboard graph

► setting paths' weights appropriate for learning styles

► selecting and grouping LOs best suited for given learning style and student knowledge level

► distributing each group of LOs onto pages of a work path in the storyboard graph

► setting inter-page links' annotations and thresholds at control points

Fig. 4. Methodology for adaptive course design

- Construction of storyboard graph has to imply development of sufficient working (learning) paths covering different polymorphic learning characters, i.e. different combinations of style levels for reflector, theorist, activist and pragmatist. It is not realistic to cover all the possible combinations of such style levels, however, even after developing paths for the four quadrants of fig. 1 the adaptation control engine will be able to select the path mostly suitable for predominant styles of given individual learner character. During the next step, the instructor should define a set of weights for each of these paths, where the set comprises four values showing appropriateness of the path for each learning style;
- Disposal of LOs appropriate for given learning character (combination of learning styles) should be performed after following a pedagogical strategy. The methodology does not fix or restrict such a strategy, thus, instructors are free to select upon their preference;
- Setting appropriate annotations of inter-page links makes possible the adaptation control engine to display them in order to inform the learner about all other possible opportunities for navigation from given course page, different from the next page for

the path determined for delivery by the engine. Thus, the engine does not restrict the learner to follow exactly the path selected as best path for the learner; he/she may leave this path and return to it latter or, otherwise, reach the next control point via another path. In any case, the engine will track all the pages traversed by the learner, in order to select at the next control point questions about LOs delivered at these pages. Note, there are also other details about tuning of the adaptation control, such setting tuning rules for selection of LOs with complexity level appropriate for learner assessment grade shown in the previous control page.

Some steps of the methodology described here may be used for management of the storyboard during the adaptive delivery, as well. For example, changing the weights of the working paths in a graph and/or the threshold's values at the control points may be executed during run time while tracking learning process and assessment results.

Designing curriculum and shaping the course are two aspects of an iterative and incremental process that are consistent with the learner model. Once content is created by the author, it must be linked appropriately in the course by the instructor and adapted according to the goals, knowledge, learning style, etc. These two aspects have a great influence on the efficiency of adaptive e-learning methods. The process of creating LOs of the curriculum refers to the subject domain, while the process of designing a course storyboard is determined by the applied adaptation model.

4.2 Design of a field trial using ADOPTA

One of the main objectives of the experimental field trial consisted in evaluation of courseware delivery using ADOPTA offering adaptation to both learning style and student knowledge level. Thus, the field trial was focused on realization of adaptive course in XML technologies using the ADOPTA platform which is a joint effort of content authors, course instructors and learners' supervisors. The process workflow involved the steps of the methodology for adaptive course design shown in fig. 4. Authoring of content about XML technologies domain supposes creation of LOs of various types such as narrative LO (lesson), exercise, project, essay, problem solving, games and others, in order to be used next by instructors when designing course storyboard graphs by means of the instructor tool. Fig. 5 gives a distribution of learning objects types to learning styles of Honey and Mumford found by the authors during a decade of practical experiments in e-learning (Bontchev and Vassileva, 2009). LOs of type game, essay, project, problem-solving, comparative analysis and observation task can also be used to assess learner's knowledge as well as classic tests. LOs for assessment are given in the figure as yellow ellipses and may be used for self, peer and teacher assessment as presented in the legend. Finally, the LOs are to be annotated and organized within domain ontology as described in (Bontchev and Vassileva, 2011).

Construction of adaptive course storyboard may be based either on using strongly connected storyboard graphs or on parallel branches (Vassileva and Bontchev, 2011). The approach using parallel branches has two main streamlines (i.e., work paths) – one with educational content intended for theorists and another designed for opposite learning style - activists. As shown in fig. 6, each of these two main WPs is divided at several places symmetrically of two other paths which merge again. Thus, design in parallel branches produces two sets of WPs - one containing all the WPs for activists and other containing all WPs for theorists. Therefore, it is possible for predominant activists or theorists to add also LOs appropriate for pragmatists or reflectors (according distribution of types of LOs shown in fig. 5).

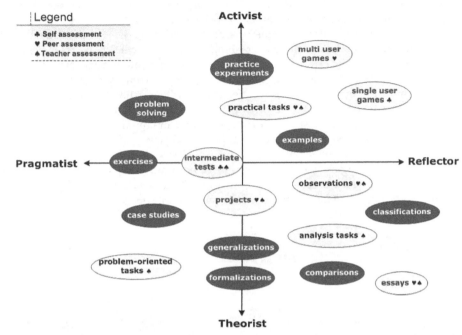

Fig. 5. Appropriateness of learning objects types to learning styles of Honey and Mumford

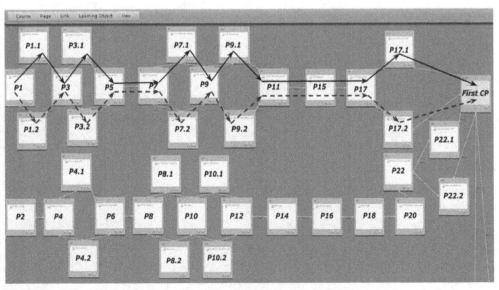

Fig. 6. Partial view of a narrative storyboard graph in the ADOPTA instructor tool (Vassileva and Bontchev, 2011)

After designing and tuning of the storyboard of an adaptive course, the adaptation control engine is able to deliver paths and LOs appropriate respectively to individual learning character and learner's knowledge level. For this purpose, the learner is supposed first to pass the Honey and Mumford survey for assessment of the learning character (styles) and, next, to start the adaptive course. If, at the first control point, the learner assessment grade will surpass the threshold defined at that threshold, then the learner will be able to continue through the path selected by the engine or to navigate to another page making part of another path - by using the annotated link to that page referred as outgoing link. Fig. 7 presents a view of the initialization of the weights of WPs in the Instructor tool, for the developed adaptive course in XML technologies. Each working path consists of a list of pages and has weights for activist, reflector, theorist and pragmatist (when using styles of Honey and Mumford). In contrast with this adaptive navigation, adaptive content selection is possible by placing at each page of the path several LOs with different complexity levels. The adaptation control engine will select LOs with appropriate complexity for given learner depending on his/her last assessment grade received at the previous control point and, as well, according tuning rules for selection of LOs with complexity level appropriate for that grade.

WP ID	WP name ▼	List of pages	activist	reflector	theorist	pragmatist
347	YES_T_R	1, 1.2, 3, 3.2, 5, 5.2, 7, 9, 9.2, 11, 11.2, 15, 17, 19, 19.2, Exam 1	41.5556	94.4444	87.3333	51.5556
443	YES_T_R	Exam 1, 21, 23, 25, 27, 29, 29.2, 31, 31.2, 33, 33.2, 35, Exam 2	30	70	70	30
410	YES_T_P	1, 1.1, 3, 3.1, 5, 5.1, 7, 9, 9.1, 11, 11.1, 15, 17, 19, 19.1, Exam 1	30	40	70	80
454	YES_T_P	Exam 1, 21, 23, 25, 27, 29, 29.1, 31, 31.1, 33, 33.1, 35, Exam 2	30	40	70	80
444	YES_A_R	Exam 1, 26, 28, 30, 32, 34, 36, 36.2, 38, 38.2, 40, 40.2, 42, Exam 2	81.1429	93	35.5714	45.5714
411	YES_A_R	2, 2.2, 4, 6, 6.2, 8, 10, 10.2, 12, 12.2, 14, 16, 18, 20, 22, 24, 24.2, Exam 1	70	60	30	40
458	YES_A_P	Exam 1, 26, 28, 30, 32, 34, 36, 36.1, 38, 38.1, 40, 40.1, 42, Exam 2	70	40	30	80
442	YES_A_P	2, 2.1, 4, 6, 6.1, 8, 10, 10.1, 12, 12.1, 14, 16, 18, 20, 22, 24, 24.1, Exam 1	94	52	42	104

Edit WP weights for learning styles — Refresh — Edit

Fig. 7. Initialization of the weights of WPs in the instructor tool

5. Assessment results

The chapter presents results of evaluation of courseware delivery using the ADOPTA platform offering both learning style and knowledge level adaptations. The experimental field trial was conducted by using the adaptive course in XML technologies specially designed for this purpose. 84 four-year students of the bachelor program in Software engineering took participation in practical experiments. These students were divided into two groups with equal number of participants and equilibrated in terms of average student performance demonstrated in previous assessments of the same students. The first, so called control group passed course modules of a traditional, non-adaptive course in XML technologies given by the Moodle platform, while the experimental group took the same modules using ADOPTA where the course was adapted to individual learning styles and student performance shown at intermediate assessment test. Thus, each student of the experimental group obtained learning materials, which are most suitable for her/his individual learning character and knowledge level between two control points.

Students from both the control and experimental group had passed through the same assessment tests and received grades in percentage from 0 to 100%. The assessment results of both student groups are given in fig. 8 by interpolated curves in order to express better dynamics and changes. The eloquent difference between these two curves shows in a clear way that students of the experimental group (taken the adaptive version of the same course) have demonstrated rather better performance, with average result of 77,89% while average result of the control group is 67,14%. As far as both the student groups consisted of the same number of students (42 for a group) with equal average performance shown in former assessments, we conclude the adaptive delivery of the same course is more effective than the traditional one and, thus, the adaptation to style of learning and student performance makes learning more appealing and productive.

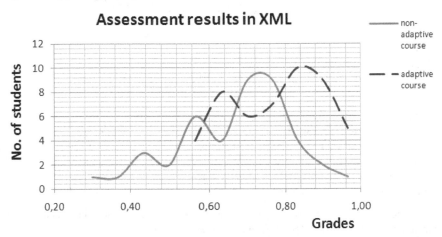

Fig. 8. Assessment results for non-adaptive and adaptive courses in XML technologies

In order to assess the effectiveness of adaptivity to learning styles, a special survey was conducted among the students of the second group after the end of the adaptive course in XML technologies. The questions asked for students' opinions about the quality of adaptive courseware delivery. Fig. 9 presents students' answers using 5 levels Likert scale with the levels: 1=strongly disagree, 2=disagree, 3=not sure, 4=agree, and 5=strongly agree, for the following questions presented in the form of statements:

1. Learning objects delivered within the course fit your learning style presented by values for theorist, pragmatist, reflector and activist).
2. The ADOPTA platform does really adapt the courseware to my learning style.
3. The assignments, exercises, topics for essays and games were interesting and valuable for me.
4. The ADOPTA platform effectively adapts the learning courseware to my knowledge level.

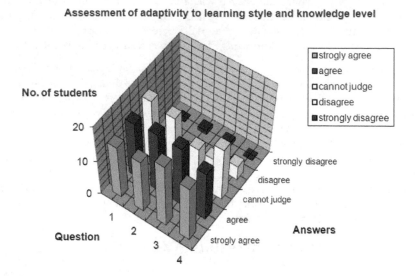

Fig. 9. Results about assessment of adaptiviy to students learning styles and knowledge level

The results presented in fig. 9 show a rather positive feedback on the effectiveness of platform adaptivity to learning styles (questions 1 and 2) as well as to student knowledge level (questions 3 and 4). The majority if students do agree on the effective adaptation of courseware according to the student character issues such as learning style and knowledge. Though they are some students who cannot judge on this, learners regard learning objects delivered to them by the platform as valuable and useful for individual learners.

Next four questions (statements of the survey) regard the issue of preference of adaptive platform to non-adaptive one. They are given below:

1. I prefer an adaptive e-learning platform to non-adaptive one with similar implementation.
2. Adaptive learning does lead to greater knowledge and results compared with non-adaptive learning.
3. I would use this adaptive learning system again.
4. I would recommend this adaptive learning system to other students.

Fig. 10 provides results about general assessment of ADOPTA as an adaptive e-learning system. It is important to underline students recognize the benefits of adaptive systems concerning obtaining greater knowledge and results compared with non-adaptive learning. The majority of them agree on the fact the adaptive learning does lead to greater knowledge and results compared with non-adaptive learning, which has been proven by this field trial (see fig. 8). There are few students who are not sure. In general, the majority of students regard adaptive learning as a more arguing and effective way of technology-enhanced learning than the traditional non-adaptive one.

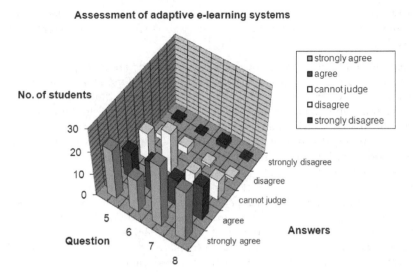

Fig. 10. Results about a general assessment of ADOPTA

6. Conclusion

Adaptive hypermedia platforms continue being a challenge in modern development of technology enhanced learning. This chapter addressed practical approaches for design and construction of courseware delivery with adaptation on one hand to learning style and, on the other hand, to knowledge level (i.e., to student performance). The approaches were implemented using the ADOPTA platform, together with a field trial aiming at general evaluation of the platform and assessment of effectiveness of the adaptation to learning style and knowledge. While adaptivity to learner style is achieved on the base of explicit learner pre-tests and adaptive navigation within the storyboard graph, adaptivity to learner's performance is implemented via adaptive content selection by using assessment results at each control page of the course in order to select LOs with appropriate level of complexity for a given learner. Both the types of adaptation are managed by the adaptation control engine of the ADOPTA platform.

The presented results obtained from the field trial are based on questionnaire about realized adaptivity to students learning styles and knowledge level. They reveal a rather positive students appreciation of achieved level and quality of adaptivity and show adaptive courses are an appeal and challenge for students to learn better and more. Here, implementation of the storyboard graph for adaptive course delivery is of crucial importance. The instructor has to select types of LOs appropriate for given polymorphic learning style by taking in consideration distribution of LOs types to learning style as shown in fig. 5 or a similar one. As well, to tune the engine to select at each non-control page of the course LOs with complexity level adequate to assessment results shown by the learner.

Finally, authors have to underline that presented results are context-dependant – they are obtained by conducting an adaptive course with bachelor students in Software Engineering. During the experiments, it has been found these students have in general a learning character where reflectors and theorists are the predominant learning styles. They are quite possible other results for adaptive course delivery to students with different predominant learning styles.

Though experimental results gained by the initial case study are quite positive, there should be mentioned some shortcomings of the chosen approach. First at all, learning style of an individual is not fixed forever but may evolve with time, even during delivery of a course. Therefore, learning style should be assessed not only by a pre-test in the very beginning of the course but also at some latter points. However, filling up several times the same questioner containing decades of questions for determining individual style would be tedious and boring for learners. A much better approach for the practice will be determining learning style implicitly during the e-learning process, e.g. by an intelligent agent tracking learner behaviour and choice of types of learning objects. Therefore, this should be a starting point for our future works. On other hand, optimizations could be introduced to work process of instructors, as well. For the moment, they should develop paths for adaptive e-learning within the course graph and, next, to set weights of these paths for different learning styles of the chosen style family and to place on pages of the paths and to tune various LOs of different level of complexity. Another, much easier and faster approach would be to set appropriateness of LO for learning styles together with LO complexity level while authoring learning ontology and course content by means of the authoring tool. Next, the instructor should only select within the ontology the order of partitions of the ontology to be delivered to learners. Then, the adaptation control engine will start traversing these ontology partitions in the selected order and will choose LOs appropriate for particular learner style and performance. For sure, such an approach misses ordering and annotation of individual LOs according an advance pedagogical strategy for a specific learner character, however, it would be much easier for practical usage and therefore should be considered for future design and experimental works.

7. Acknowledgment

This work is supported by the ADOPTA project funded by the Bulgarian NSF under agreement No. D002/155.

8. References

Bontchev B., Vassileva D. (2009). Adaptive courseware design based on learner character, *Proc. of Int. Conf. on Interactive Computer Aided Learning (ICL2009)*, 23-25 Sept., 2009, Villach, Austria, pp.724-731.

Bontchev B., Vassileva D., Chavkova B., Mitev V. (2009) Architectural Design of a Software Engine for Adaptation Control for the ADOPTA E-learning Platform, *Proc. of Int. Conf. on Computer Systems and Technologies (CompSysTech' 09)*, Ruse, Bulgaria, Vol. II.11, ACMBUL, ISSN: 1313-8936, pp.1-6 (best paper award).

Bontchev, B., Vassileva, D. (2011). Adaptive assessment based on learning styles and student knowledge level, *Proc. of the CSEDU Special Session on Assessment Tools and Techniques for e-Learning (ATTeL 2011)*, Noordwijkerhout, The Netherlands, May 7-8, 2011, ISBN 978-989-8425-50-8, Vol.2, pp.449-454.

Brusilovsky, P. (1996). Methods and techniques of adaptive hypermedia. *Journal of User Modeling and User-Adapted Interaction*, Vol. 6 (2-3), pp. 87-129.

Conlan, O. (2003). *State of the Art: Adaptive Hypermedia*, M-Zones Deliverable 1, pp. 47-57.

Collis, B., Strijker, A. (2002): New pedagogies and reusable learning objects: Toward a new economy in education. *J. of Educational Technology Systems*, Vol. 30 (2), pp. 137-157.

Dagger, D., Wade, V., Conlan, O. (2005). Personalization for All: Making Adaptive Course Composition Easy, *Special issue of the Educational Technology and Society Journal*, IEEE IFETS.

De Bra, P., Houben G.-J., Wu H. (1999). AHAM: A Dexter-based Reference Model for adaptive Hypermedia. *ACM Conf. on Hypertext and Hypermedia*, ISBN:1-58113-064-3, Darmstadt, Germany, pp. 147-156.

De Bra, P., Smits, D., Stash, N. (2006). Creating and Delivering Adaptive Courses with AHA! *Proc. of the first European Conference on Technology Enhanced Learning EC-TEL*, Crete, October 1-4 2006, Springer LNCS 4227, pp. 21-33

DCMI. (2009). Dublin Core Metadata Initiative Overview, July 2009, available online at: http://dublincore.org/documents/dces/

Friesen, N. (2005). Interoperability and learning objects: An overview of e-learning standardization, *Interdisciplinary Journal of Knowledge and Learning Objects*, 1, pp. 23-31.

Grimón, F., Monguet, J. M., Ojeda, J. (2009). Knowledge Based Information Retrieval with an Adaptive Hypermedia System, LNCS, ISBN 978-3-642-02263-0, pp. 457-463.

Hartmann, J., Palma, R., Sure , Y., Suárez-Figueroa, M.D.C., Haase, P., Gómez-Pérez, A., Studer, R. (2005): Ontology Metadata Vocabulary and Applications. *Proc. of Int. Conf. on Ontologies, Databases and Applications of Semantics*, Springer, pp. 906-915.

IEEE LTSC. (2004). Learning Object Metadata, *IEEE LTSC Working Group 12*, available online at: http://ltsc.ieee.org/wg12/index.html

Karagiannidis, C., Sampson, D. (2002). Accommodating Learning Styles in Adaptation Logics for Personalised Learning Systems, *Proc. of World Conf. on Educational Multimedia, Hypermedia and Telecommunication*, pp. 1715-1726.

Kolb, D. (1984). *Experiential learning: experience as the source of learning and development*, Englewood Cliffs, New Jersey: Prentice Hall.

Lindsay, E. K. (1999). *An analysis of matches of teaching styles learning styles and the uses of educational technology*, Doctoral dissertation, North Carolina State University, Raleigh.

Munoz-Seca, B., and Silva Santiago, C. (2003). Four Dimensions to Induce Learning: The Challenge Profile, *IESE Working Paper No. D/520*.

NISO. (2004). Understanding Metadata. *NISO Press*, ISBN: 1-880124-62-9, available online at: http://www.niso.org/publications/press/UnderstandingMetadata.pdf.

Paramythis, A., Loidl-Reisinger, S. (2003) Adaptive Learning Environments and e-Learning Standards, *Proc. of Conf. on e-Learning (ECEL2003)*, Glasgow, Scotland, pp. 369-379.

Rey-López, M.,Fernández-Vilas A., Díaz-Redondo R., Pazos-Arias J. (2002), Providing SCORM with adaptivity, *Proc. of the 15th Int. Conf. on World Wide Web*, ISBN:1-59593-323-9, pp. 981-982.

Sadler-Smith, E. (1997) Learning Style: Frameworks And Instruments, *J. of Educational Psychology*, Vol. 17, Issue 1.

Vassileva, D., Bontchev, B., Grigorov, S. (2009) Mastering Adaptive Hypermedia Courseware, *Acta Electrotechnica et Informatica*, ISSN: 1335-8243, Vol. 9, No. 1, 2009, pp. 57–62.

Vassileva, D. (2010). Storyboard Design for Adaptive E-learning Based on Learning Styles, *Proc. of Second Int. Conf. S3T*, September 11-12, 2010, Varna, Bulgaria, ISBN 978-954-9526-71-4, pp. 22-29.

Vassileva, D., Bontchev, B. (2011). Storyboard Design for Courseware Adaptation to Learner Style and Knowledge, *Proc. of IADIS Int. Conf. e-Learning 2011*, Rome, Italy, 20-23 July 2011, ISBN: 978-972-8939-38-0, pp.157-164.

Velsen., L. (2008). User-centered evaluation of adaptive and adaptable systems: a literature review, *The Knowledge Engineering Review Journal*, Cambridge University Press, Vol. 23:3, pp. 261–281.

Weber, G., Hans-Christian, K., and Weibelzahl, S. (2001). Developing Adaptive Internet Based Courses with the Authoring System NetCoach, Hypermedia: Openness, Structural Awareness, and Adaptivity, *LNAI, Vol. 2266*, ISBN: 978-3-540-43293-7, pp. 226-238.

2

Learning Performance and Satisfaction on Working Education

Chun-Ling Ho and Tsung-Han Chang
Kao Yuan University
Taiwan

1. Introduction

The emerging Internet and World Wide Web (WWW) brought about fast variations in the development of the learning process in the past ten years. There are various forms for learning, such as Computer-Aided Instructions (CAI), Intelligent Tutoring System (ITS), to Web-Based Learning (WBL), and e-learning systems. In present fast changing electronic world (e-world) knowledge is the key to maintaining the appropriate impetus and momentum in organizational and academic environments. In this situation continuous, convenient and economical access to training and qualifications assumes the highest priority for the ambitious individual or organization. With the booming development of Internet and information technology, the Internet has broken the limitation of time and space. Information and Communication Technology (ICT) have recently affected strongly on every field in the society; especially in recent years, e-learning is being applied widely in the areas of training around the world.

Generally speaking, e-learning is a mode of education that builds on a network technology-based and also uses a mix of computer and other ICTs, across time and space restricted to deliver instruction and provide access to information resources. It can be included delivery systems such as videotape, interactive audio-video, CD-ROMs, DVDs, video-conferencing, VOD, e-mail, live chat, use of the Web, television, satellite broadcasts and so on. It also includes the delivery of contents through Internet, intranet/extranet, audio and videotape, satellite broadcast, interactive TV, and CD-ROM". Access to these resources means that students can do homework at a time they feel free and convenience, therefore learning may conduct synchronously or asynchronously.

E-learning can provide content and knowledge as valuable as like traditional training environment. Conventional learning often requires learners to travel to different locations and gather in various classrooms at specific time, but e-learning has no such restrictions. Meeting face-to-face is no longer necessary and learners just need to meet with each other via electronic modes of delivery (e.g., chat rooms, discussion boards, instant messaging). The benefits of e-learning are not only to learners but also the organizations when they learned form this education training mode.

Taiwan in 1999 had the "Fundamental Science and Technology" concept to establish fundamental principles and directions for the development of science and technology. The same year the government approved NTD 40 million within a 5-year period for the "National Science and Technology Program for e-Learning". Firms are aware of the need to become learning organizations and increase workers' skills in order to accommodate new technologies. The e-Learning offers not only the way for anytime, anywhere, flexible learning online, but is also a cost effective and flexible method, and one the public and private sectors have taken as a useful tool to train and educate the workforce.

For enterprises, e-Learning could be savings, increasing worker productivity, driving operational efficiencies, and streamlining corporate training. e-Learning initiative Basic Blue program in IBM, it would save $16 million in 2000. And after cooperating with their e-Learning management system-Platue Systems, the American Red Cross saved more than $10 million in seven-years. About Toyota Motor Sales USA in 2002 declared that the use of the Learning System to strengthen training, it would save more than $11.9 million in five years. Worldwide revenues in the e-Learning market will reach US$ 500 billion by 2010, and the growth of e-Learning market is expected to multiply by 6.

Learning Environment online is one of key factors that increase the learning satisfaction. e-Learning platform should include Content Management System (CMS) and Learning Management Systems (LMS). Modular Object-Oriented Dynamic Learning Environment (MOODLE) is a free and open source e-learning software platform and is designed to help educators create online courses with opportunities for rich interaction. It opens source license and modular design that people can develop additional functionality. Basing on MOODLE, e-learning system provides help and supports to learners through diverse technologies including real-time chat, messages boards, email, lecture material files, and so on. According to Clark and Mayer (2003), e-learning was defined as instruction delivered on a computer by way of CD-ROM, Internet, or Intranet with the following features:

- Includes content relevant to the learning objectives.
- Uses instructional methods to help learning.
- Uses media elements to deliver the content and methods.
- Linked new knowledge and skills to learning goals and to improved organizational performance.

This chapter proposes a theoretical model based on working safety training in construction and integrates the adoption and satisfaction of e-learning by labors. The objective are threefold:

1. To conceptualize a theoretical structural model based on e-learning.
2. To identify the factors affecting using e-learning system.
3. To make sure how factors in the proposed model influence labors' learning in working safety training of e-learning.

This chapter attempts to construct a conceptual model and then integrate the some external factors into the proposed model. The objectives/questions include the following:

Question 1: What are the factors that significantly influence labors using the technology in e-learning environments?

Question 2: How does the proposed model explain the variances of satisfaction?

2. Working safety training

In the face of no decrease occupational injuries, attaining a high and consistent level of safety-health management system is becoming an important issue for manufacturers and industry. According to the statistics, the major occupation accident rate of construction has been the highest among all industries. In Taiwan, the percentage of deaths from the construction professional accidents between 2001 and 2010 is around 0.031%, much higher than that during the same period in advanced countries in Europe, America and the UK, indicating that the situation of construction professional accidents in construction has become a very serious problem. Thus it's imperious to improve the construction worker safety management, in order to decrease the construction accident occurrence.

On the other hand, the working injury statistics revealed by Council of Labor Affairs in Taiwan, 75% of the casualties were caused by worker's unsafe behavior, and 75% of the unsafe behavior related injured workers were not properly trained by the employers on safety. It means working safety training will lower injuries and plays most significant role in reducing unsafe behaviors. Therefore, how to improve the effect of safety training is one of the key factors to reduce working injuries.

The general safety training courses in most companies still follow traditional oral teaching method and lack of discussion, practice, and simulation drill. And in order to reduce training cost, most of instructors are in-house employees that provide the boring courses. It will decrease the effect of training. This chapter derives the training and e-learning for labor safety and by analyzing the survey and setting up the e-learning procedures, it also establishes a good labor safety training planning and implementation mechanism which can be conformed the requirements of laws and regulation in construction.

3. Proposed model and hypotheses

3.1 Sample

This chapter obtained the valid samples from A construction and the purpose is to explore the relationship among education training and the relationship after training by e-learning. There were totally 185 questionnaires issued in this chapter, and 178 questionnaires are valid (effective sample rate is 96.2%). First, responses from the questionnaires were gathered and entered into SPSS 16. The significance level chosen for this study was .05. Descriptive statistics on all the data provided frequencies, percentages, means, and standard deviations.

The characteristics of this sample were calculated including age and gender of using e-Learning for labor working safety training by SPSS that also conduct Descriptive statistical analysis, Factor analysis, Reliability analysis, Analysis of variance, T-test, Duncan multiple T-comparison, and Regression analysis to probe this study. The reliability of data also assessed by computing Cronbach's alpha.

The sample consisted of 178 workers with 43.6% female and 54.4% male. For age, 12.3% of total respondents were over 50 years old, with about 28.6% in the age of 50-40 years old, about 38.9% in the age of 40-30 years old and about 20.2% in 30-20 years old.

3.2 Instrument development

On the questionnaire, four predictors-user interface, rich content, platform function, learning support to satisfaction on e-learning training, and two labor variables-age and gender were selected for further investigation. Figure 1 depicts the hypotheses of three groups. Every group shows the hypotheses to examine the effect of perceptions.

H1: System design (user interface, rich content, platform function, learning support) are positively related to satisfaction on e-learning training.

H2: System design (user interface, rich content, platform function, learning support) are correlated with labor variables of age and gender.

H3: Satisfaction on e-learning training is correlated with labor variables of age and gender.

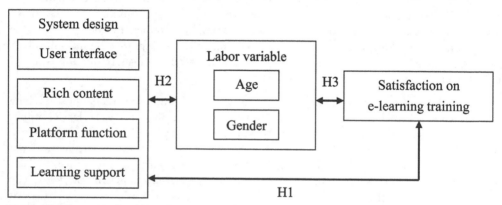

Fig. 1. The framework of Satisfaction on e-learning training

Team	Item	Measure
User interface	U1	Easy to use
	U2	Friendly interface
	U3	Colorful elements
Rich content	R4	Multi-media for design
	R5	Suitable training content
	R6	Tools for fast learning
Platform function	P7	Function with well done
	P8	Playing easily
	P9	Good network connection
Learning support	L10	Given learning direction
	L11	Help function design
	L12	Supporting online tutor
Satisfaction on e-learning training	S13	Increase the learning times by myself
	S14	Intensive training effect

Table 1. Variable Definition

A survey questionnaire was developed to measure the relevant constructs. Table 1 summarizes the operational definition as well as the references for each construct. A five-point Likert-type scale asked the subjects to rate the degree to which they agreed with the statements on a 1 to 5 scale-1 represented "strongly disagree" and 5 "strongly agree". And Table 2 presents the items and the respective loadings of the instrument.

4. Data analysis

4.1 Reliability and factor analysis

In verifying the scale for measuring these constructs, Cronbach's alpha was used to assess the reliability. The coefficient alpha values for user interface, rich content, platform function, learning support were 0.92, 0.81, 0.90, 0.93 and 0.87. Because the Cronbach's alpha values were above the conventional level of 0.7 (Nunnally, 1978), the scales for these constructs were deemed to exhibit adequate reliability.

It conducted a confirmatory factor analysis (CFA) to test the convergent validity of each construct. The loadings of items against the construct being measured were tested against the value 0.7 on the construct being measured and table 2 showed the results obtained for the loadings in relation to the latent variables. The factors structure in factor analysis went well with the structure of the questionnaire.

Item	Component				
	1	2	3	4	5
U1	0.8912				
U2	0.8673				
U3	0.3767				
R4		0.9022			
R5		0.7891			
R6		0.5236			
P7				0.7816	
P8				0.8603	
P9				0.7928	
L10			0.6156		
L11			0.8993		
L12			0.8762		
S13					0.7837
S14					0.8619

Table 2. Initial values of loadings

Based on the criteria that item loadings greater than 0.70, we analysis of the cognitive absorption construct shows that all items, and then U3, R6 and L10 are much lower than acceptable. These two items were dropped from the final model.

Once all the items that did not load satisfactorily had been removed, the model was rerun. Table 3 shows the results of testing the measurement model in the final run. The t-values for model loadings show that model loadings are all above 1.96 and significant.

T Statistics	SD	Item	Component				
			1	2	3	4	5
8.9035	0.0357	U1	0.8912				
7.0981	0.0218	U2	0.8673				
12.4582	0.0563	R4		0.8972			
7.0972	0.0371	R5		0.7633			
14.3156	0.0936	P7				0.7655	
22.9064	0.0367	P8				0.8413	
25.0673	0.0655	P9				0.7836	
10.3528	0.0887	L11			0.8763		
13.7835	0.0523	L12			0.8359		
14.3196	0.0348	S13					0.7837
9.3681	0.0762	S14					0.8619

Table 3. Final values of loadings

4.2 The relationship between System design and labor variables

For understanding the relationship, in case between gender and user interface, rich content, platform function, learning support by using T-test. The result showed both gender had significant to perceived each mean (p-value), and the result revealed that male (mean=5.03) and female (mean=4.34). It is indicates in Table 4.

	Mean			
	User interface	Rich content	Platform function	Learning support
Male	4.09	6.12	5.73	4.36
Female	4.35	5.02	4.63	4.17
t-statistic	3.26	4.15	3.87	4.56
df	212.95	214.33	214.76	214.28
p-value	0.00	0.00	0.00	0.00

Table 4. The relationship between system design and gender

As illustrates in Table 5, age level had many significant influence on the user interface, rich content and platform function (p-value = 0.00), and 20-50 years old generally make more interesting of all means.

	Mean			
	User interface	Rich content	Platform function	Learning support
Over 50 years old	1.13	4.89	5.26	0.57
50-40 years old	4.36	5.02	4.63	4.17
40-30 years old	5.39	5.36	5.14	4.06
30-20 years old	5.17	5.89	4.37	4.82
t-statistic	4.69	4.12	4.33	-0.86
df	57.63	57.09	57.82	51.87
p-value	0.00	0.00	0.00	0.68

Table 5. The relationship between system design and age

4.3 Structural model evaluation

The analyses of data include descriptive statistics and Structural Equation Modeling (SEM). SEM with LISREL 8.5 will be used to analyze the data from the respondents. It has a number of advantages over multiple regressions which is commonly used to validate aspects of the theory. The SEM consists of two parts, and they are the structural model and the measurement model. The structural model shows potential causal dependencies between endogenous and exogenous variables, and the measurement model shows the relations between the latent variables and their indicators. The structural model was evaluated using the following criteria:

a. Ability to explain variance
b. Significance of path coefficients

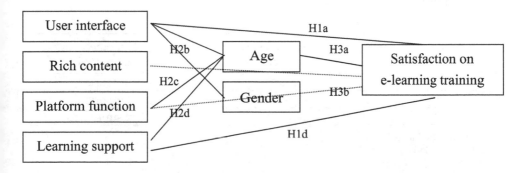

Fig. 2. Model with T-value path coefficients

The structural model was tested with the data from the entire data sample and each of labor variables respectively. The comparison of path coefficients are between system design and satisfaction on e-learning training, labor variables and satisfaction on e-learning training, system design and labor variables (shown as Fig.2). The significance of difference was calculated in Table 6 and Table 7. Following the figure show the results of SEM, include standardized, estimated and T-value model, as well.

Hypotheses	Effects	T-values	Result
H1a	user interface<-> satisfaction on e-learning training	3.256***	Supported
H1b	rich content <-> satisfaction on e-learning training	4.012***	Supported
H1c	platform function <-> satisfaction on e-learning training	3.763***	Supported
H1d	learning support <-> satisfaction on e-learning training	3.002***	Supported
H2a	user interface <-> age	4.786***	Supported
H2b	rich content <-> age	3.267***	Supported
H2c	platform function <-> age	-0.162	Not supported
H2d	learning support <-> age	0.268	Not supported
H2e	user interface <-> gender	0.157	Not supported
H2f	rich content <-> gender	2.767***	Supported
H2g	platform function <-> gender	-2.031	Not supported
H2h	learning support <-> gender	0.365	Not supported
H3a	age <-> satisfaction on e-learning training	4.629***	Supported
H3b	gender <-> satisfaction on e-learning training	1.903	Not supported

*p <0.05 (one-tailed test)
**p <0.01 (one-tailed test)
***p <0.001 (one-tailed test)

Table 6. Hypotheses test

Model hypotheses	Standardized Path Coefficients	Hypotheses Supported
H1	0.721**	Supported
H2	0.893**	Supported
H3	0.126	Not supported

*p <0.05 (one-tailed test)
**p <0.01 (one-tailed test)
***p <0.001 (one-tailed test)

Table 7. H1 to H3 hypotheses test results

It can be seen in the above figure, the T-value for eight factors are more than 1.96 suggested by Byrne (2001). H1a, H1b, H1c, H1d, H2a, H2b, H2f, H3a are supported by the data and the other hypotheses (H2c, H2d, H2e and H3b) are rejected. Significant differences were found in two groups of H1 and H2. Significant differences appeared in the path coefficients of all, they are system design and satisfaction on e-learning training, user interface and age, rich content and age, rich content and gender, age and satisfaction on e-learning training.

The results found in fact, for satisfaction on e-learning training, it has a substantially greater effect on system design. Both of their coefficients are significant, validating H1. H3 assumes the perceptions of labor variable are positively related to satisfaction on e-learning training. In this case illustrate partly influence between them, thus the results do not provide support for H3. H2 posit that system design attitude would have an affect on labor variable. However, findings illustrate only perceived "user interface and rich content" shows significant coefficient. Therefore, the findings do not totally support H2.

5. Factors influence labors' satisfaction of e-learning in working safety training

This section summarized some major findings which were discussed with the aims of the chapter:

- Majority of respondents on age of labor variable, it were between 30-50 years old with positively related to satisfaction.
- This case study found no direct effect on gender satisfaction and system design, but only a significant effect on rich content of system design. The non-significance of the direct effect is consistent with other recent researches.
- System design demonstrated much significant influence with satisfaction on e-learning training, such as user interface, rich content, platform function, learning support. These finding are also consistent with the prior studies.
- Based on e-learning satisfaction, it identified strongly four significant predictors of system design in the structural model of the SEM test: user interface (T-value=0.35***), rich content (T-value=4.012***), platform function(T-value=3.763***), and learning support (T-value=3.002***).
- H1 posit that satisfaction and system design would have a positive relation to e-Learning systems.
- H2 posit that system design and labor variable would have a positive relation to age of labors.
- H3 posit that labor variable and satisfaction would have no relation to e-Learning systems.

6. Discussion on e-Learning and working training

Recently, e-Learning has become an important teaching method, and to implement an e-learning system can make the whole training process to go through it smoothly without any limitation of time and space. Therefore, e-Learning has become the revolution in the 21st century, and it is not only the learning tendency in the future, but also the important part to come into economic knowledge. Learning for people will become more self-initiated and individualized.

Internet already starts to change the industry of education. By the characteristics of instant and without boundary, Web-Based Training (WBT) has become an important trend for the enterprises' education and training. The e-learning training mode is one of WBT and popular for enterprises. For the limitation of cost and time, e-learning has become an important trend on training, and many enterprises build an e-learning system as employees' training tool. Some companies do not know how to implement e-learning step by step or what is the factor keys to success, especially in construction fields. The critical factors of enterprise e-learning are still unclear for them.

This chapter is attempted to establish an implementation model that may help construction understand the critical factors of e-learning for effective plans. Based on e-learning, it tries to find out those critical success factors influencing over implementing and performance. Furthermore, this found that if the learning quality is increased by conducting e-learning mechanisms that can achieve the goals of reducing cost and increasing the efficiency in working training.

Since e-Learning is one of the best tools to increase value on working training, the purpose of this chapter is to understand how constructions in Taiwan implement e-learning system, what key factors to effect the adoption and processes for the implementation. In the implementation procedure, there are effective factors– course, teaching materials, instructional design, multi-media technology and infrastructure, which affect the results of achievement and learning. Therefore, this research focuses on the user's satisfaction by investigating the e-Learning mode and the training ways. However, studies of user satisfaction when using e-learning systems are very limited. This study will discuss a comprehensive model and instrument for measuring learner satisfaction with e-learning systems.

After this, we set up three groups in accordance with the result of the different learning elements on learning satisfactory investigation. During data collection and analyze, it will carefully examine evidence of reliability, content validity, criterion- related validity from the samples of a case with e-learning system. The procedures used in conceptualizing the survey, generating items, collecting data, and validating are described. To further analyze the data, statistical methods such as T-test, Correlation Analysis, and Structural Equation Modeling could be conducted.

The findings and conclusions were made based on the analyzed data and related certification Hypothesis:

1. Different system design will influence learning motivation.
2. The labors could accept the e-Learning technology that depends on age and rich contents of e-learning.
3. The good system design of e-learning significant effects on grade satisfaction.
4. The exploration of satisfaction in e-learning based on different labor variables and items of learning system attitudes.

e-Learning also brings advantages of flexibility and low cost for working education so that the strong strength can not be ignored. Nevertheless there are no the theoretical essentials to how to create the learning management system according to the characteristic of the enterprises. The chapter applied SEM to explore the relation among satisfaction, labor variables and system design by analyzing factors in the e-learning environment. First of all, it will analysis the system style, such as user interface, rich content, platform function, learning support. Then we had conducted an experiment to compare the learning performance between e-learning teaching and the conventional teaching.

To promote the training satisfaction and performance, this chapter highly suggests that the construction should understand learning characteristics and learning behavior from workers with safety classes to fulfill the needs from learner. Therefore, the three basic principles in conducting evaluation are based on system design (user interface, rich content, platform function, learning support), labor variables (age and gender) and satisfaction on e-learning training.

The major findings of this chapter are as follows:

1. System style significant effects on grade and attitude towards the e-Learning.
2. The e-learning system should be based on labors' attitudes and different subjects.
3. The most efficient learning pattern will be explored in construction of working education.
4. The key factors for positively-correlated effect are between satisfaction and system design.
5. For good training program, to make the e-learning cost-efficient and to integrate information to suit for construction is important.

According to the chapter, a successful e-learning system is integrated with the application of technology and the design of system. Therefore, this chapter will provide valuable reference to the construction adoption of an e-learning system.

7. References

Chin, W. W., and Todd, P., 1995, On the use, usefulness, and ease of use of structural equation modeling in MIS research: a note of caution, MIS Quarterly, 19 (2), pp.237-246.

Clack R. C., Mayer R. E., 2003, E-learning and the Science of Instruction, Jossey Bass Pfeiffer.

Ma, Q., Liu, L., 2004, The technology acceptance model: a meta-analysis of empirical findings, Journal of Organizational and End User Computing, Vol.16, pp. 59–72.

Masiello, I., Ramberg, R. & Lonka, K. P. O., 2005, Attitudes to the application of a Webbased learning system in a microbiology course. Computers & Education 45, pp.171-185.

Nunnally, J. C., 1978, Psychometric theory, New York: McGraw-Hill.

Ong, C. S., Lai, J. Y. and Wang, Y. S., 1994, Factors affecting engineers' acceptance of asynchronous e-Learning in high-tech companies, Information and Management, 41(6), pp.795.

Raaij, E. M. V., Schepers J. J. L., 2008, The acceptance and use of a virtual learning environment in China, Computer & Education, Vol. 50, pp. 838-852.

Wang, K. H., Wang, T. H., Wang, W. L. & Huang, S. C., 2006, Learning styles and formative assessment strategy: enhancing student achievement in Web-based learning. Journal of Computer Assisted Learning 22, pp.207-217.

Wilson, B. G., 1996, Constructivist Learning Environments: Case Studies in Instructional Design, Educational Technology Publication, Englewood Cliffs, New Jersey.

3

Assisted On-Job Training

Cláudio Teixeira and Joaquim Sousa Pinto
University of Aveiro
Portugal

1. Introduction

When dealing with critical systems that users must comprehend to take full advantage of their functionalities, deployment and support teams must take special care with users' training. Even when the development process takes in consideration testers' feedback, there is always the need for more users' hands-on training.

Of course, this is easier said than done. Users tend to be overloaded with regular tasks and finding time to assist a regular formation course is difficult, if not impossible in most cases.

This chapter presents the work being done in Cape Verde relating this subject. We have been developing an information system, named SIPP, to be used in the Courts of law in Cape Verde. SIPP stands for *Sistema de Informação do Processo Penal* (Criminal Proceedings Information System). SIPP is a joint initiative, sponsored by the Ministry of Justice of Cape Verde and developed from scratch by the University of Aveiro and University of Cape Verde. The SIPP has been in testing phase since June 2010 and will be put in production phase on October 2011.

Being a project developed from scratch, there were some barriers (cultural, practical and technical) that we had to overcome to succeed in the project.

One of our main concerns was to help users apprehend how the system works; so, along with online and printed material, we have developed a teaching system that simulates the different actors and automatically checks if the right information was collected from a given textual document, giving feedback to the users about the task's outcome.

To do so, we've deployed a training platform with the same web interface, but different data. On this platform, users could rest at ease on regards of the correctness of the information inserted. Moreover, this was a controlled scenario, so we could monitor and act accordingly when the actions made by the user were distinct from the expected ones. This chapter explains briefly the overall information system and explains in depth the workflow architecture used to deploy the assisted learning process.

From the preliminary results, there are a few key aspects worth mentioning:

- Being a country divided in 10 islands, regular user's training, using traditional classroom approaches is very expensive (mainly due to the country's geography) and bothersome, mainly due to the shear amount of regular court work left behind during training stage;

- Computer illiteracy had to be tackled first
- When users started working with the assisted on-job training, the overall opinion was that such system enabled them to understand the several available options faster and without worries of destroying real life work due to incorrect system operation.

The remainder of this chapter is organized as follows: section 2 briefly presents the state of the art on the On-job training subject, while section 3 presents an overview of SIPP. Section 4 contextualizes SIPP in Cape Verde and Section 5 details the assisted on-job approach in SIPP. Finally, section 6 presents the conclusions of the presented work.

2. Online on-job training – State of the art

Considering the online training and e-learning platforms, several different approaches have been followed, from simple online tutorials, to adaptive context-aware (Bahreininejad & Yaghmaie, 2011) and platforms based on semantic infrastructures context-aware (Yu, Zhou, & Shu, 2010).

With web 2.0, these e-learning applications evolved to social networking applied to e-learning (Abel et al., 2010; Angelaccio & Buttarazzi, 2010).

Regardless of the information model underneath the e-learning process, useful skills and knowledge, resulting from the investment in human capital has been preconized as a distinctive factor for employees and employers alike (Schultz, 1961). Life-long learning is considered an important aspect for both employees and employers (Wu & Huang, 2007).

On-job training contributes to the enhancement and development and human capabilities, according with the trained topic (AlAli, 1997). More importantly, continuous on-job training helps users feel more satisfied with their current position (Georgellis & Lange, 2007).

However, as pointed out by (Borchardt & Grap, 2010), e-learning systems are usually targeted at traditional learning institutions and at big enterprises. This is mainly due to the costs per trainee of developing the information structure with the specificities and particularities of each small and medium enterprise.

2.1 E-learning in higher education

In more traditional education environments, like higher education institutions, e-learning frameworks have been in use for decades. Most of the e-learning platforms available have the ability of presenting information in terms of single lectures or courses.

According to (Lokken, Womer, & Mullins, 2008), the most used e-learning frameworks in the US in 2007 were Blackboard, Angel and Moodle.

Blackboard (Blackboard Inc., 2011) is a commercial e-learning solution, featuring options for almost all requirements in teaching. Course materials, work deliveries and discussion forums and amongst the most used features.

Angel was acquired by Blackboard in May 2009, so its features became an integrant part of the Blackboard's core.

Moodle (Moodle Trust, 2011) is an open source Learning Management System, that has been gaining momentum and supporters throughout the academic community. Again course materials, work deliveries and discussion forums are amongst the most used features.

In (Thibault, 2011) authors compare both e-learning platforms. Two of the most widely used Learning Management Systems are almost identical in terms of functionality (roughly 95%). The author states that with added plugins and extensions, it is possible to obtain 100% coverage of site's functionality.

2.2 On-job training – Final thoughts

Considering our scenario: teach users how to use a specific application, besides the approach of (Borchardt & Grap, 2010), no other approach seemed to benefit the teaching of SIPP's functionalities. Therefore, we started developing a model where users could not only practice, but also learn to use the system. This will be discussed in later sections.

3. SIPP overview

SIPP is a web-based information system, developed to support the digital workflow of law case files in the Courts of Cape Verde. With this system, the different may interact with the case files.

SIPP's users are the Court's administrative staff, Judges, District Attorneys, Lawyers, the Court's Presidents and Members of the Supreme Councils.

SIPP is an N-tier system, composed, in fact by two distinct applications: a web-based application and a service-oriented workflow engine. Figure 1 outlines SIPP's architecture.

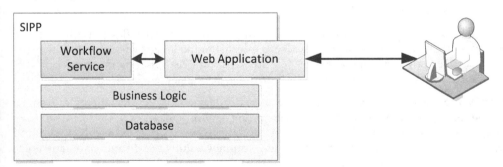

Fig. 1. SIPP Overview

Each user will access the application and expects to be able to execute the same tasks as it would on Court. This means that access to sensitive information within the case files must be handled with care: each user cannot access more data that it would on the paper case files.

3.1 Database and business logic

The database layer consists of a high availability SQL Server cluster. This cluster holds database records and stored procedures for better query performance on complex queries.

The business logic consists of a set of classes and transformations for simpler queries and for regular CRUD (Create, Retrieve, Update and Delete) operations. Enhanced retrieve operations (information of related objects, complex cross table queries, etc.) is also handled on the business logic layer. All database handling is processed by this layer. This enables a one point entry for audit and log tracking of operations. Also, security enforcement mechanisms are in place at this layer, to prevent erroneous or misbehaved application or user access.

3.2 Workflow service

The workflow service is deployed on an application cluster, enabling high availability of the service. The service is built upon Microsoft.Net Workflow Foundation (Zhu, 2010). Service communication is built upon Windows Communication Framework (Resnick, Crane, & Bowen, 2008).

To orchestrate and manage the information flow from the handling of case files, we decided to use a workflow engine. This seemed like a natural step towards the dematerialization of the case files. Workflow engines are capable of handling long running processes. In this particular case, a single process may stretch for several years, depending on its complexity and number of appeals. One other feature that we intended to explore using workflow engines was the dynamic update of a given workflow. When referring to laws and systems that must adhere to the strict regulation of laws, if significant changes in the law are made, then systems must be updated. However, the updating method must consider the specificities of running processes and how these should be treated: in some cases, the new laws will only apply to new case files, in other cases the new laws will apply to all new case files and to some (or all) running process. The use of a workflow service enables us to handle these specificities and more.

SIPP's workflow service is based on several smaller services and workflows, as illustrated in Figure 2. Most of the workflows in place are internal to the service, meaning that they are only available for communication with other workflows. The main entry point of communication with the overall workflow service is the Versioning Service.

Versioning Service – This workflow handles document edition. Documents are edited online, using the web application. The versioning service handles any kind of data, from simple document edition to N-step forms. At any given time, users may save their work and resume it when needed. If required, they may continue editing the document on any given saved version (actual or older).

Request and Decision – This workflow handles the basic process of submitting the request (by any party in the case file) and decision of the request (usually by the judge of the case). Judges may also issue decisions with no pending request. This workflow is used on both cases. Workflow actions are triggered by the reception of completed documents from the versioning service. This workflow mimics most of the traditional (manual) information process. However, given the inability for computer systems to accurately understand textual documents and automatically extract meaningful information from it, we have added an extra step (when comparing with the traditional paper version) to the workflow: after the decision document is received, the administrative staff must extract the meaningful information from the document, "explaining" to the application what to do with the decision received earlier. Despite seeming as an additional and cumbersome task, it is vital for the correct functioning of the entire system. The top-level workflows (*Habeas Corpus*, Regular Process and Appeals) are triggered based on the information extracted by the administrative staff. The upside of this extra step is the ability to latter extract a series of reports and statistical information from the entire system, at no extra cost. Request and decision workflow consists mainly of three events: request received, decision received and explanation received. Each event is triggered by a different actor.

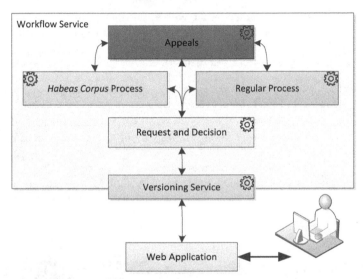

Fig. 2. Detailed view of the workflow service

Habeas Corpus **Service** – This workflow handles the entire process related with *Habeas Corpus* case files. It receives events triggered from the request and decision workflow and from the Appeals workflow.

Regular Process Service – This workflow handles the regular court case files, regardless of the process' complexity. Regular Court process case files are divided into four categories, depending on the nature of the crimes and the Judge's decision. It receives events triggered from the request and decision workflow and from the Appeals workflow.

Appeals Service – This workflow handles the case files on Higher Court instances. It receives events triggered from the request and decision workflow, from the Habeas Corpus and from the regular process workflows.

3.3 Web application

User-wise, the web application is the single point of interaction with the system. For security reasons, the communication between the workflow service and the web application is restricted to just that; users may not directly communicate with the workflows.

The web application enables users to access the system and work on their tasks and portfolio. In this scenario, portfolio refers to the active case files of a given user.

Workflow usage was kept to the minimum, meaning that only effective workflow-like tasks were to be deployed as workflow services. The remaining information access is done by reaching directly to the business logic layer. When triggered, the workflow layer processes information and permanently stores it in the database, through the business logic layer. Therefore, it is possible to assess all information by using the business logic layer. Besides giving a faster access to information, it lessens the load on the workflow engine, making it available to other requests.

1. Figure 3 presents the look and feel of the web application, with 8 areas marked:
2. User's location: enables the user to rapidly identify the currently working area;
3. Main menu: this area controls the top level sections available to each user. Depending on the user's roles, the available options may differ.
4. User's control panel: the area holds the user's identification and session termination options. It also enables the access to the user's control panel, where he may edit personal information.
5. Portfolio case file holder: this section lists the user related court file process in progress.
6. Court file process information: the information about any given process is organized in tabs, for easier reading.
7. Case file tasks: lists all pending tasks related to a given process.
8. Pending actions: lists all on-going user tasks related to a given process. These are organized by vertical tabs. On-going tasks are usually related to versioning documents and decision processes.
9. System and page loading information.

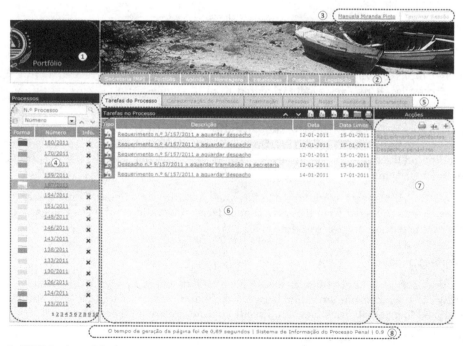

Fig. 3. SIPP look and feel

As mentioned, the process of detailing or dissecting the information within a decision was called a "Decision explanation". In this stage, the user (usually an administrative Court staff member) must extract meaningful information to feed the system. This means that for each type of considered meaningful information there is an explanation form associated. Figure 4 presents the explaining form of a final sentence on a case file. In this case, the accused was found guilty as charged and condemned.

In Figure 4 this information as already submitted by the user. The next step is to fill out the information related to the Crimes (on which was the user found guilty on which was he found not guilty) (1), the main sentence (2) with information on days in prison, fine amount, etc., accessory sentences (3) as inhibition to drive, and finally, information regarding civil damages (4).

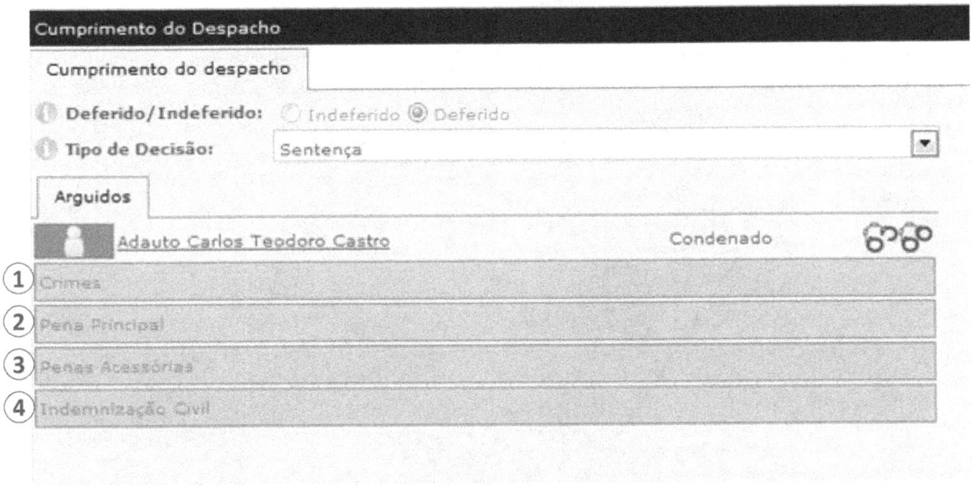

Fig. 4. Decision explanation

4. Demographics and regional concerns

Cape Verde is an archipelago of 10 islands that cover around 4,000 square kilometres of ground. Across these islands, there are 16 regular Courts and 3 higher instance Courts, where this application must be available, and with which the District Attorneys, Judges and Court staff must be at ease. These 16 regular Courts are unevenly divided, with most of the islands with just one Court, consisting of less than 10 users per Court.

Communications wise, the government sponsors a public network, available for all the country's public services, Courts included. Figure 5 depicts such network. All communications converge to the main island, Santiago. Most of the national online services are based on Santiago and, more importantly, it is through Santiago that all International network traffic flows. Inter-island communication links are usually saturated at about 95%, during working hours. Despite this obstacle, regular internet communication is feasible from almost every public office, thanks to strong cache mechanisms and quality of service rules imposed by the network administrators.

Along with the heavily packed inter-island network, one other technical difficulty usually arises: power outage. Given its archipelago nature, each island must be able to produce its own electricity. From time to time, due to generator problems, excessive demand and other reasons, an island region is left in the dark. With no electricity there is no communications and therefore, no web services. This holds true not only for the physical location (Court, lawyer's office, etc.), but for power outages along the network routing to the datacentre. This means that, depending on the outage location, a region or the entire country may unable to access any given web service.

These conditions mean that any given online system deployed in these conditions, to be considered "environmentally full proof", must be able to support off-site processing. In this case, the option was to go back paper trail and later proceed with the digitization of the record produced during the inaccessibility period.

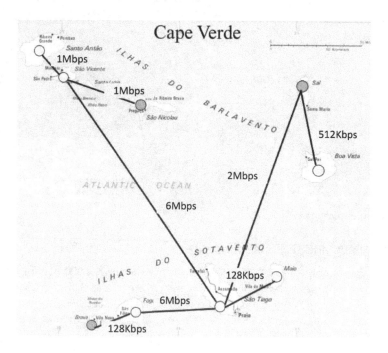

Fig. 5. National network for public services (Monteiro, S., & Teixeira, 2010)

Adding to these tough conditions, the familiarity of the court's staff with computer systems is below the desirable level. Most of them have, in fact, a computer standing in their desks. And most do use them for work tasks (and received training to do it). However, the regular usage usually involves repetitive tasks, consisting on text edition and printing. Given the overload of case files per Court, staff usually does not have the on-job time (or at ease) to pursue on practicing, discovering and learning additional features.

5. Assisted on-job training using SIPP

Considering the concerns that were raised on the previous section, we had to devise a way to overcome the staff related problems and to mitigate the impact of the infrastructural problems. As mentioned, the infrastructure problems were mitigated by enabling users to post-process documents.

The staff related problems, however, posed a new set of challenges. How could we guarantee a satisfactory level of basic computer skills to all Court staff, Judges and District Attorneys? How could we teach them to use a new application, with minimal downtime of the Court's service? Considering the different social stratus amongst the Court staff, how could we ensure a teaching service where each person would feel comfortable to reach out and express his difficulties, without being judged by others?

To ensure a satisfactory level of computer skills, the University of Cape Verde was put in charge of an ambitious program of teaching all Courts' administrative staff on basic computer skills. These sessions were conducted in several islands, giving the opportunity to the staff to refresh or learn basic computer skills, as scanning, text processing, spread sheet processing and web browsing.

5.1 Human assisted on-job training

Following this learning program, users apprehended most of the skills required to the next level: SIPP specific training. Considering the responsibilities of each person and the available features for each role, we were required to perform different learning sessions, covering the different features assigned to the different roles.

When the first prototype was deployed, still on early testing phase, we started the training of the users and the validation of the prototype concept. After each round of testing and training, we delivered to the development team a set of results and opinions of the users about the system. This way, we could try to improve the perceived usability of the system to the next round. The first rounds, until the interface concept was considered stabilized by the users, were done with the same participants. This way they could better understand the impact of their opinions in the system.

As mentioned, in most islands there is just on Court of law. In each Court, there are at least one Judge, one District Attorney and four administrative staff elements working every day. This meant that we would either move all personnel to common facilities during the SIPP training, or we would take the teaching team in a visit to all Courts. Due to the country's geography and considering the shear costs of transporting all the Court's personnel to a common location, the choice of having an itinerant teaching team prevailed. This team would perform one-to-one on-job sessions, with no need to close the Court to the public, since this would be done based on pre-set scheduling, adjusting regular tasks with this additional task.

This on-job, one-to-one teaching method, proved to be extremely effective. Trainees were at ease to pose any question they felt like, for more basic that it would seem to them. This could only be achieved in such personalized and private environment as the user's office or desk. This way, we could assess the effects of the basic skill learning program: based on the ease revealed during SIPP training and based on their technical questions.

SIPP's human assisted on-job training consisted of two separated phases: an overall user related explanation of features (done by the teacher) and a hands-on experience, where the teacher would observe and ask for the fulfilment of a set of given tasks. On every session, this was the stage where most of the time was spent. During the first iterations, teachers often had to assist users and walk them through the required task. The session was considered as terminated when users were able to execute a fair amount of tasks without the teacher's intervention. During the entire process, teachers would take notes referring to the user's interaction. These notes were then reported to the development team, for user interface refining.

Even before the first SIPP on-job training session, a new set of questions were raised. How will users keep their learnt skills? How often can we make this kind of intervention? The answer to the last question was easy: if possible, never again. Just one visit per Court was planned. Despite being cheaper than closing the Court for two or three days and moving everyone to different places, with the intrinsic costs on travel, accommodation and meals, this approach still has the cost of having the teaching teams on the field. To answer the first question, we deployed a testing web application, similar to the online system, where users could exercise what they had learnt and continue exploring the application. This testing application will still be available when SIPP enters production phase.

As always, this led us to a new question: How to assess and validate the users' training without human supervision?

5.2 Computer assisted on-job training

To answer the question raised in the last section, we developed a computer assisted on-job training agent, an inspector, that could overcome the lack of human supervising and, at the same time, reassure users about the outcome of their practice.

This inspector is bounded to the main workflows: Habeas Corpus Process, Regular Process and Appeals. To validate the information state of a given electronic case file, we partially adapted our unit test framework, so that we could validate on the fly the information being inserted (resulting of the decision's explanation) with the expected information.

Every time a decision is explained and an event on these workflows is triggered, this agent inspects the outcome of the explanation, and compares it to the expected outcome. In the event of mismatch, the agent triggers a new decision for that process, explaining to the user his mistake, and what to do to correct it. When the outcome of the explanation matches the expected outcome, the agent signals the main workflow to proceed the information processing.

Figure 6 shows the overhead processing in the workflow engine to support the computer assisted training. It represents a triggered event, the reception of the explained decision of

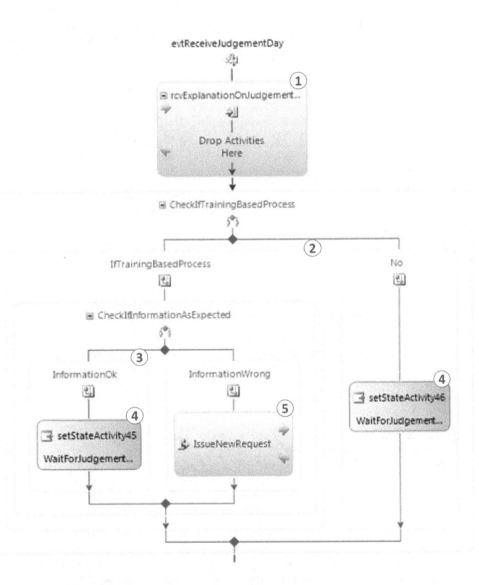

Fig. 6. Inspector bounded in the workflows

setting a judgement day for the case file (1). Upon reception, we check whether the process is a training case file or a regular case file (2). Being a training case file, we make a second check, to compare the information received with the expected information (in this case, this would be the time, date and place for the judgement, along with the defendant lawyer (if necessary) (3). If everything is as expected, or if this process is not a training case file, then the inspector allows the workflow to continue (4). Otherwise, it will not allow the workflow to continue and will issue a new request/decision, stating what was wrong and how to correct it (5).

5.3 Case file generator

The final piece for this puzzle was a case file generator, where we could define training session parameters, like the number of case files to open, the case file state (according to the main workflows), the initial process information and a set of requests and/or decisions (depending on the user's role) for users to process.

We developed a model-based random text generator that would open case files, submit requests and decisions and, most importantly, record the expected outcome of the request or decision.

Pending user's action, the inspector agent compares both data and decides whether to allow the workflow's execution or not.

This case file generator is used during all training phases (teacher assisted and computer assisted). This way, users were already familiarized with the generator's way of producing textual requests and decisions when they started using the computer assisted on-job training application.

The case file generator was inspired on our internal testing mechanisms. Besides single unitary tests, we also need to test the workflow as a hole. However, it is impossible to test the same case file with all the options available at the workflow. To handle this challenge, we developed a testing tool that simulates the web application, communicating directly with the Business Layer and with the Workflow Service.

The test tool would issue new case files, inquire on the available state options to trigger and selectively choose one event to trigger. Testing would continue until the case file was terminated. The test tool was preloaded with a set of rules and conditions to guarantee that we had covered nearly all options within the workflows. These rules and conditions could be in the form of probabilistic influence (when in state X give an $N\%$ probability to event Z) or the form of closed pathways (when in state X, proceed with event Z).

The test tool also served another important aspect: assessing the overall system performance. Since the testing tool, workflow service and database were detached modules, these could be executed from different computers. This way, we could test the limitations of our approach and proceed accordingly, early on the development phase.

5.4 Case file planner

Along with the case file generator, we developed the case file planner. After the case file generator publishes a new process, for every process state change triggered, the case file planner inspects the current process execution phase and acts accordingly, impersonating the remaining parties of case file. It is up to the case file planner to devise the actual traversed workflow for any given process.

As with the case file generator, the planner was also inspired by our internal testing mechanisms.

More than simply generating random case files using pre-defined situations and models, we needed users to experiment the full length of the process, according to their responsibilities. This way, users could help us assess the validity of each workflow and propose modifications, if required.

A simple path for a case file would be, for example: 1) when the judgement day is marked, issue a new witness request; and, 2) on the judgement day, issue the final judgement act, with the final decision about the accused party. As with the testing tool, probabilistic pathways could also be defined, providing a wider range of training options, with the same amount of supervision preparation.

Each request/decision issued will then be validated by the inspector agent previously presented.

The case file planner is an iterative agent that prepares tasks according with user's expertise on the system. To do that, it needs to understand the user's evolution so, as in a computer game, it ranks users' achievements. This way, it may plan more complex case file paths to more experienced users and more simple tasks to users starting their training or struggling with the system.

The user interaction is recorded jointly by the planner and the enforcer, allowing the supervising team to personally compare the expected outcome with the actual outcome produced by the user. This additional debugging feature

6. Conclusion

When we started this process, users were apprehensive about what to expect as an outcome. This was the third attempt that the government had made to implement such a system and users who had participated on previous attempts were reluctant to start yet another project. The project's initial risk was in fact high. The fear factor associated to a new system combined with the perception of a possible "Big Brother", working for the Ministry of Justice and against the Justice personnel, were more than enough to put us in an uncomfortable starting position.

We managed to get around the user's initial misbeliefs by presenting them the advantages (and disadvantages) of such system. These presentations have shown us that people were eager to use an electronic system to support their work, as long as the infrastructural and technological problems were solved and the security and privacy concerns could be verified at all times.

The development process included elements of each perceived role in the Court. This benefited the overall result, since these members were the first to see the developments, to comment and propose new directions on what they felt was incorrect. More importantly, they would comment with their colleagues on the developments of the system and on the possibilities that the system already possessed. This information dissemination generated a positive expectation wave along the users. This was indeed observed when the general testing and training phase started.

Throughout the training process, we realized that some users were still struggling with basic computer skills. To help them overcome this situation, a new computer course was proposed, more specific and focused on the user's difficulties.

We produced printed and electronic versions of the system's manual, adapted to each user's roles. Along with this help, we pursued on a one-on-one on-job teaching methodology. With this approach, users were more collaborative than on initial group sessions. Moreover, they would feel comfortable enough to pose questions relating both SIPP and general computer subjects.

In this chapter we presented SIPP and explained in detail the workflow architecture used to deploy the on-job assisted learning process. The on-job assisted training was performed on two separated phases: one-on-one human assisted training and computer assisted training. The first phase helped users understand the insights and working mechanisms required by the SIPP. The second phase helped users gain confidence about their autonomy and ability to use the system.

To give users the proper feedback, even on the second training phase, we developed an inspector agent. This agent had the responsibility to assess user's submitted information and instruct the main workflows on the outcome of such information. In the event of erroneous information submitted, the agent would also issue a new request/decision, impersonating the requestor/judge of the case file. With such feedback, users were reinsured that the training would produce the desired results.

The case file planner enabled us to understand where some unforeseen problems were. When several users struggle to perform a planned task or work plan, the planner informs the management team to further investigate on the roots of the problem. It may be an interface deficiency, a programming bug or a modelling fault.

The training application inherited most of the features we had in place internally for testing purposes. This way, the training application was relatively cheap, since it consisted of refactoring the test framework and deploying a series of agents, for inspecting and for producing test information.

Trainees found that this training application was helpful to understand the several available options faster and without worries of destroying real life work due to incorrect system operation. The project managers, however, found that most of the trainees (Court staff) lacked on sufficient computer usage knowledge. This was an important assessment that triggered an initial course on computer usage for all Court staff, prior to launching this application.

The initial goal for this project was met: deploy an on-job assisted learning application, with the same look and feel of the "real" application, where users could try all the application's features without worries of doing things wrong.

After the initial training, we monitored user's activity in the system, and realized that users were in fact using and testing the system on their own. Some users were just exploring the SIPP's features, while other were in fact doing their homework, working on the case files generated for training purposes. Despite being on-job training, some users were actually accessing the system from their homes, since the system is available online.

However, the amount of users actively using the system after the initial training started to decay around two weeks after the one-on-one training. Despite being a relatively normal situation, since users cannot neglect their regular tasks, it is far from the desired usage patterns. With low usage patterns, users tend to forget, at least partially what they had already learnt about the system. We expect that with the paced adoption of the system on all Courts during the next months, users will find time to refresh their SIPP's knowledge.

7. References

Abel, F., Bittencourt, I. I., Costa, E., Henze, N., Krause, D., & Vassileva, J. (2010). Recommendations in Online Discussion Forums for E-Learning Systems. *Ieee Transactions on Learning Technologies, 3*(2), 165-176. doi: 10.1109/Tlt.2009.40

AlAli, S. (1997). An assessment of on-job training programmes in Kuwait. *International Journal of Educational Development, 17*(1), 83-90.

Angelaccio, M., & Buttarazzi, B. (2010). A Social Network Based- Enhanced Learning System. *19th Ieee International Workshops on Enabling Technologies: Infrastructure for Collaborative Enterprises (Wetice 2010)*, 94-95. doi: 10.1109/Wetice.2010.59

Bahreininejad, A., & Yaghmaie, M. (2011). A context-aware adaptive learning system using agents. *Expert Systems with Applications, 38*(4), 3280-3286. doi: 10.1016/j.eswa.2010.08.113

Blackboard Inc. (2011). Blackboard - Home Retrieved 30th of June, 2011, from http://www.blackboard.com/

Borchardt, U., & Grap, F. (2010). E-Learning Application Support for SME. *Perspectives in Business Informatics Research, 64*, 62-72.

Georgellis, Y., & Lange, T. (2007). Participation in continuous, on-the-job training and the impact on job satisfaction: longitudinal evidence from the German labour market. *International Journal of Human Resource Management, 18*(6), 969-985. doi: 10.1080/09585190701321112

Lokken, F., Womer, L., & Mullins, C. (2008). Tracking the Impact of E-Learning at Community Colleges, 2007 Distance Education Survey Results: Instructional Technology Council.

Monteiro, A., S., P. J., & Teixeira, C. (2010). *E-government services in scarce bandwidth locations.* Paper presented at the CENTERIS 2010 - Conference on Enterprise Information Systems Viana do Castelo, Portugal.

Moodle Trust. (2011). Moodle.org: open-source community-based tools for learning Retrieved 30th of June, 2011, from http://moodle.org/

Resnick, S., Crane, R., & Bowen, C. (2008). *Essential Windows Communication Foundation (WCF): For .NET Framework 3.5* (1st ed.): Addison Wesley.

Schultz, T. W. (1961). Investment in Human-Capital. *American Economic Review, 51*(1-2), 1-17.

Thibault, J. (2011). #Blackboard 9 vs #Moodle 2.0: A Head to Head Comparison Retrieved 30th of June, 2011, from http://www.lmswatch.com/2011/blackboard-9-vs-moodle-2-0-a-head-to-head-comparison/

Wu, H. J., & Huang, S. C. (2007). A dynamic e-learning system for the collaborative business environment. *7th IEEE International Conference on Advanced Learning Technologies, Proceedings*, 46-50.

Yu, Z. W., Zhou, X. S., & Shu, L. (2010). Towards a semantic infrastructure for context-aware e-learning. *Multimedia Tools and Applications, 47*(1), 71-86. doi: 10.1007/s11042-009-0407-4

Zhu, A. (2010). *Microsoft Windows Workflow Foundation 4.0 Cookbook* (1st ed.): Packt Publishing

4

Self-Directed Learning Readiness Factors in Physicians for Implementing E-Learning in the Continuing Medical Education Programs

Tahereh Eslaminejad[1] and Nouzar Nakhaee[2]

[1]*Educational Development Center (EDC), Kerman University of Medical Sciences, Kerman Medical University (KMU),*
[2]*Neuroscience Research Center, Kerman University of Medical Sciences, Kerman, Iran*

1. Introduction

The implementation of e-learning as part and parcel of the delivery mechanism for training and education requires tremendous amount of investment on the part of an organization or institution. However, in this highly-computerized age, learning needs are dynamic and e-learning is one of the many responses to the society's thirst for efficient, effective and appealing strategy for delivering information and knowledge. As a result, e-learning opens new ways of teaching and learning, leading to new methods of thinking and organizing learning content (Askar & Halici, 2004). One of the natural settings for e-learning is in the area of continuing education. In considering a large number of the adults as learners in an e-learning setting or in any traditional classroom for that matter, it is necessary to plan the needs of the employee, the educator and the organization involve in the learning process. Goldstein and Ford (2001) argued that more organizations are progressively considering continuous learning as an important factor in maintaining their competitive advantage. Borotis and Poulymenakou (2004) believed that e-learning initiatives can be considered as the proper solution for delivering continuing educational programs at a lower cost with ubiquitous offering of a wide range of information and knowledge that are different from the traditional approach. Also Hall (2001) posed that e-learning can be an effective method of learning for adults who have busy schedules or live in remote areas, and unable to attend an everyday traditional classrooms. This innovation allows the learners to learn at their own pace, saving time and money, and they can pursue continuing education on computers in the workplace or in the home (Randell, 2001).

In the area of Andragogy, it is argued that adult learners need to know why they have to learn something before undertaking it. At the same time, they are motivated to learn only to the extent that they perceive the knowledge will help them perform tasks they confront in their life situations (Knowles, 1987). Since the learners are ready and willing to take the responsibility for their own learning, the participants' learning style is a factor that may affect learner readiness for e-learning process. Rosenberg (2001) argues that willingness to learn and motivation for successful training and learning are very important and suggests that creating the right incentives can encourage participation. Sound time management is another important factor that should be considered imperative for effective e-learning, Frankola (2001) states if participants do not have time or motivation and willingness to take the given time off for learning, e-learning will not succeed.   Knox (1986) delineates several characteristics of adult learners in four categories: enhancing proficiencies, development and learning, influences on participation, and the importance of active learner participation that can enable educators to plan and organize learning activities around adults' background and aspirations. In addition Rogers (1986) identifies four characteristics of this adult natural learning process and pointed out that, in pursuing self-directed learning, each adult adopts one own learning style and a range of strategies employed is typical of adults than by other group of learners. He increased, since self-directed learning is directed toward specific goals, adult learning tends to focus on how to cope with the particular situation rather than the general principles. Thus, one of the characteristics of the individual that allied itself to the benefits and success of online learning is self-directed or autonomy in learning. Self-directedness involves the learners taking the initiative to identify their own learning needs and goals, selecting and using the learning strategies that work best for those needs and is able to use basic skills, organize time, and develop a plan for completing work given to them. A self-directed learner is responsible for development of her/his learning skills and deciding when and how she/he going to learn. The benefits of self-directed learning include having a greater control over learning and an increase in self-concept, motivation, and sense of self-control, since the learners are expected to function without an instructor (Knowels, 1975). Most literature (for example, Bernard et al., 2000; Chen & Lin, 2002; Clark & Mayer, 2002; Urdan & Weggen, 2000) concurs with Guglielmino (2003) in considering learners as an important factor in e-learning readiness.

Self-directed learning (SDL) is related to independence or autonomy in learning; it is a logical link for readiness for e-learning. A self directed learner accepts responsibility for own learning and view problems as challenges and not obstacles (Guglielmino, 1977). Self-direction in learning refers to two distinct but related dimensions. The first of these dimensions is a process in which a learner assumes primary responsibility for planning, implementing, and evaluating the learning process. The second dimension refers to as learner self-direction, centers on a learner's desire or preference for assuming responsibility for learning. Therefore, self-direction in learning refers to both the external characteristics of an instructional process and the internal characteristics of the learner, where the individual assumes primary responsibility for a learning experience (Brockett & Hiemstra, 1991). In this study based on the ongoing works on self-directed learning readiness for SDL investigate four categories involves self knowledge, attitudes, skills, and habits as self-directed learners.

1.1 Self-directed knowledge

Self-knowledge is a philosophical concept of self awareness person, understanding him or herself. It is also commonly referred to knowledge of one's particular mental states, including one's beliefs, desires, and sensations. The learners with self directed knowledge have the ability to be aware of "self." This attribute is closely related to some of the executive processes identified with metacognition. It enables learners to be aware of their learning processes, of their weaknesses and strengths, to know if they can call up additional powers of concentration,

Self-Directed Learning Readiness Factors in Physicians for Implementing E-Learning in the Continuing
Medical Education Programs

53

to know of their ability to use a different approach, to know how and what is distracting in their environment, to know the importance of a given learning activity, to know when they need assistance, to have a realistic perception of their ability to achieve their learning goal. Self directed knowledge can be accomplished through reflection and usually self directed learning enhance by knowledge of one's preferred learning style (Guglielmino, 2003).

1.2 Self-directed attitude

Several studies have suggested that attitudes may be an important element in teaching computers (Woodrow, 1991). Todman & Dick (1993) for example, suggested that the teacher's attitude towards computers may have an effect on the quality of experience a child has with computers in the school. Many researchers reported that children like computers and are positively motivated to use them (Shade, 1994).

A review of the literature on attitudes toward computers by Lawton and Gerschner (1982) showed that children found computers to have infinite patience, never to get tired, never to forget to correct or praise, to be impartial to ethnicity and gender, and to be great motivators. In the same review, it was shown that students liked computers because they were self-paced, gave immediate feedback, and did not embarrass them when they made mistakes. The early studies found that negative attitudes and fears about computers were exhibited mostly by teachers, not children, thus general teacher attitude plays an important role in the educational process (Muller, Husband, Christou, & Sun 1991). Mason and Weller (2000) found that children do not see computer technology as a science but as a tool to be used in everyday life. The learners who have self directed attitudes usually have characteristics such as able to make decision and doing it successfully, to have positive thoughts about their potential for success in their plans, are independent learning, prefer to work alone, go to new activities, to reach new levels of performance, and learning online, are open mind, and try to learn anything they need.

1.3 Self-directed skills

The fundamental skills are needed for effective self-directed learning. Guglielmino (2003) state a self directed learner usually is skilled at identifying and analyzing its learning needs. The individual has a moderate allocation of the identified personality attributes and the skills appear to be particularly important in successful self-directed learning. They also may have limited observational skills that inhibit their ability to determine what is important in their learning environment. Therefore, some effort is often required to develop these skills before a person becomes a successful self-directed learner. Thus, when working with people with little experience in self-directed learning, careful attention should be given to helping them to imagine possible outcomes of results of their learning, and then encouraging them know how and why to choose from among multiple desirable goals (Long, 2006). Gugilielmo (1977) cited in Griffin (1989) has developed a self-directed learning readiness scale, she considered factors such as openness to learning opportunities, self-concept in an effective learner, initiative and independence in learning, informed acceptance of responsibility, love of learning, creativity, future orientation, and ability to use basic study skills and problem-solving skills. Some skills related to meeting learning needs include the using learning methods, making decision for effective learning new skills, able to engage in divergent thinking, writing skills, reading skills, using online tool for working with others, able to collecting require data from various sources, to able organize, analyze, and evaluate data for answering to question, set goals, effectively planning for activities, and translate learning needs into learning goals.

1.4 Self-directed Habits

The positive habits are very important in use of various technologies that used for e-learning and their development can be streamline and anchor the effective e-learning. Guglielmino (2003) posed that one of the most important habits on self directed learning is persistence; it is emphasizing on doing a work or reach a goal. Also the reflective individual and environmental scanning from own performances are worth emphasizing. Habits include such things as to be self-discipline, willingness try to search and know new idea, steadiness for completing works and own decisions, trying out how to find work problem, resistance and stability in analyzing material, and constantly expressing thoughts and idea to writing.

This paper attempts to identify the various concepts related to self-directed learning and also the various components of the doctors' self directed learning readiness which influence the successful adoption of e-learning in the field of continuing medical education

2. Methodology

This descriptive study examines the self-directed learning (SDL) readiness for e-learning in the physicians who participate in CME programs in Iran.

The research questionnaire consist of statements regarding factors about self directed learning readiness for e-learning in four categories and was distributed to 461 medical doctors who participated in the CME programs. All items were measured on a five-point Likert scale, with 5 indicating "strongly agree" and 1 indicating "strongly disagree".

Factor analysis, correlations, and ANOVA were the main methods of data analysis. Factor analysis was conducted to extract major factors that influence the e-learning readiness with using Varimax rotation with Kaiser Normalisation. In the factor designation, individual loadings of 0.5 or greater were used to interpret the results and factors with Eigenvalues equal to or greater than one were extracted.

3. Findings and discussion

The analysis of this study was the identification of factors influencing the nedical doctors' self-directed learning readiness for e-learning. By Principal Component Factor Analysis (PCFA) extracted factors and labels are suggested for each of factors according to their statements.

There were four domains for the learner's self directed learning for e-learning readiness namely Knowledge, Attitude, skills, and habits. Each item in each domain contained relevant statement pertaining to e-learning readiness, followed by a five-point Likert scale ranging from "strongly disagree" to "strongly agree". The average mean of SDL readiness was 3.35±.43 with a maximum mean of 3.83 for SDL attitude readiness and SDL habits having the lowest mean of 2.79 as summarized in Table 1 Further analysis is given in the next section.

Most participants evaluated their SDL readiness moderate (38%). Thirty six percent assessed themselves as good and 10% excellent. Only 16% claimed they were weak and very weak. Regarding doctors' attitude, 71% of the respondents had positive attitude toward e-learning.

Self-Directed Learning Readiness Factors in Physicians for Implementing E-Learning in the Continuing
Medical Education Programs

55

Domains	Mean	SD
Knowledge	3.44	.60
Attitude	3.83	.35
Skill	3.35	.63
Habit	2.79	.43
Total	3.35	.43

Table 1. Mean and SD in learners' SDL readiness

The majority (87%) claimed that they prefer learning through independent project or research instead of structured assignment and 72% prefer to conduct research activities to reach new levels of performance or find new ways to learn anything. Doctors also said they believe that high quality learning can take place without having face to face interaction. For knowledge, skills, and habits of self directed learning most of doctors were in an intermediary range (between 2.79 and 3.44). Only 8% reported that they had no adequate knowledge and less than 20% are not well skilled in self directed learning.

Concerning identifying factors that influence self directed learning readiness in learners, in this study Exploratory PCFA process on the knowledge domain extracted factors in self need assessment; components included diagnosing their learning needs, formulating learning goals, identifying human and material resources for learning, choosing and implementing appropriate learning strategies, and evaluating learning outcomes. Having knowledge to guide and direct their own learning, enable learners to control their own processes of learning making their learning more effective. Being familiar with self directed learning principles are important components in self need assessment. It may reduce the number of misunderstandings, lead to a deeper understanding of the subject or domain in question, and may further integrate new knowledge on the basis of their previous understanding. Knowles (1987) pointed out; clinicians in SDL first identify a clinical problem, then pursue the learning task, next acquire the new knowledge or skill, and finally practice the new knowledge or skill. Also in SDL attitude, respondents emphasized on factors such as comfortable with independent study, innovation in learning and comfortable with relevant and applicable subjects. These findings are also supported by other studies. Knowles (1975) argued there is convincing evidence that people who take the initiative in learning (proactive learners) learn more things, and learn better, than do people who sit at the feet of teachers passively waiting to be taught (reactive learners), because they enter into learning more purposeful and with greater motivation. This is because they retain and make use of what they learn better and longer than do the reactive learners. Further he claimed that learning is maximized when it is self-directed, because learners study material that is most relevant to them.

The analysis of the readiness factors in SDL skills domain, brought up by the respondents was ability to self evaluate and self develop. Adult learning theory posits that adult learners can identify their learning needs, find solutions to problems, base learning on experience, and self-direct their education. Knowles (1987) also stated an essential aspect of self maturing is developing the ability; it is increasing responsibility for their own lives - to become increasingly self-directed. Shin and Haynes (1993) also demonstrated that learning behaviors taught during medical school will have an effect on practice; therefore, medical educators should emphasize self-directed learning skills during residency training.

In the area of SDL habits, learner identified two important factors that included: self discipline and to self motivate learning. These factors contain components such as self discipline, motivation to try and search for new idea, steadiness for completing projects and expect to succeed in own decisions, try to find work problem and constantly express thoughts and idea to writing, accustomed to search for new idea, techniques, equipments, and programs, assess performance and initiate learning. Regarding the importance of positive habits on SDL, Guglielmino (2003) posits one of the most significant habits on SDL is persistence, it emphasized doing work to reach a goal.

Some research regarding enhancing learning in SDL emphasized that skills and habits play a critical role in learners' success. For example Sparling and Lewis (2001) stated that students need to be able to ignore distractions, and concentrate on their work. In addition, learners may need to use your basic academic proficiencies, such as skimming for information and then reading the important portions more carefully because reading a textbook is quite different from reading a newspaper.

To be self-disciplined and self motivate are critical factors in online programs, since in an online class, there is no instructor standing to monitor progress. If learners are not a self-disciplined person, it might be very difficult to have an efficient and effective e-learning process. It is often really difficult to make up for lost time. Online learners particularly doctors need to rely on their own problem solving abilities. They must know what resources are available to assist them, for instance, online help, tutorials, or telephone hot-lines. In this regards Wolfgang and Dowling (1981), and Kuh and Cracraft (1986) found that self motivation in nontraditional learner is one of the most significant factors which foster the personal growth and influence academic achievement. Therefore learners who have the ability of self motivation and are self discipline, identify their learning needs and also find solutions for problems, support their learning on experience and practice and finally direct their education. In this regard, doctors use problem-based learning, because their patients become the impetus for their learning experience and clinical practice. These characteristics will prepare them to be ready for e-learning and learner's readiness is one of the most important factors for having an efficient and effective e-learning process. The summary of the findings related to extracted factors on learners is presented in Table 2.

Domain Category	SDL Readiness Factors
Knowledge	- Familiar with self need assessment
Attitudes	- Comfortable with innovation in learning
	- Comfortable with self development
	- Comfortable with independent study
Skills	- Ability to use online learning
	- Ability to self develop
Habits	- Accustomed to be serious and critical learning
	- Get used to be Initiate own learning
	- Accustomed to be performance evaluation

Table 2. Factors extracted by Category in SDL readiness domain on learner with Interpretative Labels

4. Conclusion

Self directed learning (SDL) readiness domain as one of the critical characteristics of online learning is that learners can control the pace of their own learning. The most important

Self-Directed Learning Readiness Factors in Physicians for Implementing E-Learning in the Continuing
Medical Education Programs

57

factors that learners identified in this domain were; familiarity with learning need assessment, comfortableness with independent study, innovativeness in learning, the relevant and applicable subjects, self evaluation ability, self development ability, self discipline in learning, and so accustomed to be self motivation in habits domain. Concerning self-directed learning is an important aspect in the adult lifelong learning. Thus, university of medicine turn toward the implementation of e-learning for the training of doctors are needed a particular model to assess and identify factors that influencing on self directed learning readiness to improve them because the self-directed adults will learn more, learn better, retain, and make better of learning than do reactive learners and so have more power in creating their own path in the journey of continuous learning throughout their life.

5. Acknowledgments

We thank the physicians in Kerman Iran, who participated in this study, and all our colleagues in university of medical sciences in Kerman, Iran, who helped us particularly Associate Professor Dr. Ali Akbar Haghdoost for their expert statistical advices.

6. References

Askar P., & Halici U., (2004) E-learning as a catalyst for educational innovation, In C. Ghaoui (Ed). E-education applications: Human factors and Innovative Approaches. IGP publishing, USA

Bernard, R. M., Rojo de Rubalcava, B., & St-Pierre, D. (2000). Collaborative online distance learning: Issues for future practice and research, Distance Education. 21(2), 260-277. Retrieved May 31, 2007, from http://clp.cqu.edu.au/offline_articles_A-K.htm

Brockett, R.G., and Hiemstra, R. (1991). Self-Direction in Adult Learning: Perspectives on Theory, Research, and Practice. London and New York: Routledge & Kegan Paul.

Borotis, S. Ap. & Poulymenakou, A. (2004). E-Learning readiness components: key issues to consider before adopting e-Learning interventions. Paper presented at the World Conference on E-Learning in Corporate 2004, Washington, DC, pp. 1622-1629. Retrieved November 2, 2005, from
http://www.eltrun.gr/papers/eLReadiness_ELEARN2004.pdf

Chen, N. s. & Lin, K. M. (2000). Factors affecting e-learning for achievement. [Electronic Version] from, http://lttf.ieee.org/icalt2002/proceedings/t502_icalt148_End.pdf

Clark, R. C., & Mayer, R. E. (2003). e-Learning and the science of instruction: Proven guidelines for customers, & and designers of multimedia learning, S. F., CA: Pfeiffer

Frankola, V. (2001). Why online learners drop out. Workforce, 80(10), 52-60. Journal of Education for Teaching. 4(2), 183-191. Retrieved June 15, 2001, from
http://www.workforce.com/feature/00/07/29

Guglielmino, L. M. (1977). Development of the self-directed learning readiness scale (Doctoral dissertation, University of Georgia, 1977). Dissertation Abstracts International, 38, 6467A.

Guglielmino, P. J. & Guglielmino, L. M. (2001). Learner characteristics affecting in electronic distance learning. In H. B. Long & Associates, 21st century Advances in Self-Direction Learning. Schaumberg, IL: Motorola University Press.

Guglielmino, P. J. & Guglielmino, L. M. (2003). Are your learners ready for e-learning? In G. M. Piskurich (Ed.), The AMA handbook of e-learning: Effective design, implementation, and technology solutions, New York: AMACOM, 87-98.

Goldstein, I. L., & Ford, J.K. (2001). Training in organizations (4th ed.): Wadsworth Publishing.

Hall, B. (2001). E-Learning Guidebook. Six Steps to Implementing E-Learning. Retrieved Jan. 16, 2006, from http://www.brandonhall.com/public/forms/sixstepdb

Knox, A.B. (1980). Proficiency Theory of Adult Learning. Contemporary Educational Psychology. 378-404.

Knowles, M.S. (1975). Self-directed Learning. New York: Association Press.

Knowles, M.S. (1980). The Modern Practice of Adult Education: From Pedagogy to Andragogy. (2nd ed.) . New York: Cambridge Books.

Knowles, M. S. (1987). Adult learning, Training and Development Handbook. R. L. Craig (Ed.). New York: McGraw-Hill. Ch.9.

Kuh, G., & Cracraft, L. (1986). Predicting adult learners' success in higher education. In J. A. Lucas (Ed.), The Adult Learner: Four Aspects, AIR File 27. Tallahassee, FL: Florida State University, Association for Institutional Research.

Lawton, J., & Gerschner, V. T. (1982). A Review of the Literature on Attitudes toward Computers and Computerized Instruction. Journal of Research on Development of Education, 16, 50-55.

Long, H. B. (2006). SKILLS for SELF-DIRECTED LEARNING. Available from http://faculty-staff.ou.edu/L/Huey.B.Long-1/Articles/sd/selfdirected.html

Mason, R., & Weller, M. (2000). Factors affecting students' satisfaction on a web course. Australia Journal of Educational Technology, 16(2), 173-200

Mueller, R.O., Husband, O.H., Christou, C., Sun. A., 1991. Preservice Teacher Attitudes towards Computer Technology: A Log-Linear Analysis. Mid-West Educational Researcher Vol. 4,   2, P.23-27

Randell, D. (2001). E-learning for continuing education: exploring a new frontier electronic learning, http://findarticles.com/p/articles/mi_m3230/is_8_33/ai_78057546/pg_1

Rogers, A. (1986). Teaching Adults. Milton Kaynes, England: Open University Press.

Rosenberg, M. J. (2001) E-Learning: Strategies for building online learning in the digital age. New York: McGraw-Hill

Shade, D.D. (1994). Computers in early education: Issues put to rest, theoretical links to sound practice, and the potential contribution of microworlds. Journal of Educational Computing Research 6 (4): 375–92.

Shin JH. , Haynes RB. (1993).. Effect of problem-based, self-directed undergraduate education on life-long learning. CMAJ. 1993 Mar 15; 148(6):969–76. [PubMed]

Sparling, J., & Lewis, I. (2001). Learningames: The abecedarian curriculum, 12-24 months. Chapel Hill, NC: Early Learning, Inc

Todman, J., & Dick, G. (1993). Primary children and teachers' attitudes to computers. Computers and Education. 20, 199-203.

Urdan, T. A. & We ggen, C. C. (2000). Corporate E-learning: Exploring a New Frontier, Retrieved April 14, 2001, from http://www.wrhambrecht.com/research/coverage/elearning/ir/ir_explore.pdf

Wolfgang, M., & Dowling, W. (1981). Differences in motivation of adult and younger undergraduates. Journal of Higher Education, 52(6), 640-648.

Woodrow, J. (1991). Locus of control and computer attitudes as determinants of the computer literacy of student teachers. Computers and Education, Vol. 16, 237-245

5

Facts and Fiction:
Lessons from Research on Faculty
Motivators and Incentives to Teach Online

Ruth Gannon Cook

DePaul University School for New Learning
USA

1. Introduction

By 2012, most universities in the United States and some European universities have greatly augmented their online course offerings; those courses increasingly have been taught by adjunct (also called contingent or part-time) instructors. In view of the fact that it costs less for universities to hire adjunct instructors since they receive no benefits beyond a small salary per course, it would seem that faculty would be leaping at the opportunity to teach online and be recognized for their online contributions to offset this increased use of adjunct instructors. Indeed, according to a number of universities' chief academic officers, almost 50% of faculty accepted the value and legitimacy of online education (Allen and Seaman, 2008). Yet, almost ten years after the author's first research study on this subject (Gannon-Cook, 2003), the researcher found that faculty, both tenured and untenured, were still demurring from teaching online; she was stunned to discover that the rates of faculty teaching online remained low, particularly in the United States. During that same timeframe, ten years, there had been dramatic growth of students taking online courses (one in six students in the U.S. taking online courses as of 2006 [Pope, 2006, 1]). Data gathered from the researcher's university, as well as from a number of universities in the United States and Europe, indicated that faculty online participation percentages, despite growing numbers of online courses, averaged around twenty-five to twenty-eight percent (Ansah, and Johnson, 2003; Beggs, 2002: Bender, Wood, and Vredevoogd, 2004; Brabazon, 2001; Brookfield, 1995; Cavanaugh, 2005; Chang, 2008; Elaine and Seaman, 2006; Huffman and Miller & 2001; Jones and Johnson–Yale, 2005; Kosak, Manning, Dobson, Rogerson, Cotnam, Colaric, and McFadden, 2004;Lazarus, 2002; Lin, 2003; Maguire, 2002, 2006; Murphy, 2011; Offer, Barth, Lev, and Sheintok, 2003: O'Quinn and Corry, 2003; Paloff and Pratt, 2001; Zhen, Garthwait, & Pratt, 2008). So, a question remained that, if the numbers of online courses were burgeoning and almost 50% of faculty acknowledged the value and legitimacy of online education, why were so few of the faculty teaching online?

The scope of this study was to look at which factors could positively motivate faculty to teach online, and in particular, to look at whether the use of adjunct faculty in the universities offering online courses affected the motivation of faculty to teach (or not teach) online courses. This study looked at data collected from thirty-eight studies of U.S. and European universities (see Appendix A) and found that, while the primary motivators for faculty to teach online were intrinsic, such as the desire to make college education available to students who would not, otherwise, be able to attend college, and the desire to extend course flexibility (Betts, 1998; Bower, 2002; Bruner, 2007; Chen, 2008; Gannon-Cook, 2003; Gannon-Cook, Ley, Warner, & Crawford, 2009; Johnstone, 2000; Maguire, 2002, 2006; O'Quinn, 2003; Parker, 2003; Wolcott, 2002a,2002b, 2006, 2008; Zhen, Garthwait, & Pratt, 2008), other factors, such as increased workload for online teaching, lack of credit toward tenure and promotion, and lack of extrinsic motivators, such as stipends and course releases, deterred and demotivated as much as seventy-four percent of faculty from teaching online (Beggs, 2002; Betts, 2009; Betts, & Sikorski, 2008; Bower, 2002; Chen, 2008; Gannon-Cook, Ley, Warner, & Crawford, 2009; Johnstone, 2000; Lin, 2002; O'Quinn, 2003). Similar events were also occurring in countries, such as the "bric" countries of Brazil, Russia, India, and China, and, while some research from these countries were mentioned in this research, for the purposes of this study, none were included in the thirty-eight studies utilized herein. (Because it is estimated that the United States currently serves one-third of the world's students engaged in cross-border education (Hezel & Mitchell, 2006), the majority of this research were U. S. studies). Future studies of faculty motivators and the use of adjunct instructors in online courses within these countries can be conducted as the body of research continues to accumulate on this subject.

Findings and recommendations throughout the thirty-eight studies utilized in this research cited similar proposed remedies in order to persuade and support faculty to teach online, such as encouraging faculty voice and faculty participation in university policy, practice, online decisions, online course design and delivery, research credit towards tenure, and extrinsic motivations, such as course releases or monetary stipends. It was unclear, however, as to whether any of the recommendations from those studies were adopted by the administration of those universities (Beggs, 2002; Betts, 2009; Betts & Sikorski, 2008; Birch & Burnett, 2009; Bollinger & Wasilik, 2009; Bower, 2002; Gannon-Cook, 2003; McLean, 2006a,b;O'Quinn, 2003, 2004; O'Quinn, & Corry, 2002; Panda & Mishra, 2008; Quinn, Schifter, 2000a,b; Schifter, 2002; Soldner, Lee, Duby, 2004; Trower, 2008; Wolcott, 2006).

Another important research question that needed to be asked (and was asked in a number of the thirty-eight studies) was whether the universities that used large percentages of adjunct instructors for online courses found any significant differences in student retention rates in those courses. While the increased use of adjuncts was widely acknowledged, this factor was seldom mentioned as a factor in studies about faculty motivation (or demotivation) to teach online courses, so the opportunity to look at a number of studies addressing faculty motivation would provide some insights and inferences that could be made for how to best motivate faculty to teach online. Moreover, since much of the research has not focused on whether faculty teaching online brings higher student retention and completion rates than adjunct instructors, this factor is also addressed in this study.

If the research does document higher student retention with full-time faculty instructors as opposed to adjunct faculty instructors, as the studies utilized in this research seem to indicate (American Association of University Professors, 2003; Ansah & Johnson, 2003; Benjamin, 2002; Chapman, 2011; McArthur, 1999; Schibik & Harrington, 2004; Southern Area Southern Association of Colleges and Schools, 2010; Xenos, Pierrakaes, C., & Pintelas, 2002), then it might be productive to review the recommendations of those studies to see which factors would work best to best secure and retain full-time faculty to teach online courses.

What remains clear, regardless of the research, is that the universities offering online courses continue to grow rapidly and the use of increasing adjunct faculty to teach those courses also continues to dramatically increase. It would also follow that if there were particular factors that could be singled out to shed light on how to enlist and retain faculty to teach online courses, then it would be worth distilling the research and providing administrators with that data.

Definition of Terms

While the terms distance education, online learning, and electronic learning (elearning) have similar meanings, there may be subtle differences ascribed to each in other research, but for the purposes of this study, these terms will be used interchangeably.

2. Review of the literature

This study looked at thirty-eight studies to assess which factors could positively motivate faculty to teach online; the study also looked at whether the increased use of adjunct instructors motivated or deterred faculty from teaching online courses. The findings revealed that the primary reasons that motivated faculty to teach online were primarily based on intrinsic motivators, which should come as no surprise since most faculty enter academia motivated intrinsically to teach and help others. But later studies, after 2003, pointed to extrinsic motivators having more positive effects on influencing faculty to teach online courses.

In the studies of faculty motivation to teach online that were conducted in the early twenty-first century, it was found that the majority of faculty choosing to teach online were motivated for largely altruistic reasons, similar to the same reasons they chose to teach (Betts, 1998; Schifter, 2000 a, b; Johnston, Alexander, Conrad, & Fieser, 2000; Gannon-Cook, 2003; Maguire, 2002; Parker, 2003; Schifter, 2000a, b; Wolcott, 1996, 2002). Of these, the two intrinsic motivators most often identified by faculty in those studies were: "ability to reach new (student) audiences that could not attend classes on campus; and, greater course flexibility for students" (Gannon-Cook, p.137). In addition to these primary motivators, early adopters also enjoyed learning new technologies and having the opportunity for personal growth through the experience of teaching online (Betts, 1998; Bower, 2002; Bruner, 2007; Chen, 2008; Gannon-Cook, 2003; Gannon-Cook, Ley, Warner, & Crawford, 2009; Johnstone, 2000; Maguire, 2002, 2006; O'Quinn, 2003; Parker, 2003; Wolcott, 2002a, 2002b, 2006, 2008; Zhen, Garthwait, & Pratt, 2008).

While intrinsic motivators continued to prevail over the last ten years as the primary motivators, many of the early adopters no longer chose to teach online after a short length of time teaching online courses. The residual effects of early adoption often included faculty sharing their feedback with colleagues about their online experiences, their stories that told of many hours spent handling hundreds of emails, extra time spent answering emails, posting to discussion conferences, and helping students learn how to navigate online courses, all of which often deterred rather than encouraged other faculty to join their online teaching ranks (Betts, 1998; Bower, 2002; Johnston, Alexander, Conrad, & Fieser, 2000; O'Quinn, 2003; Southeast Missouri State University, 2001, Wolcott, 2002, 2006). For early adopters the added incentives included the opportunity to lead the cause of online teaching as role models, although, after heavy investments of time and energy teaching online, they often did not often remain teaching online, and in some cases, actually discouraged other faculty from teaching online (Bower, 2002; Chang, 2007; Culp, Riffee, Starrett, Sarin, & Abrahansen, 2001; Distance Education Report, 2001; Jacobsen, 2000; Jones, Johnson-Yale, 2005; Lazarus, 2003; Lin, 2002; Kosak, Manning, Dobson, Rogerson, Cotnam, Colaric, & McFadden, 2004;Maguire 2002; O'Quinn & Corey, 2002; Paloff & Pratt, 2001; Wolcott, 2002a; Zhen, Garthwait, & Pratt, 2008).

There were also other factors that were demotivating and deterred faculty from teaching online. In some cases teaching online actually posed real threats to faculty quests for tenure, factors such as the increased workload involved in online teaching, the lack of credit toward tenure and promotion for online teaching, and the lack of other incentives, such as raises, or course stipends. So, while administration in many universities touted as much as fifty percent of faculty being interested in teaching online, in truth, as much as seventy percent of faculty in the studies still declined to teach online (Beggs, 2002; Betts, & Sikorski, 2008; Bower, 2002; Chen, 2008; Gannon-Cook, Ley, Warner, & Crawford, 2009; Johnstone, 2000; Lin, 2002; Murphy, 2011; O'Quinn, 2003; Parker, 2003).

The recommendations throughout these studies repeatedly cited remedies to provide faculty with incentives to teach online that did not involve large investments of monies, such as the encouragement of faculty voice, the inclusion of faculty in university policy and practice decisions, and the awarding of online teaching credit towards tenure (Ansah, & Johnson, 2003); Betts, 1998; Betts, 2008; French, 2001; Gannon-Cook, Ley, Warner, & Crawford, 2009; Maguire, 2006; Schifter, 2000a,b, 2002; Soldner, Lee, Duby, 2004; Wolcott, 1996, 2002a,b; Zhen, Garthwait,& Pratt, 2008). The recommendations also included the awarding of extrinsic motivators that would incur increased administrative costs, such as course releases or monetary stipends, but could also prove to be a profitable investment if it resulted in higher student retention and online course completion rates (Betts & Sikorski, 2008; Betts, 2009; Bollinger & Wasilik, 2009; Johnston, Alexander, Conrad, & Fieser, 2000; Maguire, 2002, 2006; McLean,2006b; O'Quinn, 2002, 2003; Quinn, 2008; Parker, 2003; Wolcott, 2006, 2008; Zhen, Garthwait, & Pratt, 2008).

Some of the factors that received the largest number of responses from faculty in those thirty-eight studies were extrinsic, and those factors would provide distinct benefits to faculty teaching online courses. So, while intrinsic factors may have first inspired participation in online teaching, research studies, such as those conducted by Beggs (2002), Bowers (2002), Gannon-Cook (2003), Stevens (2001), and Wolcott (2002a,b), reported that faculty participating in continued online teaching were often supported by extrinsic factors, such as increased salary, course releases, and credit toward tenure.

Lack of incentives has become an increasing barrier to institutional growth in offering distance education. Studies, such as that of the Distance Education Report (2001), Southeast Missouri State University (2001), Zhen, Garthwait, & Pratt (2008), found that issues related to faculty were of greater relevance to faculty teaching online than technological issues. While technological issues could become a concern, they were often not elevated to a level of anxiety by faculty members until they had taught online at least one or more times. But once faculty members began teaching online, they often assessed the time invested and, despite their commitment to be of help to the students, started to take inventory of the time demands required to teach online courses. Since salaries often do not keep pace with the rising costs of living, these faculty members were often faced with basic physiological needs that must still be met, such as rent, and food (Gannon-Cook, 2010). When faced with the increased demands of teaching online for their home universities, several studies even indicated that there were faculty choosing to teach online for other universities instead of teaching online for their home universities (where they were employed full-time) because there was no additional compensation for teaching online at their home universities (Bowers, 2002; Gannon-Cook, 2003; Johnston, Alexander, Conrad, & Fieser, 2000, Maguire, 2002; Parker, 2003; Wolcott, 2006).

The use of increasing adjunct faculty to teach online courses will also continue, largely because there is such a strong need for instructors for online courses and programs in the rapidly expanding world of virtual education. But there are other reasons too for this trend that are more bottom line: adjuncts do not require benefits, such as insurance, and adjuncts can be paid far less than faculty. With these savings apparent to university administrators, there is often a rush to the use of adjunct instructors in online courses, and in fact, the trend to hire more or all adjunct instructors is the case of many for-profit universities. Without a thorough investigation, there could be a lack of understanding by administration as to the costs and benefits of enlisting adjunct instructors rather than full-time faculty to teach online.

High student attrition in online courses and programs (average 40%-60%) (Betts & Sikorski, 2008; Gannon-Cook, 2003; United States Distance Learning Association, 2001, 2007) could end up costing universities more than the costs associated with employing full-time faculty. A look at what student attrition costs universities would be worth the time invested, particularly since online attrition rates (in the United States) range from 40% to 50%, and can be as high as 70% to 80% (Betts & Sikorski, 2008; National Center of Educational Statistics, 2010, 2011). Attrition can be even higher in online programs, often losing 40-60% of first year students (Betts, 2008). Further research into student retentions and course completions might provide alternative administrative solutions that reap greater financial benefits. Even the retention of one or two students in each online course could add up to a cumulative effect in the overall retention rates of students which, in turn, could also have significant bottom line ramifications financially for the university in both course and degree completions (National Center of Educational Statistics, 2010, 2011). According to the National Center of Educational Statistics (2010, 2011), if university retention rates in online courses and programs could be raised to the average 78.6% retention rate reported for traditional universities, or even if the financial bottom line could be improved by five to eight percent in revenues with these retention increases, this could translate to several million dollars over a several-year period for the university.

These numbers could be very compelling to administrators looking for ways to increase revenues and retain students and worth further investigation at their universities. The American Association of University Professors (AAUP), an organization co-founded by John Dewey to provide a criterion of quality higher education academic standards, cites.

The dramatic increase in the number and proportion of contingent faculty in the last ten years has created systemic problems for higher education. Student learning is diminished by reduced contact with tenured faculty members, whose expertise in their field and effectiveness as teachers have been validated by peer review and to whom the institution has made a long-term commitment. Faculty governance is weakened by constant turnover and, on many campuses, by the exclusion of contingent faculty from governance activities. (American Association of University Professors, 2011, p.2)

While there are other factors that contribute to student attrition in online courses, such as family responsibilities, job requirements, and other personal factors, attrition can still be reduced with careful attention, such as advising, mentoring, and nurturing, and all these can generate university allegiance, but do prove more challenging for universities without strong cores of full-time faculty (Allen & Seaman, 2010; Betts, 2008; Howell, Laws, & Lindsay, 2004; Southern Area Southern Association of Colleges and Schools, 2010). Interactivities beyond discussion boards and drop boxes can create bonds based on "human interaction fostered through instruction, programming, and personalized engagement" (Betts, 2008, p.399). Adjunct instructors can do these kinds of interactivities, but, like their students, they too have other responsibilities, such as full time jobs elsewhere, or a multiple of universities where they teach online. So, while they may teach effectively, they don't have time to get to know their part-time employers' university cultures, nor do they have much time to mentor and nurture, or generate university allegiance in their students when they don't have that allegiance themselves. Full time faculty members' careers revolve around not only teaching, but service and research, and they can nurture their students with consistency and follow through with their students that is less possible with adjunct instructors. There are some studies that look at whether the consistency of full-time faculty teaching online courses increases student retention and completion rates in online courses (Benjamin, 2002; Betts & Sikorski, 2008; Bower, 2002; Bruner, 2007; Chapman,2011 Gannon-Cook, 2003; Johnston, Alexander, Conrad, & Fieser, 2000, Luzer, 2011; Maguire, 2002; Wolcott, 2006]). To-date, however, the trend towards the use of adjuncts in teaching online courses continues and so does the growing argument in many universities against full time faculty.

In the United States and in the European countries, the standards established by accrediting agencies like the Southern Association of Colleges and Schools (2003), and by organizations, like the American Association of University Professors (2010), state the university should maintain a parity of adjunct instructors to full-time faculty. For example the Southern Association of Colleges and Schools (2010), which monitor accreditation standards for most southern states in the United States, requires a parity of no more than one full-time faculty to four adjunct instructors; moreover, it also mandates that "at least 25 percent of the discipline course hours in each major at the baccalaureate level (must be) taught by faculty members holding the terminal degree" (p.28). Due to the high demand for online instructors, it may become increasingly more difficult to maintain this parity without enlisting more university faculty to teach online or disregarding accrediting agency guidelines, and this again raises the question of how faculty can be motivated to teach these growing numbers of online courses.

While a number of the studies still maintained a need to intrinsically motivate faculty with "atta boys" (verbal or written compliments) for their teaching online (Ansah & Johnson, 2003; Beggs, 2002; Bruner, 2007; Cavanaugh, 2005; Jacobsen, 2000; O'Quinn, 2003; Schifter, 2000a, b; Wolcott, 2006; Zhen, Garthwait, & Pratt, 2008), studies conducted in the last seven - eight years have pointed to the need for extrinsic motivators to enlist and keep faculty involved in teaching online. Among those studies recommending extrinsic motivators, there was some argument about which incentives worked best, but the primary extrinsic motivators in a number of studies were reduced teaching load or release time (Betts, 1998, 2009; Bower, 2002; Schifter, 2000a,b; Gannon-Cook, 2003; Johnston, Alexander, Conrad, & Fieser, 2000; Wolcott 2002a, 2002b); faculty training (Bebko, 1998; Beggs, 2002; Betts, 2009; Clarke, Butler, Schmidt-Hansen, & Somerville, 2004; Culp, Riffee, Starrett, Sarin, & Abrahansen, 2001; Donovan, 2004; Edwards, 2004; French, 2001; Lin, 2002; Twigg, 2000); and money, such as stipends, raises, or additional payments for teaching online (Betts, & Sikorski, 2008; Bower, 2002, Bruner, 2007; Gannon-Cook, 2003,2009; Gannon-Cook, Ley, Crawford, Warner, 2009; Wolcott, 2002ab, 2006).

But there were also studies that looked at negative motivators to teaching online: (Akbulut, Kuzu, Latchem, Odabasi, 2007; begs, 2002; Betts, 1998; Bower, 2002; Bruner, 2007; Gannon-Cook, 2003; Johnston, Alexander, Conrad, & Fieser, 2000; Kwoumka & Gannon Cook, 2003: Lin, 2002; O'Quinn, 2003: Parker, 2003; Schifter, 2002; Twigg, 2000; Wolcott, 2002a, b). The studies' findings suggested that there were factors that could put off faculty from even considering teaching online (Beggs, 2002; Betts, 1998; Bruner, 2007; Gannon-Cook, Ley, Crawford, Warner, 2009; Maguire, 2002, 2006; O'Quinn, & Corry, 2002; Schifter, 2000a, b; West, Waddoups, & Graham, 2007; Wolcott, 1996, 2002a, b); each study contained similar findings, but there were slight variances in the factor rankings. The majority of the studies listed the factors as:

lack of salary;
lack of merit pay;
lack of credit or promotion;
lack of recognition and award;
lack of royalties;
lack of release time;
concern about faculty workload;
lack of technical support;
lack of support from colleagues;
lack of support from Dean and university administrators

Many of those studies also cited several intrinsic deterrents that were voiced by faculty reticent to teach online; the two intrinsic factors most often cited were:

concern over the quality of instruction for online students; and concern over the quality of online courses

Since each study's findings related to the university where that study was conducted, findings could not be generalized, but the repeated mention of the above-listed deterrents, both extrinsic and intrinsic, throughout the studies, pointed to the strong likelihood that these factors represented at least a representative number of faculty members' feelings about teaching online.

While the findings mentioned above were the most cited in the studies researched herein, there were also some surprising findings that surfaced in a number of studies that might also be worth looking at when considering which factors would best motivate faculty to teach online. There were other factors that were not singled out as meaningful to faculty, but that may have been because the factors were not understood by faculty who had not previously taught online. Perhaps the reasons may have been that those faculty were just becoming aware of the potential time commitments required for online teaching (faculty who had previously taught online were quick to share their online teaching experiences with fellow faculty members, but there still seemed to be a general lack of awareness of the time involved in teaching online classes). In addition, little or no evidence may have been available to the faculty participating in these studies that would provide insights into time required to create the content and deliver course materials in online environments, or the time to work with the instructional designer or design teams that would co-create the online courses with the faculty serving as content matter expert for the online course(s). The steps involved in designing, implementing, and teaching online extended beyond traditional in-class preparation time, largely because online courses required more online interactivities, more graphic representations, and more attention to cultural implications, all while there were additional considerations, such as how the course materials would be housed within the learning management system, and how the technology would be utilized inside and outside the course (Ansah, & Johnson, 2003; Betts, 1998; Bender, Wood, & Vredevoogd, 2004; Cavanaugh, 2005; Chang, 2007; Chang 2008; French, 2001; Harley, 2002; Jacobsen, 2000; Lazarus, 2003; Weller, 2006).

A surprising finding was how low the ranking was over the factor of copyright ownership rights, and in some studies this factor was not even a consideration by faculty who had participated in the studies. Few faculty seemed to be concerned over copyright ownership rights, or royalties, at least as of the latest studies reviewed for this research (Betts, 2009; Gannon-Cook, Ley, Warner, & Crawford, 2010; Quinn & Trower, 2008; Wolcott, 2006; Zhen, Garthwait, & Pratt, 2008). (Concern over royalties was listed as one of the deterrents to faculty participating online in a number of the studies used in this research, but this factor ranked at most, fourth on the list of factors that could affect participation in online courses (Gannon-Cook, Ley, Crawford, Warner, 2009; Maguire, 2002, 2006; O'Quinn, & Corry, 2002; Schifter, 2000a, b; Wolcott, 1996, 2002a, b). Part of the reason for the lack of faculty interest or concern about ownership or royalties may have been because many faculty usually designed their own on-ground (traditional classroom) classes as a part of their teaching duties for the university; they did not generally copyright their courses, nor did they receive any royalties, or additional compensation for their courses. So it would follow that faculty that had not taught online would not think about copyrights or the potential problems that could surface with respect to contracts for designing courses that could either include payments for the design of courses and royalties, or "work for hire" courses designed for the university without any royalty rights. Without faculty being presented with the pros and cons of online course contracts, it would make sense that faculty who had not taught online previously would not pay attention to this factor when responding to surveys requesting their prioritizing of copyright considerations in designing online courses.

Another factor that was mentioned in many studies (Beggs, 2002; Betts, 1998, 2008; Bollinger & Wasilik, 2009; Bower, 2002; O'Quinn, 2003; O'Quinn & Corry, 2002; Quinn & Trower, 2008; Wolcott, 2006; Zhen & Pratt, 2008) was "lack of support from dean and university administrators" and that factor was ranked in the top ten factors in the list of motivators (or demotivators) to participate in distance education. Since there was no clear interpretation of what would constitute greater support from the deans or administrators, it was hard to parse out what that would mean, but the studies cited generally indicated that "support" seemed to mean that the dean and administration understood the faculty member's commitment's to teaching online with accommodations, such as teaching load adjustment for teaching online, updated technology training and software updates, or simply by providing positive administrative support. In some comments generated from faculty it seemed that a number of respondents felt that faculty should be included in university decisions, particularly with respect to curricular and design decisions that affected both faculty and students. Other considerations, such as credit toward tenure, could also fall under the category of "support" and would also acknowledge the work involved in teaching online.

This study did not look at trends in other countries, so research will need to be conducted to see if the recommendations from studies, such as the ones cited herein, would be applicable to universities offering online courses and programs in those countries. For universities seeking to provide cross-border education, it would make sense to consider the cultures and traditions of those countries first and implement measures that honor those priorities, then conduct studies, similar to the ones cited here, that address the use of adjuncts and full-time faculty, and the bottom-line cost comparisons of using more adjuncts or full-time faculty to teach online courses.

One Taiwanese study of online students pointed to a lack of adequate mentoring or advice from experienced and knowledgeable faculty as one of the most frequently cited sources of delay in completing their degrees (Kuo, 2011). It was also mentioned in several Chinese studies (Chang, Martin, Schellens, 2010; Huang, Dedegikas, Walls,2009; Zhang, Zhang, Duan, Fu, Wang, 2010) that it was important for the university to be aligned with its mission and that "Chinese students are used to the classroom teaching style. The reason for this situation could be that the traditional face-to-face class is still the main style of teaching in China" (Khou, 2011, p.6). Questions were also raised about whether the universities studied articulated global learning as a goal for its undergraduates; there were also questions about how faculty were rewarded for their teaching and scholarship (Chapman, 2011) and there were comments that cross-border providers may not meet each country's priorities, and perhaps these locales are better served by their local universities than by foreign providers that more frequently deliver what they already have developed elsewhere.

A review of research on Brazilian universities (Abrahão & Malanga, 2010) revealed universities have been undergoing a turning point in Brazil's brief history of higher education (the first Brazilian university, the University of Sao Paulo, was only founded in 1934). Therefore, the analysis has evidenced that "public policies for higher education must signal if they want to provide professional teaching in higher education, geared toward the job market, or rather, teaching from a real university, thus basing its mission, ethos and episteme in the 21st century on knowledge production and transmission" (p.43). No doubt if the choice is the latter, then there will be a strong need for full-time tenure-track and tenured faculty. While Brazil is also turning more to online education, it appears that there will be an emphasis placed on a "real university" experience which may necessitate traditional university standards and faculty, and will include the enlistment of faculty to teach online, so motivating faculty will become more important as the universities continue to grow. Future studies may reveal the progress of online courses and degree programs throughout the major Brazilian universities over the next decade.

In summary, there were a number of factors cited in the thirty-eight studies that could enlist and retain faculty to teach online courses and also allow the universities to best focus on their student populations and financial needs. If some of these recommendations have been adopted in the universities studied, then perhaps there can be follow-up studies that can generalize the findings so that they can be extended to other universities and to online cross-border education, or replicated in universities in other countries.

3. Analysis

This section describes the methods used to investigate variables that could motivate or inhibit faculty to teach and remain teaching online courses. This study utilized a qualitative, postpositivist methodology which conducted historical research to review over thirty-eight studies to uncover data that could reveal which factors best motivated faculty to participate in teaching and designing online courses. The analysis included thick description in order to uncover as much data as possible that could identify "reasonable implications for practice from their findings" (Gall, Borg, Gall, 1996, p.748).

In addition, the actor-network theory was also introduced as a viable methodology for this study since it is primarily used to study social, economic, and cultural effects, particularly in science and technology studies (STS), and to apply the STS principles across academic disciplines to higher education. (STS has already been documented effectively in disciplines other than science, most notably in organizational analysis, economics, sociology, and anthropology (Callon, 1986; Latour, 1987, 2005; Law & Hassard, 1999; Law, 1992). The relationships among technological innovations, faculty, and higher education administration are viewed in socially embedded contexts so as to get a more comprehensive look at how the findings and recommendations from the studies on faculty motivation could be utilized effectively.

Historical Analysis

In an effort to better understand how faculty, as an important element in student retention and successful completion of online courses, can be motivated to teach and remain teaching online courses, extensive research into studies on faculty motivation was undertaken by the researcher; at least 36 studies on faculty motivation were found which utilized a variety of quantitative and mixed-method methodologies. In addition a thorough literature review (see Review of Literature) supplemented the data provided from the studies. Repeatedly, intrinsic motivation was cited as an important contributor to faculty motivation to teach online, primarily because teaching online allows students to take courses and pursue a degree when they may not, otherwise, have access or opportunity to do so; and the desire to be helpful, along with the chance to contribute to the betterment of mankind, assures the inclination of faculty to take up the challenge of teaching online. Studies prior to 1999 (Bonk, 2001; Bower, 2002; Johnston, Alexander, Conrad, & Fieser, 2000; Maguire, 2002; O'Quinn, & Corry, 2002; Schifter, 2000a, b; Wolcott, 1996) included a larger number of early DE adopters who were more intrinsically motivated to participate in DE. (An early adopter is someone who takes on or embraces an innovation in the early phases of implementation). These respondents reported that the intrinsic rewards of accomplishment were enough incentive to participate in DE (Bonk, 2000; French, 2001; Husman & Miller, 1999; Johnston, 1999; Wilson, 1999). However, surveys conducted after 2000 included responses from more late adopters of DE (a late adopter being someone who has reservations about implementing the innovation and refrains from adoption until he/she is more comfortable with the innovation), and these respondents were more motivated by extrinsic rewards (Beggs, 2002; Bower, 2002; Johnston, 2000; Bollinger & Wasilik, 2009; Bruner, 2007; Cavanaugh, 2005;

Gannon-Cook, Ley, Crawford, Warner, 2009; Maguire, 2006; McLean, 2006b; O'Quinn, & Corry, 2004; Panda, & Mishra, 2008; Wolcott, 2006; Zhen, Garthwait, & Pratt, 2008).

Maslow stated there were two basic levels of human needs that motivated humans: lower level needs, such as physiological, security; and, higher level needs, such as esteem of self and others, and self-actualization (Maslow, 1970). Once the lower level needs are met, those needs become less important and the motivation rises towards the higher level needs, yet the physiological and security needs must be met, or primal survival fears surface. Work has been modern human's way of earning the means of meeting the physiological and security needs, and without a feeling of some degree of security in that work, it is hard to move up to the next order of higher level needs. Extrinsic motivation emphasizes that satisfaction from an activity is contingent upon a reward; and extrinsic motivators include a variety of offerings for faculty, such as salary increases, merit pay, course overloads, tenure or university recognition in the form of lab space, and monetary stipends (Gannon-Cook, 2010).

If a large number of studies recommend that universities give faculty more extrinsic rewards and include faculty in major decisions, such as their distance learning, then why have so many universities remained intransigent about implementing these recommendations and offering these incentives to faculty? The answer is that, usually, college presidents, deans, and administrators of universities would respond with two words: "the economy." But avoiding, or worse, refusing, to consider faculty concerns or motivations, particularly about teaching online, could result in problems that could be avoided if university administrators addressed some of the important questions and concerns of faculty. So, what are the true savings and what are the potential costs of failing to consider the recommendations of the many studies that addressed faculty concerns about teaching online?

In truth, some of the extrinsic factors with the highest rankings in the studies cited in this research (See Appendix A) would not cause the university to substantially increase its faculty budgets. These were: training, reduced teaching load, and support and encouragement from the dean or administration (Betts, 1998; Gannon-Cook, 2003; Johnston, Alexander, Conrad, & Fieser, 2000; Wolcott, 2002a, b). But highest on the list of factors that would positively influence faculty to teach online were: increase in salary, job security (credit towards tenure), and monetary support/stipends; these would all substantially add to the university's expenses. However, it bears reviewing the costs incurred for offering extrinsic rewards to the costs to enlist and retain faculty, particularly in online teaching. It might be worth exploring, particularly compared to the costs of not only the increased costs of offering any or all of these extrinsic motivators, but to also look at the costs of adjunct salaries, possible costs of lost opportunities for increased online course offerings, or, worse, the costs of student attrition or lower student enrollments due to unavailability of full-time faculty (Bender, Wood, & Vredevoogd, 2004; Benjamin, 2002; Florida, State of, 2011; McArthur, 1999; McLean, 2006a; Xenos, Pierrakaes, & Pintelas, 2002).

Actor-Network Analysis

The actor-network theory is utilized to study social, economic, and cultural effects across academic disciplines, including higher education. (Callon, 1986; Latour, 1987, 2005; Law & Hassard, 1999; Law, 1992; Schibik, Harrington, 2004; Xenos, Pierrakaes, & Pintelas, 2002).

Actor-network theory (ANT) is a type of methodology which looks at the agency of nonhuman issues and the effects of technology and other research factors upon humans and it has been used primarily in the fields of science, but has expanded in its applications across many other academic disciplines.

The basic premise of actor-network analysis is that no environment exists in a vacuum; in higher education, factors that affect faculty also affect higher educational administration, and both affect and are affected by technologies. Socially embedded contexts provide insights into the big picture—and how all of these factors converge to influence the entire environment and how the outcomes of decisions made with respect to each factor, are in turn, affected. In this research, the studies on faculty motivation that were reviewed provided invaluable insights into how their findings and recommendations could be utilized effectively.

Actor-network theory looks at how environments and networks act as a whole. An example, in the higher education elearning environment, students in an online course are encouraged to share their sociocultural backgrounds in their introductions, thus incorporating their cultural histories into their student experiences. They post their introductions via the learning management system; they share their experiences from their lives with the instructor and students in the class; and they integrate their experiences into the context of the online discussion using the technology and learning management system (LMS), yet another interface. All of these different environments and elements are brought together into a network to form a coherent whole.

According to actor-network theory, such actor-networks are potentially transient, existing in a constant making and re-making. This means that relations need to be repeatedly "performed" … (The teachers need to come to work each day, and the computers need to keep on running.)…Networks of relations are not intrinsically coherent, and may indeed contain conflicts (there may be adversarial relations between teachers/children, or computer software may be incompatible). Social relations, in other words, are only ever in process, and must be performed continuously (Wikipedia, 2011 http://en.wikipedia.org/wiki/Actor-network_theory)

In the research conducted in this study, factors addressed intrinsic and extrinsic factors that motivated or de-motivated faculty to participate in online courses; few addressed nonhuman issues. None addressed nonhuman issues in any detail, such as the effects of technology, learning management systems, and other research factors, such as online course development and design factors. Yet, no environment exists in a vacuum; factors that students affect faculty; factors that affect faculty affect higher education administration; both affect and are affected by technologies; and, all of these factors affect students and student retention. Socially embedded contexts provide insights into the big picture; by introducing a search for actor-network factors the researcher was able to take a look at how the dynamics of diverse student learners, their interaction with the technology and LMS, with each other, and with the instructor, and all of the observed participants' interactions in each module's discussions of the course's subject matter, provided a big picture perspective of the course and participants. Too often the instructor is so busy juggling the course materials, the technologies, the internal and external email student correspondences, the discussion posts, and their other faculty responsibilities, that they have little time to take a minute while in situ to look at patterns that are occurring in the course. They may not even realize there were problems experienced by students until long after the course when they receive their course evaluations, particularly if students don't put them on notice about their questions or concerns during the course. (Depending on the online environment and personalities of the students, they may not feel comfortable enough to voice concerns while in the class unless the instructor has made concerted efforts to encourage an open collaborative environment.)

The students may also be experiencing cognitive load issues associated with added stress from being in an online environment, from having to go outside the course to wikis or Wimbas, or VOIP (voice over internet protocol) sites where they must participate and post their feedback or assignments (Paas, Renkl, & Sweller, 2003; Sweller, 1994, 1999).

Cognitive load.

Cognitive load issues can be important considerations in online courses (Gannon Cook & Crawford, 2009). The learner can easily become overwhelmed with information and requirements, therefore, the online course should be structured simply to present information that progressively develops a cognitive and conceptual framework of understanding on the part of the learner. The learner must develop a knowledge base before moving on to the next bit of knowledge; a new learner may take a longer period of time to understand and develop an understanding of the subject than a learner with prior knowledge and understanding of the subject matter. "Then, once expertise is gained the newly crowned expert can reinvest the extra cognitive load into other things" (Wilson, 21 July 2008, ¶ 3). To-date, while the topic of cognitive load has been extensively discussed, there are few studies that have provided sufficient data so as to show there is a significant cognitive load impact on students participating in online courses, likely due to the fact that affective factors vary by student, such as the diverse student knowledge and skill levels (Paas, Renkl, & Sweller, 2003), as well as a number of other factors that could affect or not affect student cognitive loads in online courses.

Other factors.

In addition to cognitive load, other factors, such as the factors of cultural backgrounds, socioeconomic status, technological proficiency, and learning styles on the part of the students; and, content materials, online course design, learning management systems, as well as philosophical beliefs on the part of the teachers, there are yet other factors that are seldom even mentioned in the studies reviewed in this research. For example, language considerations could affect learning abilities of first-generation students; same for cultural courtesies that may keep some students from participating more fully.

Because there are so many unexplored factors that could contribute to the big picture of faculty motivation, the actor-network approach was utilized in this study to see if there were any consistent factors that could point to interactions with faculty teaching online in the courses researched, with design features, or with other actor-network factors that could shed light on faculty teaching online. The hope was that inferences could be made from these studies on which factors best motivate faculty participation in online courses. But without conducting more studies that parsed out individual factors that could have significant impact upon both online students and the faculty teaching or considering teaching those courses, it would be difficult to assign any attribution to actor-network factors in the assessment of what motivated faculty to teach online. Further research could shed more light on best elearning practices to contribute to the lessons learned on faculty motivators and incentives to teach online.

The research in these thirty-eight studies that could identify "reasonable implications for practice from their findings" (Gall, Borg, Gall, 1996, p.748) for faculty considering or teaching online seemed to revolve around the preponderance of courses that cited first intrinsic motivation as the top motivator, particularly referencing faculty members' desires as teachers, to be helpful to their students, and help students find ways to take advantage of online courses to advance their education. The availability of online courses and programs and convenience were intrinsically encouraging to teachers who want to see students who may, otherwise, not be able to go to college have a way to earn their degrees. These reasons seemed to be de facto motivators for faculty who had entered the teaching profession to be of service to others, the studies, never the less named them as the primary motivators.

But many faculty already carry full or overload teaching and administrative workloads, so pride of helping students achieve and personal accomplishment and might not sustain continued DE instruction without the reinforcement of some type of external motivation. There needed to be some other factors that could better assure faculty participation and retention in teaching online courses.

Universities often take the stance that DE will be integrated into traditional curricula, requiring faculty to teach DE and e-courses as a part of their teaching load. However, the researcher wanted to look at this stance, particularly with respect to second and third generation DE faculty. Since the preponderance of the studies indicated that, after early adopters had taught online they often demurred from teaching again (Beggs, 2002; Bower, 2002; Betts, 2009; Betts & Sikorski, 2008; Birch, Burnett, 2009; Bruner, 2007; Gannon-Cook, Ley, Crawford, Warner, 2009; Johnston, Alexander, Conrad, & Fieser, 2000; O'Quinn & Corry, 2002, 2004; Panda & Mishra, 2008, Parker, 2003; Quinn, Trower, 2008), it seemed that finding which factors that could not only incentivize faculty to participate in teaching online, but to continue teaching online, could prove informative.

Some collaborative approaches between administration and faculty could create ongoing dialog for enlisting and retaining faculty teaching online courses and set the tone for future stability of faculty teaching online courses. The "carrot and stick" motivation was explored in several studies (Betts, 1998; Schifter, 2002; Wolcott, 1996), with the intention of exploring which key incentives were successful as rewards for teaching online. The results in the majority of the studies had indicated extrinsic motivators were ranking the highest, even as the intrinsic motivators had shown to be powerful, but the keys to getting and keeping faculty engaged and enlisted in teaching online seemed to rest with extrinsic motivators (Beggs, 2002; Bower, 2002; Betts, 2009; Betts & Sikorski, 2008; Birch, Burnett, 2009; Bruner, 2007; Gannon-Cook, Ley, Crawford, Warner, 2009; Johnston, Alexander, Conrad, & Fieser, 2000; O'Quinn & Corry, 2002, 2004; Panda & Mishra, 2008, Parker, 2003; Quinn, Trower, 2008; Wolcott, 2002). Extrinsic rewards consisting largely of monetary rewards, primarily salary, course releases, and course stipends; it also included the reverse, demotivators, such as insufficient rewards (inadequate or no salary increases, course releases, or stipends); these seemed to be the key motivators (or demotivators) to faculty to participate in teaching online. As much as one-fourth (25%) of these combined motivators and demotivators in the studies suggested these factors weighted greater than their individual factor loadings, thus raising the likelihood these motivators could provide successful motivation (Gannon-Cook,

Ley, Crawford, Warner, 2009; Johnston, Alexander, Conrad, & Fieser, 2000; Wolcott, 2002). Factors that had next motivated faculty had been: technical and administrative support (which included not only technical support, but the ability to have their faculty voices heard), and job advancement (administration recognition of faculty efforts invested in teaching online).

Interestingly, while tenure and promotion were discussed in a number of the studies, it did not rank high in the rankings of motivators to faculty in any of the studies cited in this research, perhaps because many faculty did not see it as a factor that should be included in consideration of teaching online. It may also be that faculty felt that many universities have been moving away from tenure as a part of the university structure, but the reasons for the low ranking of tenure consideration in teaching online was not clear from the studies cited in this research.

4. Summary

While the thirty-eight studies researched herein did not address how non-human factors could have effects on faculty motivation to teach online, the need for future research in this area was put forth in this study. A look at the big picture and the effects of these non-human factors on faculty motivation to teach online could provide important insights into not only faculty motivation, but also on student retention. Research, such as the study of actor-network approaches could yield thick data that could benefit higher education administrative bottom line decisions and yield positive long-range plans for universities that seek further research in this arena.

The facts, thus far, shed light on the fiction that faculty will teach online happily just because it is their nature to be facilitative as teachers. Lessons learned from the thirty-eight studies in this research on faculty motivators to teach online provide strong indicators of which factors are the most successful in enlisting and retaining faculty to teach online.

In the end, the fact remains that online courses will continue to grow and students will increasingly be attracted to the convenience of online learning. Universities are competing with other universities around the world, so the challenges to enlist and retain online faculty that were addressed in this study reflect what universities all over the world either are or will be experiencing in the near future. Whether there are a small or large number of faculty members participating in online teaching may depend largely on whether faculty members feel valued in their online efforts and that their voices are heard.

There does not seem to be a "one size fits all" solution as regards faculty motivational factors as regards participation in DE. The trend for universities to continue to expand DE courses, due to increased consumer demand and cost effectiveness will continue. "Higher education is no longer a sanctuary against a global marketplace for educational products" (Gannon-Cook, 2010, p.135); and institutions of higher education must meet the demands of its clients. As universities move past the introductory phases of elearning, and into a culture of integrated online course delivery, research that takes into consideration the entire picture of the university environment should be considered. Administrators must not only meet the demands for DE, but also the needs of its faculty, higher education's most important assets. Higher education must address faculty needs, so as to more appropriately support faculty efforts' in teaching online courses.

Paying some attention to at least a few of the extrinsic motivators mentioned in this study may offer solutions that prove cost-effective to meet the burgeoning needs of online learning. The price to universities who take the time to address faculty motivators may be well worth the investment.

5. Appendix A

List of Thirty-Eight Studies Researched in This Study (Also See Study References)

Facts and Fiction: Lessons From Research on Faculty Motivators and Incentives to Teach Online:

Akbulut, Y., Kuzu, A., Latchem, C., Odabasi, F. (2007)
Allen, I. E. and Seaman, J. (2008)
Beggs, T. A. (2002
Bender, D., Wood, B., & Vredevoogd, J. (2004).
Betts, K. (1998).
Betts, K. S. & Sikorski, B. (2008)
Betts, K. S. (2009)
Birch, D., Burnett, B. (2009)
Bollinger, D. U., Wasilik, O. (2009).
Bower, B. (2002)
Bruner, J. (2007)
Cavanaugh, (2005)
Chang, C. L. (2008)
French, R. C. (2001)
Gannon-Cook, R., Ley, K., Crawford, C., Warner, A. (2009).
Halawi, L. and McCarthy, R. (2007).
Husmann, D., & Miller, M. (2001)
Jacobsen, D., M. (2000)
Johnston, T.C., Alexander, L, Conrad, C, & Fieser, J. (2000).
Johnstone, S. M. (2001, February).
Jones, S. and Johnson-Yale, C. (2005).
Kwoumka, S. & Gannon-Cook, R. (2003)
Kosak, L., Manning, D., Dobson, E., Rogerson, L., Cotnam, S., Colaric, S., & McFadden, C. (2004).
Maguire, L.L. (2002).
McLean, J. (2006)
Neuhauser, C. (2002)
Ngu, B. H. (2002).
O'Quinn, L., & Corry, M. (2002)
O'Quinn, L. R., & Corry, M. (2004)
Panda, S. & Mishra, S. (2008).
Parker, A. (2003).
Quinn, K., Trower, C. (2008).
Schifter, C. (2000a),
Soldner, L.B., Lee, Y.R. Duby, P.B. (2004)
West, R. E., Waddoups, G., & and Graham, C. R. (2007)
Wolcott, L. L. (1996)

Xenos, M. Pierrakaes, C., & Pintelas, P. (2002)

Zhen, A. Garthwait, A., & Pratt, P. (2008)

6. References

Akbulut, Y., Kuzu, A., Latchem, C., Odabasi, F. (2007), November). Change readiness among teaching staff at Anadolu University, Turkey (EJ777873), *Distance Education*, v.28n3 p335-350 Nov 2007.

Allen, I. E. and Seaman, J. (2008) Staying the course: Online education in the United States, 2008. Needham MA: Sloan Consortium. Retrieved on March 14, 2011 from http://sloanconsortium.org/sites/default/files/staying_the_course-2.pdf

Allen, I. E. & Seaman J. (2010). *Class differences: Online education in the United States, 2010*, Retrieved from Sloan Consortium website: http://sloanconsortium.org/publications/survey/pdf/class_differences.pdf

American Association of University Professors. (2003). Contingent appointments and the academic profession. Published by the American Association of University Professors. Retrieved on July 30, 2011 from http://www.aaup.org/AAUP/pubsres/policydocs/contents/conting-stmt.htm

Ansah, O. A., & Johnson, T. J. (2003). Time will tell on issues concerning faculty and distance education. *Online Journal of Distance Learning administration, 6(4). Retrieved February 22, 2007, from* http://sloanconsortium.org/sites/default/files/staying_the_course-2.pdf

Beggs, T. A. (2002). Influences and barriers to the adoption of instructional technology. Carrolton, GA: State University of West Georgia. Retrieved on March 10, 2011 from http://www.mtsu.edu/~itconf/proceed00/beggs/beggs.htm

Bender, D., Wood, B., & Vredevoogd, J. (2004). Teaching time: Distance education versus classroom instruction. *The American Journal of Distance Education, 18* (2), 103-114.

Benjamin, E. (2002). How over reliance on contingent appointments diminishes faculty involvement in student learning, *Peer Review* (February 2002), 4–10.

Betts. K. (1998). Factors influencing faculty participation in distance education in postsecondary education in the United States: An institutional study. Unpublished doctoral dissertation, George Washington University, Washington, DC.

Betts, K. S. & Sikorski, B. (2008). Financial bottom line: Estimating the cost of faculty/adjunct turnover and attrition for online programs. *Online Journal of Distance Learning (11:1)* Spring, 2008. Retrieved August 14, 2009 from http://www.westga.edu/~distance/ojdla/spring111/betts111.html

Betts, K. S. (2009). Online human touch (OHT) training & support: A conceptual framework to increase faculty engagement, connectivity, and retention in online education, Part 2. *MERLOT Journal of Online Learning and Teaching*. Retrieved August 10, 2009 from http://joolt.merlot.org/vl5no1/betts_0309.htm

Birch, D., Burnett, B. (2009). Bringing academics on board: Encouraging institution-wide diffusion of e-learning environments. *Australasian Journal of Educational Technology*, 25(1), 117-134. Bold, M., Chenoweth, L., Garimella, N. (2008). Brics and clicks. *Journal of Studies in International Education*, 5-25.

Bollinger, D. U., Wasilik, O. (2009). Factors influencing faculty satisfaction with online teaching and learning in higher education. Distance Education, 1475-0198, Volume30, Issue 1, 2009, pp. 10-116.

Bonk, C. J., Kirkley, J.R., Hara, N., & Dennen, V. (2001). Finding the instructor in post-secondary online learning: Pedagogical, social, managerial, and technological locations. J. Stephenson (Ed.), *Teaching and learning online: Pedagogies for new technologies* (pp.76-97). London: Kogan Page.

Bower, B. (2002). Distance education: Facing the faculty challenge. Retrieved November 23, 2003, from www.westga.edu/~distance/ojdla/summer42/bower42.html

Brookfield, S. (1995). *Becoming a critically reflective teacher.* San Francisco: Jossey–Bass, p. 6.

Brabazon, T. (2001, June 4). Internet teaching and the administration of knowledge. *First Monday*, Volume 6, Number 6. Retrieved on March 13, 2011 from http://firstmonday.org/htbin/cgiwrap/bin/ojs/index.php/fm/article/viewArticle/867/776.

Bruner, J. (2007). Factors motivating and inhibiting faculty in offering their courses via distance education. *Online Journal of Distance Learning Administration*, Vol. X, II, Summer 2007. Retrieved from http://www.westga.edu/~distance/ojdla/summer102/bruner102.htm

Callon, M. (1986). Some elements of a sociology of translation: Domestication of the scallops and the Fishermen of St Brieuc Bay. In John Law (ed.), *Power, Action and Belief: A New Sociology of Knowledge* (London: Routledge & Kegan Paul).

Cardoso, V., & Bidarra, J. (2007, March). Open and distance learning: Does it (still) matter? *European Journal of Open, Distance and E-Learning, 2007*(I). Retrieved June 21, 2007, from http://www.eurodl.org/materials/contrib/2007/Cardoso_Bidarra.htm

Cavanaugh, J. (2005). Teaching online - A time comparison. *Online Journal of Distance Learning Administration, 8(1). Retrieved February 22, 2007, from* http://www.westga.edu/~distance/ojdla/spring81/cavanaugh81.pdf

Chang, C. L. (2008). Faculty perceptions and utilization of a learning management system in higher education. Unpublished doctoral dissertation for Ohio University, retrieved on March 15, 2011 from http://etd.ohiolink.edu/send-pdf.cgi/Chang%20Chinhong%20Lim.pdf?ohiou1210864179

Chang, T. S. (2007). The relationship between faculty perceptions of teaching difficulties and their characteristics. Paper presented at the Annual Meeting of American Educational Research Association, held in April in Chicago, IL. Dalsgaard, C. (2006). Social software: E-Learning beyond learning management systems. *European Journal of Open, Distance and E-Learning, 2006*(II). Retrieved June 18, 2007, from *http://www.eurodl.org/materials/contrib/2006/Christian_Dalsgaard.htm*

Chang, Z., Valcke, M., Schellens, T. (2010, May). A cross-cultural study of teacher perspectives on teacher roles and adoption of online collaborative learning in higher education, *European Journal of Teacher Education*, v33 n2 p147-165.

Chapman, D. (2011, Fall). Contingent and tenured/tenure-track faculty: Motivations and incentives to teach distance education courses, *Online Journal of Distance Learning Administration*, Volume XIV, Number III, retrieved on September 5, 2011 from http://www.westga.edu/~distance/ojdla/fall143/chapman143.html

Creswell, J. W. (1998). *Qualitative inquiry and research design: Choosing among five traditions.* London: SAGE Publications Ltd. Florida, State of. (2011). Guidelines on Florida for effective use of part-time faculty. Retrieved on July 31, 2011, from http://www.fldoe.org/CC/policy/cc_gpm.asp

French, R. C. (2001). Encouraging participation in college and university distance education programs. Unpublished doctoral dissertation, State University of New York at Buffalo. Gall, M. D., Borg, W. R.,

Gall, J. P. (1996). Educational research. White Plains, New York: Longman Publishers.

Gannon-Cook, R. (2003). Factors that can motivate or inhibit faculty participation in distance education: A study conducted at a major public university in the southwestern United States. ProQuest Dissertation Abstracts International. University of Houston, Houston, TX.

Gannon-Cook, R., Ley, K., Crawford, C., Warner, A. (2009). Motivators and inhibitors for university faculty in e-learning. *British Journal of Educational Technology.* 40(1) p. 149-163. Malden, MA: Blackwell Publishing.

Gannon-Cook, R., Crawford, C. (2009). Addressing learner needs within online learning environments: Learner needs, instructor aptitude and proficiency, socialization within the learning community, and design of the learning environment. In *Case Studies of Interactive Elearning*, B. Olaniran (Ed.). Brian Station, TX: IGI Global.

Gannon-Cook, R. (2010). *What motivates faculty to teach in distance education? A case study and meta-literature review.* Landham, MD: University Press of America, Inc.

Halawi, L. and McCarthy, R. (2007). Measuring faculty perceptions of blackboard using the technology acceptance model. *Issues in Information Systems, 8*(2), 160-165.

Harley, D. (2002). Investing in educational technologies: The challenge of reconciling institutional strategies, faculty goals, and student expectations.

Hezel, R. (2005). Global e-learning opportunity for U.S. higher education: Introduction to Asia. *Journal of Asynchronous Learning Networks, Volume 12: Issue 1* Available from http://www.hezel.com/globalreport/IntrotoAsia.pdf

Hezel, R.T., & Mitchell, J. (2006). *Developing an elearning program: From conceptualization to implementation.* Syracuse, NY: Hezel & Associates, LLC.

Huang, S.X., Dedegikas, C., Walls, J. (2009). Using multimedia technology to teach modern Greek language online in China: Development, implementation, and evaluation. *European Journal of Online and Distance Learning*, retrieved on September 9, 2011 from http://www.eurodl.org/?p=current&article=417

Howell, S., Laws, D., & Lindsay, N. (2004). Reevaluating course completion in distance education: Avoiding the comparison of apples and oranges. *Quarterly Review of Distance Education, 5* (4), 243-252.

Husmann, D., & Miller, M. (2001). Improving distance education: Perceptions of program administrators. *Online Journal of Distance Learning Administration, 4*(3). Jacobsen, D., M. (2000). Examining technology adoption patterns by faculty in higher education. *ACEC2000: Learning Technology.* Retrieved February 21, 2007, from http://www.ucalgary.ca/~dmjacobs/acec/

Johnston, T.C., Alexander, L, Conrad, C, & Fieser, J. (2000). Faculty compensation models for online/distance education. Retrieved June 8, 2002, from http:www.mtsu.edu/~itconf/proceed00/Johnston.html

Johnstone, S. M. (2001, February). Perception versus reality: Differences in faculty at virtual and traditional institutions. *Syllabus*, 16.

Jones, S. and Johnson-Yale, C. (2005). Professors online: The Internet's impact on college faculty. *First Monday*, volume 10, number 9, Retrieved April 17, 2009 from http://firstmonday.org/htbin/cgiwrap/bin/ojs/index.php/fm/article/view/127 5/1195,

Kuo, Y.H. (2011, February). Applying a proposal guideline in mentoring English major undergraduate researchers in Taiwan. *International Journal of Evidence Based Coaching and Mentoring* Vol. 9, No. 1, p. 76.

Kwoumka, S. & Gannon-Cook, R. (2003). Methods matter: A comparison of four studies on distance education and why the results varied among those studies. Unpublished manuscript.

Latour, B. (1987). *Science in action: How to follow scientists and engineers through society* (Milton Keynes: Open University Press).

Latour, B. (2005). *Reassembling the social: An introduction to actor-network-theory* (Oxford: Oxford University Press). Law, J., & Hassard, J. (eds) (1999). *Actor network theory and after* (Oxford and Keele: Blackwell and the Sociological Review).

Law, J. (1992). Notes on the theory of the actor network: Ordering, strategy, and heterogeneity. Retrieved on July 28, 2011 from
http://www.lancs.ac.uk/fass/sociology/papers/law-notes-on-ant.pdf

Lazarus, B. D. (2003). Teaching courses online: How much time does it take? *Journal of Asynchronous Learning Networks, 7* (3), 47-53.

Lin, D. H. (2002). Perceived differences between classroom and distance education: Seeking instructional strategies for learning applications. *International Journal of Educational Technology, 3* (1), 20-32.

Lucchesi, M. A. S., & Malanga, E. B. (2010, June). Perceptions of higher education in Brazil in the first decade of the third millennium, *US-China Education Review*, Volume 7, No.6 (Serial No.67), p.31-44.

Luzer, D. (2011). Online students more likely to fail. Washington Monthly College Guide, retrieved on September 10, 2011 from
http://www.washingtonmonthly.com/college_guide/

Kosak, L., Manning, D., Dobson, E., Rogerson, L., Cotnam, S., Colaric, S., & McFadden, C. (2004). Prepared to teach online? Perspectives of faculty in the University of North Carolina system," *Online Journal of Distance Learning Administration*, volume 7, number 3, accessed September 10, 2010 at
http://www.westga.edu/~distance/ojdla/fall73/kosak73.html.

Maguire, L.L. (2002). "Literature review – faculty participation in online distance education: Barriers and motivators," *Online Journal of Distance Learning Administration*, volume 8, number 1, retrieved on July10, 2011 from http://www.westga.edu/~distance/ojdla/spring81/maguire81.htm

Maguire, L. L. (2006). Literature review: Faculty participation in online distance education: Barriers and motivators. *Millersville University*. Retrieved February 16, 2007, from http://www.westga.edu/~distance/ojdla/spring81/maguire81.htm.

Maslow, A. (1970). *Motivation and personality* (2nd ed.). NY: Harper and Row. McArthur. A. (1999).Comparison of grading patterns between full- and part-time humanities

faculty: A preliminary study. *Community College Review* / Winter, 1999. Retrieved on July 22, 2011, from
http://findarticles.com/p/articles/mi_m0HCZ/is_3_27/ai_60498502/

McLean, J. (2006a). Forgotten faculty: Stress and job satisfaction among distance educators. Retrieved on August 1, 2011 from
http://www.westga.edu/%7Edistance/ojdla/summer92/mclean92.htm

McLean, J. (2006b). Survey of faculty compensation models. Retrieved May 18, 2011, from http://cstl.seo.edu//itfrr

Milem, J. (2006, Fall). *Our underachieving colleges: A candid look at how much students learn and why they should be learning more, The Review of Higher Education* - Volume 30, Number 1, pp. 81-83.

Murphy, D. (2011). Conversation with the Associate Dean of Technology about the number of faculty who teach online at DePaul University's School for New Learning.

National Center for Education Statistics. (2003). *Distance education at degree-granting postsecondary institutions: 2006-2007*. U. S. Department of Education, National Center for Education Statistics Report, retrieved on March 20, 2011 from http://nces.ed.gov/pubsearch/pubsinfo.asp?pubid=2009044.

National Center for Education Statistics (2010, December). *Persistence and attainment of 2003–04 beginning postsecondary students: After 6 years: First look*. Alexandria, VA: Walton Radford.

National Center for Educational Statistics. (2011, February). Enrollment in postsecondary institutions, fall 2009; Graduation rates, 2003 & 2006 cohorts; and financial statistics, fiscal year 2009: First look, Laura G. Knapp, Janice E. Kelly-Reid, Scott A. Ginder, Eds. Washington, D.C: U.S. Department of Education. Retrieved on February 12, 2011 from
http://nces.ed.gov/pubsearch/pubsinfo.asp?pubid=2011230

Neuhauser, C. (2002). Learning style and effectiveness of online and face-to-face instruction. *The American Journal of Distance Education, 16* (2), 99-113.

Ngu, B. H. (2002). Online instruction versus face-to-face instruction at UNIMAS. *International Journal of Educational Technology, 3* (1), 1-19.

Offir, B., Barth, I. Lev, Y., & Shteinbok, A. (2003). Teacher-student interactions and learning outcomes in a distance learning environment. *Internet and Higher Education, 6*, 65-75.

O'Quinn, L., & Corry, M. (2002). Factors that deter faculty from participating in distance education. *Online Journal of Distance Learning Administration, 5*(4). Retrieved February 22, 2007, from
http://www.westga.edu/%7Edistance/ojdla/browsearticles.php

O'Quinn, L. R. (2003, January). Factors that deter faculty from participating in distance education. *Online Journal of Distance learning Administration.* Available:
http://www.westga.edu/~

O'Quinn, L. R., & Corry, M. (2004). Factors which motivate community college faculty to participate in distance education. *International Journal of E-Learning, 3*(1), 19-30.

Paas, F., Renkl, A., & Sweller, J. (2003). Cognitive load theory and instructional design: Recent developments. *Educational Psychologist, 38* (1), 1-4. Lawrence Erlbaum Associates, Inc. Retrieved on October 7, 2008, from

http://books.google.com/books?hl=en&id=DCcSZ7GC8lAC&dq=cognitive+load
&printsec=frontcover&source=web&ots=3rCu__Aos4&sig=yzgoZmi4aTKHJD_bnd
-EFUOlmrQ&sa=X&oi=book_result&resnum=3&ct=result#PPA1,M

Palloff, R. M. and Pratt, K. (2001). Lessons from the cyberspace classroom, paper presented at 17th Annual Conference on Distance Teaching & Learning (University of Wisconsin), accessed 6 March 2011 from
http://www.uwex.edu/disted/conference/Resource_library/

Panda, S. & Mishra, S. (2008). *Faculty attitude towards, and barriers and motivators of e- learning in a mega open university.* Educational Media International. New York: Taylor & Francis.

Parker, A. (2003). Motivation and incentives for distance faculty. *Online Journal of Distance Learning Administration, 6(3).* Retrieved February 23, 2007, from
http://www.westga.edu/%7Edistance/ojdla/browsearticles.php.

Pope, J. (2006). Number of students taking online courses rises. USA Today, retrieved on September 11, 2011 from
http://www.usatoday.com/tech/news/2006-11-09-online-learning_x.htm

Quinn, K., Trower, C. (2008). Tips for recruiting and retaining faculty: What different generations want. Paper presented at the 2008 Association of Institutional Researchers (AIR) Annual Forum in Seattle, WA.

Schibik, T., Harrington, C. (2004). Caveat emptor: Is there a relationship between part- time faculty utilization and student learning outcomes and retention? *Professional File: Association for Institutional Research,* Number 91, Spring, 2004. Retrieved on July 38, 2011 from http://airweb3.org/airpubs/91.pdf

Schifter, C. (2000a, March/April) Faculty motivators and inhibitors for participation in distance education. A study conducted at Temple University by the Director of Distance Education, a doctoral dissertation. *Educational Technology, 40(2),* 43-46.

Schifter, C. (2000b) Faculty participation in distance education: A factor analysis of motivators and inhibitors. Paper presented at the meeting of the National University Teleconferencing Consortium, Toronto, Canada.

Schifter, C. (2002). Perception differences about participating in distance education. *Online Journal of Distance Learning Administration,* Volume V, Number I.

Soldner, L.B., Lee, Y.R. Duby, P.B. (2004). Impacts of internal motivators and external rewards on the persistence of first-year experience faculty (EJ795794) *Journal of the First-Year Experience & Students in Transition,* v16n2 p19-37.

Southeast Missouri State University. (2001). A rationale and set of guidelines for evaluating the use of instructional technology. Retrieved from http://cstl.semo.edu/itfrr

Southern Area Southern Association of Colleges and Schools. (2010). Distance education and the principles of accreditation: Documenting compliance. (2010). Retrieved March, 14, 2011 from http://www.sacscoc.org/

Sweller, J. (1994). Cognitive load theory, learning difficulty, and instructional design. *Learning and Instruction* 4: 295-312. Retrieved on May 29, 2011 from
doi:10.1016/0959-4752(94)90003-5

Sweller, J. (1999). *Instructional design in technical areas.* Camberwell, Australia: Australian Council for Educational Research. Twigg, C. A. (2000). *Who owns online courses and course materials? Intellectual property policies for a new learning environment.* Troy, NY;

The Pew Learning and Technology Program Center for Academic Transformation Rensselaer Polytechnic Institute.

United States Distance Learning Association. (2001). *Research information and statistics.* Washington, DC: Author.

United States Distance Learning Association. (2007). Distance learning research and praxis. Retrieved on March 31, 2008 from http://www.usdla.org/index.php?cid=107.

Weller, M. (2006). VLE 2.0 and future directions in learning environments. In R. Philip, A. Voerman & J. Dalziel (Eds.), *Proceedings of the First International LAMSConference 2006: Designing the Future of Learning* (pp 99-106). 6-8. December 2006, Sydney: LAMS Foundation. Retrieved January 3, 2008, from http://lamsfoundation.org/lams2006/papers.htm

West, R. E., Waddoups, G., & and Graham, C. R. (2007). "Understanding the experiences of instructors as they adopt course management systems," *Educational Technology Research and Development,* volume 55, number 1, pp. 1–26.

Wikipedia. (2011). Definition of actor-network theory. Retrieved on July 28, 2011 from http://en.wikipedia.org/wiki/Actor-network_theory

Wilson, B. (2008, 21 July). Expert, novices, and cognitive-load. Retrieved on February 1, 2009 from http://www.crucialthought.com/2008/07/21/experts-novices-and-cognitive-load/

Wolcott, L. L. (1996). Tenure, promotion, and distance education: Examining the culture of faculty rewards. *American Journal of Distance Education,* 11 (2), 3-18. Wolcott, L. (2002a) *Tenure, promotion, and distance education: Examining the culture of faculty rewards.* Logan, UT: Utah State University.

Wolcott, L. L. (2002b). Dynamics of faculty participation in distance education: Motivation, incentives and rewards. In Michael G. Moore (Ed.). *Handbook of Distance Education.* Majwah, NJ: Lawrence Ehrlbaum.

Wolcott, L. L. (2006). Faculty participation: Motivation, incentives and rewards. In Michael G. Moore (Ed.). *Handbook of Distance Education.* Majwah, NJ: Lawrence Ehrlbaum.

Wolcott, L. L. (2008). Discussion of research conducted by Linda Wolcott on faculty motivation and participation in distance education. Personal interview with Linda Wolcott held on March 17, 2008 in Logan, UT.

Xenos, M. Pierrakaes, C., & Pintelas, P. (2002). A survey on student dropout rates and dropout causes concerning the students in the course of informatics of the Hellenic Open University.*Computers & Education,* 39, 361-377.

Zhen, A. Garthwait, A., & Pratt, P. (2008). "Factors affecting faculty members' decision to teach or not to teach online in higher education," *Online Journal of Distance Learning Administration,* Volume 11, number 3, at http://www.westga.edu/~distance/ojdla/fall113/zhen113.html, accessed 11 January 2011.

Zhang, L., Zhang, X., Duan, Y., Fu, Z., Wang, Y. (2010, January). Evaluation of learning performance of e-learning in China: A methodology based on change of internal mental model of learners. *Turkish Online Journal of Educational Technology,* v9 n1 p70-82.

Zurita, L., & Ryberg, T. (2005). Towards a collaborative approach of introducing elearning in higher education institutions. How do university teachers conceive and react to transitions to e-learning, WCCE 2005 - 8th IFIP World Conference on Computers in Education. Stellenbosch, South Africa: University of Stellenbosch.

Part 2

E-Learning for Engineering, Medical Education and Biological Education

6

The Use of Mathematical Formulae in an E-Learning Environment

Josep Cuartero-Olivera, Antoni Pérez-Navarro
and Teresa Sancho-Vinuesa
Universitat Oberta de Catalunya
Spain

1. Introduction

The use of mathematical formulae in engineering studies is as important as the subject content itself, especially in online distance education. In engineering studies, which have a strong technical component, both students and teachers must use formulae to express and solve their doubts, prove their knowledge or even quote any given piece of support material. In addition, in online distance education, communicating mathematics is not as easy as writing on a piece of paper or on a blackboard. As well as mastering the language of mathematics to express them properly, which is a problem that also exists in on-site environments, there is the problem of *writing* mathematics mainly through text e-mails, which is the main way to communicate within an on-line environment. The data gathered for this research at the *Universitat Oberta de Catalunya* (UOC) involves 4 terms, 15 engineering-related subjects and more than 17,000 e-mails. Among this large volume of e-mails, the use of mathematical notation is present in over 4,000 of them, representing an average of 23% of the total. As this preliminary result is quite significant, the aim of this chapter is to analyse the use of all the different strategies for communicating ideas with a mathematical content through the Internet and studying the impact for each one of them in order to find usage patterns.

Regarding virtual learning environments, as it is not possible to find previous studies about the use of mathematical notation within them, this work presents research of the different methods used by teachers and students to communicate mathematics through the Internet, and the use patterns regarding different subjects and knowledge areas. In order to do so, the core of this chapter consists of exploratory research as to which are the mentioned use patterns and tries to find relationships between them.

This chapter is structured as follows: as a first step, Section 2 explains in detail the problem addressed by this research. In Section 3, different methods for expressing mathematical notation in the particular case of a virtual learning environment like UOC are described. Next, Section 4 will introduce the scenario in which this research has been conducted. After that, Section 5 will focus on the study of how every one of these notation methods is used. Some statistical measurements are presented in order to try to find behaviour patterns through the different subjects and/or knowledge areas. The chapter ends with the conclusions and future lines of work.

2. Engineering studies in a virtual learning environment

Virtual learning environments are, in general, still challenging nowadays, as they have to deal with the barriers of time and distance. This is true not only for communication from teacher to students, but also among student workgroups or for students to communicate their queries to the teacher. The challenges become greater in engineering studies, where there are additional obstacles to overcome; for example the use of laboratories (having to become virtual laboratories) or granting access to high-profile computational tools. Focusing on the issue of knowledge transfer, one of the main problems regarding engineering studies is communication among university members, as a great part of this communication implies the use of a large amount of mathematical notation.

In the case of a virtual learning environment, the issue of learning and communicating mathematics can be compared to a disability such as visual impairment. Visually impaired students can listen to the reading of a given formula by the teacher, while they cannot easily learn how it is expressed visually, even in an on-site learning environment (Fitzpatrick, 2007). In reverse, a virtual learning environment allows students to see visual expression of formulae, but traditionally does not provide them with a verbal representation, which is also a handicap for visually impaired students. In addition, in some cases there is no auxiliary tool to help express mathematical notation, for example a formulae editor. When there is no such tool available, the methods for expressing mathematics are still computer aided, but they are as rudimentary as plain text or file attachments.

The issues of the use of mathematical notation regarding information systems has previously been stated and researched. For instance, there are differences in handling math expressions in one way or another for the indexing and retrieval of mathematics educational material in a search engine (Zhao, 2008). For that purpose, the author proposes the use of links between math expressions and text keywords. In this way, a semantic expression like "area of the function cosinus" can be linked to mathematics content about the resolution of integral functions for the particular cosinus function. From a different point of view, other authors propose a five step process for the recognition and semantic understanding of mathematical formulae, basically consisting of (Chen & Okada, 2001):

- Pre-processing: In this first step, the mathematical expression is scanned to obtain an image. This image is processed in order to remove any noise and then split into mathematical symbols, digits and letters.
- Character recognition: The individual symbols, digits and letters are processed through a character recognition system and then classified into dyadic operators, monadic operators or atom characters.
- Rule base: Any ambiguity in the mathematical expression is eliminated by using a rules system. This system consists of mathematical rules, a sense-based dictionary for handling layout-dependent ambiguity and an experience-based dictionary for handling layout-independent uncertainty.
- Expression understanding: According to the layout of the mathematical expression, a layout tree is generated and parsed. This layout treecontains type and position of symbols, their sizes and centrelines and their parent-child relationships according to the expression layout. The result of this step is a semantic tree based on the mathematical rules used in step 3. This new semantic tree contains the types of symbols, their parent-

child relationships according to the expression semantics, the mathematical meaning of the combination and information about the expression constants and variables.

- Translating: In the last step, a recognized expression is produced and translated into a script or a source code suitable for being used in third-party software like TeX or Mathematica.

As we stated in Section 1, currently there is not much research into the particular context of a virtual learning environment, regarding the use of the mathematics language. The main communication method in this kind of environment is the use of e-mail, so students have to adapt their communications, including the mathematical notation within them, to this particular communication tool. Next, Section 3 shows how this is carried out by students and teachers and also explains the different available methods.

3. Writing mathematical notation within e-mails

The teaching and learning activity in a virtual campus, like in the case of UOC, is developed mainly within the virtual classroom. The virtual classroom is a space where teachers and students can communicate in a few different ways:

- Classroom forums
- Discussion boards
- Delivery board
- Private e-mail

Most of the interaction among the classroom members happens in the classroom forum or discussion board, where any of the members can send text messages and attach documents, while all the rest of members can read any of the messages and reply to them. Besides this communication space, students and teachers can also communicate by using their private e-mail address or the delivery board, where students send their due work, like continuous assessment tests. In the case of the private e-mail or the delivery board those messages are private to the sender and the recipient. However, the message format within all of these communication spaces is the same one: an e-mail written with the virtual campus e-mail editor.

As previously stated, there are several tools to improve mathematics communication in virtual learning environments, mostly formulae editors. Some of these formulae editors work as a standalone program, like the Wiris Editor (Wiris, 2011) or Microsoft Equation Editor (Microsoft, 2011), which can also be embedded into other software like Moodle. Some others are available directly on a website, like the LaTeX Equation Editor (The Number Empire, 2011) or sMArTh (sMArTH, 2011). Most of them use very common mathematical notation languages, like LaTeX (LaTeX, 2011) or the commonly known as MathML, Mathematical Markup Language (World Wide Web Consortium, 2011), which make them very feasible as plug-ins for other environments.

At UOC, such a mathematical notation tool has been available only during the last few terms, and it is still considered to be in its early stages. In fact, several tools are being tested and it is still to be decided which one is the best option. Before this tool was available, students and teachers needed to use other communication methods. These methods can range from the virtual campus e-mail editor itself -either in its plain text or Rich Text

Format versions- to more evolved tools for attaching documents like Microsoft Word or OpenOffice.org Writer –where these tools can be considered as the transfer method of the formulae itself, instead of the e-mail body.

Two main methods for expressing mathematics in web-based environments have been covered: through pictures and through coding with MathML (Yue-sheng & Jia-yi, 2008). These methods are focused on the way a formula is usually represented in a web page, from a technological point of view. Since this research though is focused on how students write formulae, it has to respond to a different classification, based on the technique used to write them. For instance, a symbol can be written with any rich text editor (for example the $\sum$ symbol), or even with a plain text editor depending on the symbol (for example the + symbol). However, the construction of a given formula is frequently not possible using only text and needs other tools to help with its visual representation, for instance as shown in Figure 1:

$$\lim_{\Delta x \to 0} \sum_{i=1}^{\infty} f\left(x_i\right) \cdot \Delta x$$

Fig. 1. Sample formula

It is also possible to cite a formula by using any simple text editor, while in the case of a formula attached to an e-mail body an external tool is needed to generate the attachment itself. Therefore, a wider classification has been used, obtained from the observation of the behaviour of students and teachers: full mathematical formulae, mathematical symbols, formulae referencing and attachment. In order to better understand the results, all these different ways of communicating are explained and delimited through the next sections.

3.1 Full mathematical formulae

The first and most common method for expressing mathematical notation is through full mathematical formulae, understanding it as an equality (i.e. a=b+3), an inequality (i.e. a+2>5), or a mathematical expression consisting of a combination of more than one mathematical symbol (i.e. sin(ln(1))). Full mathematical formulae can also be expressed in any specific syntax delivered by programming languages or software commonly used in engineering environments. These variations are also considered in this group, for example specific mark-up codes like "\sqrt", which are meaningful for the LaTeX2 editor, converting the expression \sqrt{1-e^2} into $\sqrt{1-e^2}$.

3.2 Mathematical symbols

The mathematical symbol method consists of writing just one mathematical symbol at a time, whether it is in plain text (i.e. lambda) or by using the symbol itself (i.e. λ), and exclusively when the symbol is not part of a whole mathematical formula. Numeric expressions have been considered into this group only if they are preceded (or followed) by a mathematical symbol (i.e. >10 or 10!). Hyper-index, sub-index, or commonly used abbreviations of mathematical expressions like SQR, TAN, etc. also fall into this group.

3.3 Formulae referencing

Formulae referencing is used whenever a certain formula or expression is cited within the text, whether it is in its most common way (i.e. the formula on the first paragraph of page 24) or by using a previously established citation system (i.e. formula 17).

3.4 Attachment

The last method consists of attaching a file containing the formulae referenced in the e-mail body (i.e. the attached formula is wrong), or even writing the whole body of the message in an attached file. The attachment might be an image, some kind of text document (RTF, Microsoft Word, OpenOffice.org Writer, etc.), or even a scan of handwritten formulae.

According to Zhao classification of mathematical educational resources and some math information indexing and retrieval systems analysed through his research (Zhao, 2008), mathematical expressions can be considered as syntactically math-aware whenever the retrieval system reads the syntactical structure of the math expression to be searched for. On the other hand, if the system is capable of also capturing the semantics of the expression, then it is considered as semantically math-aware. Other systems, incapable of recovering neither the math-related syntactic or semantic meaning, are considered as math-unaware. Following this classification, full mathematical formulae and mathematical symbols could be considered as syntactically math-aware, and formulae referencing as semantically math-aware. However, as we have seen, there are not many different ways of expressing mathematical notation, although as explained in this section they are quite different from one another. Therefore, the next sections address the scenario for this research and the analysis of how each method is used by students and teachers, what patterns can be found among different subjects and knowledge areas and what the possible reasons are for a particular behaviour.

4. Scenario under study

As described in section 3, there are several ways of including mathematical expressions in a digital text subject to be sent by email. As most of the communication between teachers and students takes place in the classroom forum, for this research we have only considered the e-mails sent to that communication space. Therefore, in this section an exhaustive analysis of over 17,000 e-mail messages is made in order to classify them according to the type of mathematical expression method used. These e-mail messages have been gathered from 15 different subjects, all of them related to engineering degrees.

The interaction among students at the UOC is mainly developed through the virtual campus. Therefore, it is very common to find e-mails not directly related to the subject, for example introductory messages, technical problems or Christmas greetings. In order to avoid any kind of noise in the results, all these e-mails have been carefully discarded. This cleansing leaves still more than 15,000 e-mails. In a first search through this data, it has been detected that the use of mathematical notation is present in over 4,000 of the 15,000 e-mails, representing an average of 27% containing some kind of mathematical expression. These 4,000 e-mails are the ones we are going to take into consideration for the rest of this work.

Having prepared the e-mails which are going to be processed, this work focuses first on statistically analysing the types and frequency of mathematical notation used in them. With this information, a careful search through the data will make it possible to detect any particular usage pattern or specific student behaviour depending on variables such as the subject, the knowledge area, the type of studying material and other subject-related variables. Therefore, the next section deals with processing and analysing all this data in order to explain different behaviours in different classrooms.

5. Analysis of the results

Having agreed the motivation for this study, the characteristics of the research subject and the scenario in which it is developed, this section addresses the core of the research. We will first present a basic study of the way students and teachers communicate using mathematical expressions, consisting of the use frequency for every different expression type. Afterwards, the analysis will focus on determining some similarities and differences in the usage pattern for different subjects and/or knowledge areas. Finally, and in order to be able to better explain the reasons for those patterns, some of the most significant descriptive statistics will be developed.

5.1 A basic classification

The first question arising out of this study is to what degree mathematical expressions are used, regarding the different types of notation. We must bear in mind that students are not required to use any specific notation method, so they are free to use whichever method they think is most convenient for their communication needs. As previously noted, and unless it is stated differently, this research and its calculations will consider only the 4,000 e-mails containing some kind of mathematical notation. Therefore, Table 1 gathers the use percentage for every mathematical notation type, showing that around 66% of the e-mails include full mathematical formulae. The rest of the e-mails include, in order of use frequency, single mathematical symbols (24%), formulae citation (11%) and attachments with some mathematical notation (10%). It should be noted that e-mails may fall under more than one category if they use more than one of the different methods. Full results are shown in Table 1.

Total	Formulae		Symbol		Citation		Attachment	
# e-mails	# e-mails	Total %	# e-mails	Total %	# e-mails	Total %	# e-mails	Total %
4055	2679	66	967	24	461	11	390	10

Table 1. Classification of e-mails according to the mathematical notation type used

Furthermore, we want to analyse if this same frequencies apply to individual subjects. The aim is to find out if those frequencies exist regardless of the knowledge area of a particular subject, its content or its methodology. As a first step we will analyse the data in Table 1 but this time grouped by subject. Table 2 shows these results.

As we can see in Table 2, not all the individual subjects have the same average percentages regarding the use of one or other type of mathematics expression. The overall pattern is the same, but there are subjects where full mathematical formulae is used less in favour of citation, or the use of many more mathematical symbols. This fact can be due to differences between the methodology and the study materials of every subject, or also due to different student profiles. In both cases, the results now require us to take into consideration each individual subject. Therefore, as a further step, it is necessary to find out what the patterns are for every subject, which are in turn classified under different knowledge areas. The next section takes care of this matter.

Subject	Total	Formulae		Symbol		Citation		Attachment	
	#	#	%	#	%	#	%	#	%
Algebra	332	235	71	77	23	29	9	24	7
Automata Theory and Formal Languages I	128	57	45	63	49	2	2	9	7
Computers Structure and Technology	287	175	61	101	35	6	2	11	4
Cryptography	224	155	69	49	22	36	16	10	4
Discrete Mathematics	244	158	65	71	29	29	12	12	5
Engineering Physics Fundamentals	228	107	47	52	23	127	56	10	4
Introduction on Mathematics for Engineering	194	147	76	22	11	10	5	23	12
Linear Systems	316	224	71	60	19	14	4	30	9
Mathematical Analysis	425	307	72	120	28	66	16	55	13
Mathematics I	352	250	71	48	14	12	3	54	15
Probability and Statistics	218	170	78	21	10	13	6	24	11
Statistics	331	228	69	83	25	45	14	21	6
Technological Fundamentals I	216	136	63	73	34	4	2	9	4
Technological Fundamentals II	328	203	62	78	24	64	20	31	9
Wiris Laboratory (Algebra)	232	127	55	49	21	4	2	67	29

Table 2. Classification of e-mails according to the subject and the mathematical notation type used

5.2 Different subjects, different behaviour

After these first results, and as we have observed thanks to the statistics in Table 2, the next questions deal with the behaviour of students and teachers according to a particular subject. The main goal is to find out if the same average behaviour can be applied to all of the studied subjects or, if not, what are the possible reasons why there is a different behaviour, by finding subject-related variables affecting that overall pattern.

In order to calculate the next measurements, firstly we will consider the total number of e-mails for every subject, including the ones with no mathematical notation but directly related to that particular subject. We can see there is quite a significant difference between subjects regarding the type of mathematical notation used: depending on the subject, we find 17% of the total e-mails contain mathematical notation, while it can rise to 45% for other subjects.

If we consider only e-mails containing mathematical expressions for every subject, as we previously did in Table 2, we observe differences in the use of one or other type of expression. Table 3 shows the full results of this data, but as a main result it is possible to observe that the percentages are quite different from one subject to another:

- Regarding full mathematical formulae, the results range from 45% in Automata Theory and Formal Languages to 78% in Probability and Statistics.
- In the case of single mathematical symbols, the percentage varies from 10% in Probability and Statistics to 49% in Automata Theory and Formal Languages.
- Regarding formulae citations, the percentage ranges from 2% in Automata Theory and Formal Languages, Wiris Laboratory (Algebra) or Computers Structure and Technology to 56% in Engineering Physics Fundamentals.
- For attachments containing mathematical notation, the percentages range from 4% in Cryptography, Engineering Physics Fundamentals, Computers Structure and Technology or Technological Fundamentals I to 29% in Wiris Laboratory (Algebra).

As it can be seen, there are significant differences regarding both the percentage of e-mails containing mathematical notation and the use of one or another expression method. Considering these results, the next question that arises is about the relationship between similar behaviours. As subjects can be classified within different knowledge areas, Table 3 also contains the same statistics, this time calculated for each one of those areas.

The most significant fact regarding the differences between knowledge areas is about Physics. In that knowledge area there is, compared with the other areas, quite a significant increase in overall mathematical notation use: while for Mathematics this percentage is around 28% and for Technology it is around 21%, for the Physics area it increases to 39%. Analysing this fact in detail and if we have a closer look at the different notation methods, the increase is mostly related to citations: 56% against 9% in the other areas. The reasons for this behaviour pattern are two-fold:

1. There is a well defined citation method in the subject falling under this knowledge area (Engineering Physics Fundamentals), which is responsible for this increase in the use of mathematical notation. This citation method consists of uniquely identifying with a number every single formula used within the subject. In every work document during the term, as well as within communications between students and teachers, formulae are referenced by using those unique numbers. Therefore, it can be easier and faster for both students and teachers referencing any of the formulae and thus the mathematical notation percentage increases. This same fact causes the rest of the notation types to be less used for the Physics area. Technological Fundamentals II (Circuit Theory) uses the same citation method and as we can see it is the second subject where the citation method is used more, with a percentage of 20%.
2. The subject itself: in Physics there are many formulae that students have to learn and understand. This explains the difference with Technological Fundamentals II, where the number of formulae is very much smaller.

Again, the usage figures for full mathematical formulae have an expected pattern, according to the results previously shown in Table 2. While for the Mathematics area it increases to 69%, very similar to the 62% for the Technology area, it drops to 47% for the Physics area. This behaviour is because of two main reasons: the first one is that the Technology area has a lower amount of formulae use within the subjects than the Mathematics and Physics areas.

Area	Subject	Total e-mails #	Math notation #	Math notation %	Formulae #	Formulae %	Symbol #	Symbol %	Citation #	Citation %	Attachment #	Attachment %
Mathematics	Algebra	1170	332	28	235	71	77	23	29	9	24	7
	Automata Theory and Formal Languages I	610	128	21	57	45	63	49	2	2	9	7
	Cryptography	1122	224	20	155	69	49	22	36	16	10	4
	Discrete Mathematics	1020	244	24	158	65	71	29	29	12	12	5
	Introduction on Mathematics for Engineering	726	194	27	147	76	22	11	10	5	23	12
	Linear Systems	846	316	37	224	71	60	19	14	4	30	9
	Mathematical Analysis	953	425	45	307	72	120	28	66	16	55	13
	Mathematics I	1198	352	29	250	71	48	14	12	3	54	15
	Probability and Statistics	610	218	36	170	78	21	10	13	6	24	11
	Statistics	1413	331	23	228	69	83	25	45	14	21	6
	Wiris Laboratory (Algebra)	1120	232	21	127	55	49	21	4	2	67	29
	AREA TOTALS	10788	2996	28	2058	69	663	22	260	9	329	11
Physics	Engineering Physics Fundamentals	581	228	39	107	47	52	23	127	56	10	4
	AREA TOTALS	581	228	39	107	47	52	23	127	56	10	4
Technology	Computers Structure and Technology	1665	287	17	175	61	101	35	6	2	11	4
	Technological Fundamentals I	1078	216	20	136	63	73	34	4	2	9	4
	Technological Fundamentals II	1230	328	27	203	62	78	24	64	20	31	9
	AREA TOTALS	3973	831	21	514	62	252	30	74	9	51	6

Table 3. Usage of mathematical notation types by subject and aggregations by knowledge area

The second reason is that in the Physics area the use of a citation method is favoured as we previously explained.

Still looking at full mathematical formulae and focusing on the Mathematics area, this same irregular behaviour can be verified. The average use percentage of full mathematical formulae for this knowledge area is around 69%, which is quite high, but the behaviour is not the same for all of the subjects in this area. While most of them fall into the range 65% to 75%, there are two subjects where the percentage drops dramatically to 45% and 55%. These subjects are, respectively, Automata Theory and Formal Languages I and Wiris Laboratory (Algebra). Similarly, as previously explained, these subjects do not contain as much mathematical formulae as the rest of the subjects and therefore the use percentage decreases. On the other hand, the use percentage of mathematical symbols in the subject Automata Theory and Formal Languages I is quite high, since this subject contains a high amount of single mathematical symbols instead of full mathematical formulae.

Besides these facts, as for the rest of the notation types there is no significant difference. Again, the conclusion we come to is that in some cases the use of one or other type of notation is highly dependant on the subject, depending on the content itself and on a previous agreement between teachers and students for using some specific notation method as we could see in the Physics subject. In this way, it seems that it is easier and more feasible for students and teachers to express mathematics by the use of a previously established citation system. But again, for the rest of the subjects, apparently the use of one or other method is more likely to be linked to the students' particular preferences.

In the next section we will develop more statistics in order to find yet more specific relationships between subjects and knowledge areas.

5.3 A global statistical analysis

The previous section has shown that there are significant differences in the use of notation between different subjects or knowledge areas. At this point it is important to develop some global descriptive statistics in order to better understand the links between different expression methods.

Table 4 shows the main statistical measurements, calculated for every notation type and knowledge area. For each of these groups, it shows the mean, the minimum and maximum, the standard deviation and the mode, all values represented in percentages. Regarding the special case of Physics, as there is just one subject under this knowledge area, we will not consider its standard deviation.

As it can be seen in Table 4, there are two cases in which the mean does not fall into the mode range:

- Mathematics area, formula within the e-mail body
- Mathematics area, attachment with formula

In none of these cases, though, the difference between the mean and the mode is very significant. This might only be a symptom of an abnormal distribution, and it is not surprising because as we described in previous sections there is a very different pattern in a few subjects for using one or other mathematical notation type depending on the subject and area.

The Mathematics knowledge area is the one showing a larger difference overall between the minimum and maximum percentages for every notation type. This was already explained in a previous section, the reason being there are two subjects in this area (Automata Theory and Formal Languages I and Wiris Laboratory) which do not follow the regular pattern of the other subjects because of their content type. That is also confirmed by this area having the overall highest standard deviations, especially concerning the most used notation types: full mathematical formulae (with a standard deviation of 9) and mathematical symbol (with a standard deviation of 10).

	Knowledge area	Mean	Min	Max	Standard deviation	Mode
Formula within the e-mail body	Mathematics	67	45	78	9	>= 70% - < 80%
	Physics	47	47	57	-	>= 40% - < 50%
	Technology	62	61	63	1	>= 60% - < 70%
Mathematical symbol	Mathematics	23	10	49	10	>= 20% - < 30%
	Physics	23	23	23	-	>= 20% - < 30%
	Technology	31	24	35	5	>= 30% - < 40%
Citation	Mathematics	8	2	16	5	>= 0% - <10%
	Physics	56	56	56	-	>= 50% - < 60%
	Technology	8	2	20	8	>= 0% - <10%
Attachament with formula	Mathematics	11	4	29	7	>= 0% - <10%
	Physics	4	4	4	-	>= 0% - <10%
	Technology	6	4	9	3	>= 0% - <10%
Attachment without formula	Mathematics	5	1	14	4	>= 0% - <10%
	Physics	1	1	1	-	>= 0% - <10%
	Technology	6	4	9	2	>= 0% - <10%
Attachment with graphics	Mathematics	2	0	5	2	>= 0% - <10%
	Physics	2	2	2	-	>= 0% - <10%
	Technology	5	1	10	4	>= 0% - <10%
Any kind of mathematical notation	Mathematics	28	20	45	8	>= 20% - < 30%
	Physics	39	39	39	-	>= 30% - < 40%
	Technology	21	17	27	4	>= 20% - < 30%

Table 4. Statistical analysis grouped by notation type and knowledge area

Table 5 shows the same statistical measurements groups as in Table 4, but this time regardless of the knowledge area. As it can be seen in the results, the percentages are more dispersed, showing a high standard deviation on all three most commonly used notation types: formula within the e-mail body, mathematical symbol and citation.

As it can be observed, the only group mismatching the mean into the mode range with a significant percentage is Formula within the e-mail body. But analysing the data in Table 3, we can see that it is only due to a very irregular use of mathematical formulae: while the mode stays at the range 70%-80%, the rest of the subjects not falling into this range belong to a few different ranges. Therefore, we can discard the statistics in Table 5 as they are not explanatory for this study.

	Mean	Min	Max	Standard deviation	Mode
Formula within the e-mail body	65	45	78	10	>= 70% - < 80%
Mathematical symbol	24	10	49	10	>= 20% - < 30%
Citation	11	2	56	13	>= 0% - <10%
Attachment with formula	9	4	29	6	>= 0% - <10%
Attachment without formula	5	1	14	4	>= 0% - <10%
Attachment with graphics	3	0	10	2	>= 0% - <10%
Any kind of mathematical notation	28	17	45	8	>= 20% - < 30%

Table 5. Statistical analysis grouped by notation type

Finally, Table 6 shows, according to the mode, the most popular notation types within each knowledge area. This rank also states that one or other notation type use highly depends on the subject and area, Physics being a good example of that: Mathematics and Technology areas both have formula within the e-mail body as the most commonly used notation type,

	Most commonly used	Second commonly used
Mathematics	Formula within the e-mail body	Mathematical symbol
Physics	Citation	Formula within the e-mail body
Technology	Formula within the e-mail body	Mathematical symbol

Table 6. Most commonly used citation methods by knowledge area

while Physics has citations as its preferred type. Furthermore, Physics does not have mathematical symbols in second place as Mathematics and Technology do, but formula within the e-mail body instead. This means that for Physics, when citation is not being used, the pattern reflects the one in Mathematics and Technology.

As we have seen, these main statistical measurements neither completely explain the overall behaviour of students choosing a particular mathematics expression method. More information is needed, basically in the way of a much larger e-mail sample, so it is possible to understand why a student expresses mathematics in a particular way. Therefore, this research leads us to conclude that a deeper study is needed in order to analyse different patterns linked to particular students.

6. Conclusion

In this chapter it has been shown: 1) which strategies and methods students use to communicate mathematical formulae in a web based e-learning environment, by means of the analysis of 17,000 messages; and 2) how important each method is depending on the subject and on the knowledge area.

This study has been developed exclusively using an e-mail web application that lacks a formulae editor, in order to explain the way students communicate using mathematical notation. In the course of this research, it has been seen that the use of mathematical formulae in virtual learning environments has to be carefully studied in order to provide students with better communication, as well as a better understanding of mathematics in engineering degrees.

From the study, it can be concluded that:

- Mathematical formulae appear in 30% of the e-mails for the analysed subjects. This shows that in the area of e-learning for technical and scientific degrees formulae play a key role in communication. When a technological solution is not available, which is the case, students manage to find a way to communicate mathematics. However, it has to be taken into account that this is an extra handicap for students in subjects that they traditionally find difficult. The challenge of communication, besides the inherent difficulty of the subjects, can cause some students not to ask questions.
- Mathematical expressions appear in different ways: as a symbol, as a formula written in pseudocode (LaTeX style), as a cited formula and as an attachment.
- For some subjects, the method used to communicate mathematical formulae depends on two factors:
  - The subject itself: some subjects have more formulae (like Physics) and others have more symbols (like Automata Theory and Formal Languages I). The complexity of the formulae and the role they play in the subjects will determine how much mathematical formulae will appear. Then, the overall amount of mathematical notation used by teachers and students seems to relate to the amount of mathematical notation content within the subject itself better than to some other external factors.
  - The features of the study materials: some subjects, like Physics or Technological Fundamentals II, have a very good citation method since every formula is numbered. This makes it easier for students and teachers to cite formulae by their

number and therefore causes a significant boost to the use of formulae thanks to the simplicity of the citation method. Assuming that students and teachers use (or should use) mathematical notation whenever they need to, and regarding the increase of mathematical notation use in Physics, it can be concluded that the lack of such an easy pre-established notation method causes difficulties in communication among the members of a virtual classroom community.

- There is no pattern regarding the use of mathematical formulae which is valid for all the subjects and knowledge areas. When a concrete type of notation is considered, the results show there is an overall common pattern among all the subjects, full mathematical formula, symbol and citation being the most commonly used. The exception though occurs when a certain notation method is established beforehand, in which case it seems easier and more likely to be used by students and teachers according to the increase of use observed in the particular case of the Physics subject.

- Therefore, there are signs leading to the existence of student patterns and profiles, more than an overall pattern for every subject. In some cases, when a subject offers an easy and feasible method for expressing mathematics, such is the case for citation, students and teachers tend to adopt it and in that way increase the use of mathematics content within e-mail. In the rest of cases, the student preference seems to be the main reason for the selection. In that case, we need to analyse what leads a student to choose one or other method and if that choice can be linked to a better understanding of the subject, thus a better academic performance. Or furthermore, from a different point of view, if students that have a better academic performance are linked to one particular type of mathematical expressions.

All these conclusions show the importance of mathematical notation for students of technological subjects. For some subjects, this study has detected several key points as indicators for the use of a specific mathematics expression method. For example, in certain subjects, a well-established citation system makes it easier and faster for students to use citation instead of any other method. In the same way, other features like the structure of the study materials or even its content, can also affect the behaviour of students. As for other subjects, further work has to be developed in order to find proper key indicators, which apparently can be related to particular student profile or preferences.

In spite of the large volume of e-mails processed in this research, more than 17,000, the information gathered from them is not enough to identify these student profiles. Currently, the information related to one particular student through different subjects and terms is not significant enough, statistically speaking, to be able to determine if they are following a particular pattern. Therefore, future research must bear this in mind and target particular students behaviour instead of overall subject behaviour. Once this information is available, future studies can also try to find links between the academic performance of students and mathematical expressions use patterns. For example, it is possible to find out if a specific behaviour pattern, varying from the classroom average, leads to a different academic performance, either if that performance is reflected in the students' final marks or on a higher rate of students following continuous assessment during the term. Furthermore, not only the use of the communication method chosen by the student, but the variation in the use of different methods, the usage amount of each one of them and even the content of the e-mails itself can lead us to detect different student profiles from which we could have another very interesting point of view. For example, the use of a richer language or the development and discussion of a given formula through a thread of e-mails can help teachers identify the expected performance for a particular student and therefore help them focus on the students who are not following this pattern.

According to the results of this research, the contents and structure of a subject can lead students to communicate mathematics in a particular way, sometimes more frequently than the average. However, this does not necessarily mean a better overall performance in a subject, as students would perhaps perform better if the subject was, conversely, designed according to the preferences of the students, providing them with the necessary tools for this purpose.

Finally, the use of mathematical language within a virtual classroom is a handicap for e-learning since students and teachers are only able to express themselves by the use of e-mail but, furthermore, we must take into account that this problem can be much worse for disadvantaged student groups – as for example students with visual impairments – especially when we consider the similar difficulties that both students in a virtual environment and students with visual impairments face on a daily basis (as was explained in Section 2). Therefore, these are the main aspects that will be explored in future work.

7. References

Chen, Y. & Okada, M. (2001). Structural Analysis and Semantic Understanding for Offline Mathematical Expressions. *International Journal of Pattern Recognition and Artificial Intelligence*, Vol. 15, No. 6, pp. 967-988, Sept. 2001.

Fitzpatrick, D. (2007). Teaching Science subjects to Blind Students. Seventh IEEE International Conference on Advanced Learning Technologies (ICALT)

LaTeX (2011). A document preparation system. Date of access: 01/05/2011. Available from: http://www.latex-project.org

Microsoft (2011). Microsoft Equation Editor. Date of access: 01/05/2011. Available from: http://www.microsoft.com/education/en-us/teachers/how-to/Pages/mathematical-equations.aspx

sMArTH (2011). An online equation editor for MathML and LaTeX. Date of access: 01/05/2011. Available from: http://smarth.sourceforge.net

The Number Empire (2011). LaTeX Equation Editor. Date of access: 01/05/2011. Available from: http://www.numberempire.com/texequationeditor/equationeditor.php

Wiris (2011). The global solution for maths education. Date of access: 01/05/2011. Available from: http://www.wiris.com/en/editor

World Wide Web Consortium (2011). MathML, W3C Math Home. Date of access: 01/05/2011. Available from: http://www.w3.org/Math

Yue-sheng, G. & Jia-yi, Z (2008). Uploading Strategy of the Formula in the Web-based Mathematics Testing System. International Conference on Computer Science and Software Engineering.

Zhao, J. (2008). Towards a User-centric Math Information Retrieval System. Bulletin of IEEE Technical Committee on Digital Libraries, Vol. 4, issue 2, fall 2008, ISSN 1937-7266

7

E-Learning Usage During Chemical Engineering Courses

Majda Krajnc

University of Maribor, Faculty of Chemistry and Chemical Engineering
Slovenia

1. Introduction

During the last century a lot of changes appeared within the education process. At the beginning of the 20th century, children went to school on foot. Sometimes their homes were very far from their schools, so they spent a lot of time per day just walking. Our grandmothers and grandfathers were such a generation. Sometimes sleepy and tired, they still had to listen very carefully to what the teachers said because they had to make notes for their homework. Teachers were strict and pupils had to obey them. Teachers were often the only people who gave children information about history, geography, mathematics, chemistry etc. Most the inhabitants of those times did not have a radio, and television did not exist yet. Despite this, some of the pupils of this generation went-on to universities and even became scientists. How was it possible? Did they have enough knowledge under such circumstances? They did not have computers and internet yet. In spite of all that, they had knowledge skills, and work ethics than the generations at the end of the 20th century. They spent a lot of time in libraries reading, learning and, writing about what they were learning. They discussed a lot about their problems with their colleagues and professors. They were very good listeners.

In the second half of the 20th century students, in general, did not need to go to school on foot anymore, whether they lived far from school or not. They could choose the bus or train, or even lived in student hostels. The evolution in technology also caused an evolution in the education process. The lectures became more practical. Lecturers did not only use a blackboard and chalk when lecturing but some of them started to use different technical equipment such as overhead projectors and slides for presenting the subject material to their students. Students could spend time in modern libraries, make notes in notebooks or even make copies of the course material. Many lecturers wrote their own books as course material, which students could then buy.

At the beginning of the 21st century, a group of eminent professors of chemical engineering (Felder et al., 2000) announced that in the very near future, it would be almost impossible to carry-out the education process without incorporating better teaching methods. Different study reforms would change the traditional curricula and lecturers would simply have insufficient time for explaining all the material, within the classroom. This meant that students would need to take greater responsibility for their own knowledge and non-traditional methods, such as active learning, cooperative learning, problem-based learning, project-based learning, and e-learning would be the more important activities regarding a more efficient education system (Krajnc, 2009). The solutions exist, it is upon the lecturer to decide which method to choose.

When the computer era began, computer experts started to develop information and communication technology (ICT), which created a huge revolution in the presentation of knowledge and information to the world, which then became a much smaller place with a lot more information. A basic ICT infrastructure needs computers, the internet, e-mail, and intranet. Using such structures, an electronic way of learning (e-learning) is possible and in a modern society all these tools are usually available.

E-learning could be used as part of traditional learning (blended-learning, hybrid-learning, mixed-learning) or just as online (virtual) education and incorporated into any course content i.e. the natural sciences or sociology. Maybe it is a little harder to use it in natural sciences because the mathematicians probably asses knowledge electronically less than the historian.

Nowadays, it is normal to use electronic slides, the internet, e-mails, electronic learning environments and e-course material during lectures presentation. When using ICT at lectures, it is the lecturers' responsibilities to present students with qualitative and important information. Many lecturers who use ICT say that when ICT is included within the traditional method of education, it facilitates lectures and the students' work, and the lectures became more dynamic and interesting. Different e-activities also enrich the subject content. E-learning presents an alternative for students and helps them to find a balance between their private lives, careers, and education. It is one of the more dynamic and enriching forms of learning, and reduces dependency on space and time (Paik et al., 2004). It offers both individual learning experiences, and opportunities for working together with colleagues (Peat, 2000).

A lot of statements have been made to date which have shown both positive and negative responses to e-learning. The following are some examples. Lecturers who have one hundred or more students at their lectures know that the lecturer my well spend more time on the final assessment than on lecturing, lecture preparation, and tutorials (Husssman et al.; 2004, Excell, 2004). Because assessment represents a significant part of a lecturer's workload, computer-assisted assessment has the potential for allowing an effective assessment regime to be maintained in the cases of large classes. E-learning assessment of knowledge is also of great benefit from the students' points of view. Rossiter et al. (2010) implemented online quizzes within a Chemical Process Principle Course in the freshman year. Such a new method of learning improved students' learning and success, particularly among weaker students and helped them to develop transferable skills regarding teamwork and communication. The quizzes helped them to do their homework, and to a certain extent, develop their core technical skills for problem-based learning activities.

On the one hand, e-learning brings a lot of advantages whilst, on the other, it does require the adoption of new skills and knowledge. At the beginnings of any e-learning incorporation into the education process, a lot of time is needed in order to learn new aspects regarding the adoption of new technologies, and their different tools. Some users stop using it after their initial experience. Pei-Chen Sun et al. (2008) investigated those critical factors affecting learners' satisfaction with e-learning. They discovered that learner computer-anxiety, instructor-attitude towards e-learning, e-learning course flexibility, e-learning course quality, perceived usefulness, perceived ease of use and diversity during assessments, are the critical factors. The effect of learning activities and students' satisfaction are influenced by their instructors' attitudes when handling learning activities. Active and positive attitudes do motivate students regarding e-learning usage. Pei-Chen et al. (2008) also discussed that course quality, which includes teaching material, interactive discussion, and course-scheduling, had the strongest association with satisfaction regarding e-learning. Furthermore, many e-learning users were discouraged from e-learning by those poor technologies having slow response-times or frequent technical difficulties.

Nowadays, a lot of e-tools are available for e-education e.g. internet tools (wikis), electronic or virtual learning environments (Blackboard, Webassign, WebCT, Moodle), and web labs. Through such tools the lecturers and students can communicate in two different ways: synchronous and asynchronous. A lot of experiences and supporting technologies on synchronous e-learning were presented by Granda et al. (2010). They pointed-out two major features of synchronous e-learning systems, i.e. audio and video-conferencing. The first one is used to allow participants to participate orally within learning sessions, whilst the second is used to reinforce a sense of user-presence. Floyd Smith et al. (2010) presented their experiences of a synchronous distance-education course for non-scientists, which was successfully carried out over two semesters and jointly by three universities.

Lectures and experts from many institutions worldwide who already use different kinds of e-learning tools within their education processes (Lau, 2005; Maurice, 2006; Selmer 2007; Hussman, 2004; Rodrígues et al., 2006) think that such technology stimulates and motivates students' interest in their subjects, improves their learning performances within the discipline of industrial engineering, and significantly improves the teaching and learning, whilst saving time and money regarding all aspects of the classroom. Web labs, for example, provide students with training for working with experimental equipment and help them to understand the fundamentals of unit operations e.g. distillation and drying (Dongil et al., 2009). Such laboratories drastically reduce the economic necessity of providing new equipment, and stimulate skills such as teamwork, communication, and presentation (Selmer, 2007; Le Roux et al., 2010).

Electronic tools could be successfully used in interdisciplinary learning courses in which e.g. students participate outside the classroom. Schaad et al. (2008) described such course in which students had the option of participating in either a service-learning exercise within an area ravaged by a natural disaster within Lousiana and North Carolina, or to research a topic related to natural disasters. All students attended the lecture component of the course and completed on-line quizzes on Blackboard in order to demonstrate their understanding of the presented material. The twice-weekly lectures were recorded and provided in the form of Webcasts for future reference.

Some educators use Internet tools e.g. wikis technology, to enhance creativity, communication, student interaction, collaboration, and the organization of information (Hadley & Debelak, 2009) when students work on projects, and as a replacement for traditional text-books where students add problems and edit the educational content (Richardson, 2006). When using wikis during projects, the supervisor can keep constant tabs on a student's progress, so the projects are completed on time and the results are valid.

ICT has also been incorporated into some Chemical Engineering Courses at the Faculty of Chemistry and Chemical Engineering (FCCE), University of Maribor (UM), Slovenia. At the beginning, this novelty confused the majority of the teaching staff. Some lecturers thought that the students' knowledge would decrease by incorporating e-learning into their courses. Only a few enthusiasts believed that new learning methods and tools will produce better and efficient study results, and that some activities will expand both the lecturers' and students' knowledge. The results of their efforts are described in this Chapter.

This Chapter is organized as follows: Section 2 introduces the incorporation of e-learning at the FCCE in Maribor. Section 3 illustrates the efficient tools of e-learning i.e. electronic tests for the e-assessment of knowledge and multimedia e-chapters. The students' and teaching staffs' responses to e-learning are also presented in this section. Section 4 concludes the chapter describing their experiences of e-learning usage from both the students and teaching staffs' points of view, and ends with the challenges for the future.

2. Incorporation of e-learning at FCCE, University of Maribor

E-learning at the Faculty of Chemistry and Chemical Engineering (FCCE) in Maribor was incorporated into the education process for the first time during the academic year 2004/2005. The pedagogical staff started to adopt the electronic learning environment called ELEUM, which was developed at the Faculty of Electrical Engineering and Computer Science, in Maribor. It was available to all members of the University free of charge. It was a simple but effective electronic learning environment, which could be used by all lecturers and students as a communication tool.

ELEUM advanced into the pedagogical process very slowly, because the introduction of anything new is hard and painstaking work. However, the first experiences showed that it could improve the quality of the process. Only one lecturer from one Course used it at the beginning. Only certain activities were used in the first year because this was a new method of learning, teaching and communicating. In general, lecturers put on ELEUM electronic documents of the Course material, the criteria of the Course, dates for exams and colloquiums, and information about lectures, practical work etc. Then new functionalities were added from year to year.

Although the pedagogical staff became acquainted very slowly with this new method of working, the students adopted it almost immediately. Their responses to e-learning and the ELEUM were collected by means of a questionnaire (Krajnc, 2006, 2009). The questionnaires were filled by students at the Process Synthesis Course, where e-learning was introduced for the first time at FCCE. The course was carried-out in the second semester of the third year as a professional higher programme.

The questionnaire results showed that during the academic year 2004/2005 e-learning was almost unknown to students, by the next academic year approximately one half of students knew or partly-knew e-learning, but by the 2006/2007 academic year, all the students knew it well or fairly-well. Thus, information about e-learning within the education process has advanced from year to year (Krajnc, 2009). At the beginning, the lecturer was the main source of initial information about e-learning but over the following academic years, the students received information from their friends and other colleagues who had used an electronic learning environment in previous years, too. Students thought that ELEUM was an effective tool and helped them to improve the qualities and efficiencies of their studies.

They pointed-out the following advantages:

- updated information about the Course,
- all the data collected in one place,
- electronic text-books.

Students also stated, that they could print-out, for example, solution manuals, questions for traditional oral exams, chapters of the text-books, whenever they wanted to. The lecturer could correct the data, and update the manuals and text-books.

In 2009, ELEUM was replaced by Moodle, a internationally-known open-source (course) learning management system also called "Virtual Learning Environment" (VLE) (Dougiamas, 1999). In comparison with ELEUM, Moodle was fairly sophisticated and provided more aids than ELEUM. When Moodle became available for educational purposes, it caused stress among lecturers. It was a novelty once again. For this reason, the lecturers were only capable of putting on it mainly electronic documents and exam results, as at the time of ELEUM's beginning. The Computer Centre of the University of Maribor, Department for e-learning, prepares learning workshops every year because of the problems. By such an education of the pedagogic staff, Moodle has advanced into the pedagogical process from year to year.

3. Efficient tools for e-learning

In spite of many useful electronic tools, being available online, there are some which particularly help to decrease the lecturers' workloads and increase efficiency when studying. The following, presents only two of them i.e. electronic tests (quizzes) for the electronic assessment of knowledge and multimedia e-chapter which helps students to prepare for electronic or classical assessments of knowledge.

3.1 Electronic assessment of knowledge

From almost the beginning of the ELEUM's usage, electronic tests (quizzes) were prepared for students who were willing to choose them instead of the traditional oral exam. Some people would say that creating a bank of questions takes a lot of time and effort, and the final result is a greater lecturer workload. This was true at the beginning of e-assessment but after a year or two the workload decreases because it is unnecessary to create a new bank of questions every year but only to add new or edit old questions. It is certainly true that lecturers engaged in such work have a lot of enthusiasm for their work and want to offer students new ideas.

The students' responses to e-test usage were different in comparison with other available functionalities. In this case, knowledge was assessed using an appropriate mark after finishing each e-test. For these reasons, students did not decide to use them in as greater numbers as for other tools.

The first electronic test was realized at the Process Synthesis Course during the academic year 2004/2005, and since then every following academic year without interruption. Some students have seen a lot of advantages in such a choice, such as (Krajnc, 2008):

- they can avoid the embarrassment of confronting their lecturer face to face,
- they can concentrate better on the questions,
- the results of the e-tests are known immediately.

Since the academic year 2004/2005, more and more students have chosen this assessment of their knowledge, instead of the classical oral examinations (Krajnc, 2008), as shown Fig. 1.

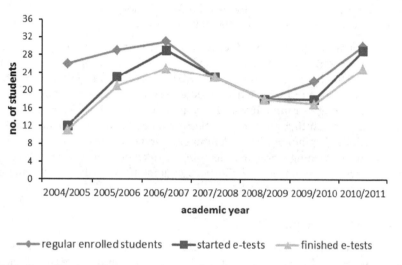

Fig. 1. Students' applications for e-tests during the Process Synthesis Course.

The middle-curve shows the interest for e-tests during the seven academic years of the Process Synthesis Course. The curve shows the increase in e-test applications until the academic year 2007/2008. The next academic year the interest stayed the same, i.e. all students chose e-tests, but in the academic years 2009/2010 and 2010/2011 some students did not choose e-tests instead of the classical oral exam. The lower curve represents the number of students who finished e-tests successfully. It can be seen, that in the academic years 2007/2008 and 2008/2009, all the regular enrolled students chose e-tests and also finished them successfully. It is evident that the number of sceptical students decreased gradually from the academic year 2004/2005 to 2007/2008 but increased again during the academic year 2009/2010. The fluctuation in e-tests applicability among students during the seven year time period was mainly about their ignorance of the new way of learning, and an unwillingness to become acquainted with the knowledge in so short a time i.e. chapter after chapter.

E-tests were prepared for each chapter of the course material separately and were composed of different numbers and kinds of questions. They were executed approximately twice a month. Students had one week to prepare for each e-test. When the e-test was turned on, they came to the Faculty's computer room.

All e-tests included about 70 questions. Students had to focus on each question very carefully since the answers sometimes seemed very similar. A student was successful if the fraction of correct answers was at least 60 %. There were different types of questions in each e-test:

a.   questions with one correct answer from two possible answers,
b.   questions with one correct answer from among several possible answers,
c.   questions with several correct answers from among many possible answers,
d.   true/false questions,
e.   the essay-type questions.

The following are some examples of those e-test questions included in the electronic assessment of knowledge during the Process Synthesis Course.

Example 1: The essay-type question

A four-component mixture is to be separated by distillation.
The boiling points and amounts of each component are presented in a table.

Component	t_b /°C	q_m /(t/h)
1	-10 (corrosive)	10
2	40 (toxic)	20
3	80	50
4	90	20

What separation sequence would you recommend and
which of the several heuristics explain the orders of separation?

Example 1 represents the essay-type question. The Table presents data for a four-component mixture which should be separated into pure components. Students need to focus on the properties of the components i.e. boiling points, corrosiveness and toxicity, and on this basis determine the appropriate separation sequence. They have to take into consideration two heuristic rules:

a.   remove the corrosive and hazardous material early, and
b.   difficult separations are best saved for last.

Their findings are written in the box below the question.

Example 2: The multiple-choice type question with one correct answer.

The following result is obtained with the Arrhenius equation:
$-E/R = -19967$ K.
The activation energy in kJ/mol is:

Izberite en odgovor.   ⊛   16,6 kJ/mol ✗   Your answer is incorrect.
                                                                      You should pay more attention to R constant unit! ☺

                                      ○   1660 kJ/mol ✗

                                      ○   166 kJ/mol ✓

                                      ○   166 000 kJ/mol ✗

Example 2 is more exact because certain calculations need to be done before selecting the correct answer. A student has to know the proper value and unit of ideal gas constant (in this case 8,314 J/(mol · K)) by heart, and then calculate activation energy. He/she must pay attention to the activation energy unit which must be in kJ/mol. When he/she establishes all the requirements, the correct answer is selected (the third one in this case). Obviously in this case the student chose the wrong answer. The message »*The answer is incorrect. You should pay more attention to R constant unit*!« reminds student as to what mistake he/she has probably made.

Example 3: True/false question.

The reaction path is a **potential** for commercialization, when the products are more valuable than the raw materials.

Odgovor: ○ Pravilno ✓

        ◉ Ne drži ✗

You did not choose the correct answer. ☺

Example 3 shows a sentence which is written correctly or incorrectly. Students have to read it word by word and very carefully because sometimes only one word has a significant meaning. After deciding the student chooses only one possibility i.e. true (if the sentence is written correctly) or false (if the sentence is written incorrectly). In this case, the student chose the second possibility i.e. false, which was the wrong decision.

Students have the interesting comments on questions with the different kinds of correct and wrong answers. They think that questions with several possible answers are the most pretentious because they have to know the theory in detail. They should focus on answers very carefully because they sometimes seem similar. If they are somewhat unacquainted with the theory of the course, they usually do not select all the correct answers.

Before starting the first e-test, the lecturer explains how e-tests are conducted e.g. that they have time-limits, the questions and answers for each implementation are mixed, how many questions are contained in each e-test, and incorrect answers are estimated with negative points. Students are usually very nervous before the first e-test. This is understandable particularly in those cases where they have not had such a kind of knowledge evaluation up to that moment. In the Process Synthesis Course, the lecturer accepts a failure in one e-test, but they must be successful in the following. The theory of the chapter, in which the student fails, would he/she passes traditional.

The non-traditional way of learning i.e. co-operative work (when doing homework and solving problems in teams) and e-learning, produced good study results during the Process Synthesis Course. Almost all students finished their course obligations within the course time or within one or two weeks after finishing the lectures. The students stated that, in such a manner, more time was left for other courses and obligations where they did not have such work opportunities.

During the academic year 2006/2007, the electronic assessment of knowledge was also incorporated in the second study year within the Process Balances and Process Calculation Courses. During this study year e-tests were prepared for the self-assessment of knowledge before the oral exam. Electronic tests were active from the 1st June until the 1st October of that year, i.e. throughout whole summer examination time. Students who passed all e-tests successfully got an extra bonus towards the final mark of the exam, as a stimulus award. Almost half of the regular enrolled students (46 %) who needed to pass the Process Balances

Course and 33 % in the Process Calculation Course took e-tests before the oral exam (Krajnc, 2009) . They said that:

- with e-tests they learned what was the essence of each chapter,
- e-tests gave them a critique about the knowledge,
- correct answers were available,
- the marks and results of the e-tests were known at once and
- they would suggest such assessment of knowledge for the following generations of students.

3.1.1 Electronic assessment of knowledge for the Bologna study-program courses

When Slovenia in 2004 became a full member of the European Union and the European University Area, the Bologna Process started, to which the members of this area are bound. It encompasses a unique model regarding studies. This has meant reassessing and changing the traditional curricula towards a single-study structure within European Universities (Krajnc, 2009).

The Bologna study programmes at FCCE started during the academic year 2009/2010. Each year the results show that a lot of students register in the first study year, which causes a lot of pedagogic workload for the staff. As the application of IC learning environments is particularly useful when a lot of students are enrolled, Moodle was incorporated within some Bologna Courses i.e. Computer Science in Chemistry Course (CSC), and Process Calculation I Course (PC I) in the first semester, and Process Calculation II Course (PC II), Chemical Calculation II Course (CC II), and Process Balances Course (PB) in the second semester. On the basis of the previous experiences from the Process Synthesis Course, the electronic assessment of knowledge was also incorporated into the mentioned Bologna courses. Lectures at all courses were given once a week (3 hours every week). The lecturer explained the main points of the material, and the students learned the rest by themselves. The following explains the electronic assessment procedures at some courses.

At the Computer Science in Chemistry Course and Process Calculation I Course of the first semester, electronic assessment was introduced to the freshman three times, half an hour before regular lectures, and in a computer room of the Faculty. Each e-test was administrated only once. It was forbidden to write down the questions on the paper. A student was successful if at least 60 % of the answers were correct.

In order to obtain freshman's feedback on the applicability, usefulness, and efficiency of e-assessment, at the end of the semester students filled-in a questionnaire and answered certain questions. It was comprised of 16 questions, 13 of which were multiple-choice type questions and three were essay-type questions. The questionnaire was classified into four parts where students gave their opinions on:

- electronic-learning environment applicability,
- reasons for e-environment usage,
- electronic-assessment and
- the new way of learning.

109 of the students filled-in the questionnaire. The results showed that 10 % of students used the electronic-learning environment Moodle every day, 82 % once a week, and the rest (8 %)

once a month. They also said that the combination of traditional and electronic method of learning suited them and that they also wanted such a kind of work in other courses.

More than 71 % of the students' replies were the same as their older colleagues in the Process Synthesis Course, i.e. that they chose the electronic-assessment of knowledge because they had to become acquainted with smaller portions of the course material at once, the other students (29 %) chose the e-test because they wanted to avoid the oral exam in the professor's office. Three quarters of the students (74 %) said that after the first e-test they could better prepare for the others because after the first one they acquired a feeling for such a kind of examination. Almost all students (94 %) thought that they had enough time to answer all the questions in the e-assessment.

The lecturer also received a significant response about the intelligibilities and difficulties of the questions. The result showed that almost half the students (42 %) thought that the questions were always clear and easy to understand, and 50 % thought they were almost always understandable. 8 % of students replied that questions were sometimes understandable and sometimes not. Furthermore, 79 % of students said that questions were medium-difficult, 13 % thought they were easy, and 8 % that they were tough questions.

In one of the questions, the students compared electronic-assessment with the traditional oral exam. Almost half of the students (46 %) thought that the electronic-assessment of knowledge was easier than the classical one, 45 % said that it was easier and of higher quality, one student said it was of higher quality but difficult, and four students replied that it was easier but of a lesser quality than the classical oral exam. More than half of the students (68 %) felt less stressed at an e-examination as they had to confront the lecturer at a classical oral exam but more than a quarter of the students did not feel psychological burdened themselves by the e-test.

For the essay-type questions students gave their opinions on:

- information about the Course activities through Moodle,
- e-test failure,
- advantages and disadvantages of e-assessing knowledge.

The students mainly said that the information was clear enough, effective, and practical. They wanted to have such information at other courses. The reasons for failures in e-tests were the lack of learning, reluctance at the exam, superficiality, difficult questions, and absence from lectures.

The advantages of the e-examination were:

- on-going learning,
- instant feedback of the results,
- less time to learn,
- you are not under stress.

The disadvantages were:

- ambiguous questions and answers,
- quickly forget the theory,
- no possibility of repeating e-tests,

- reading the question wrongly.

From among the 109 students who started the electronic-assessment of their knowledge at CSC and PC I, 78 students (72 %) finished all e-tests successfully, 19 students (17 %) resigned from electronic-assessment because of negative grades, and 12 students (11 %) resigned from e-assessment because they changed their mind about such a kind of assessment or study, in general. Some students also realised that such a kind of work is too difficult for them.

The analysis of 116 active students i.e. those who finished the experimental computer work in the computer room, after completing the lectures at CSC and PC I, showed that 78 of them completed all the e-tests successfully. The others (38 of the active students or 33 %) had to move to the classical oral exam. The results showed that the lecturers' workloads regarding oral examinations decreased by 67 %. So, what does this mean in hours regarding lecturers' workloads? When you consider that one student needs approximately half an hour for a classical oral examination, 78 students meant 39 less hours needed for oral examinations, which is almost one working week. Within such a time-period, a lecturer could do other things e.g. research work, additional notes regarding course material, prepare new problems for written exams etc. It is also important to point out that the students saved time, too. They did not need extra time at the Faculty for the examination, so they saved time and money on bus or train tickets, or fuel if they had a car.

3.2 The response of the teaching staff to e-learning

Enthusiasm for introducing new methods into the educational process is not as great amongst the teaching staff as with the students. This was already apparent at the time of the ELEUM application. The first responses from the lecturers and assistants were obtained at the end of the academic year 2005/2006, on the basis of a questionnaire which was sent to all teaching staff at the Faculty. The results showed that half of the teaching staff was completely disinterested in e-learning or they were so occupied with other duties that they had no time to answer the questionnaire (Krajnc, 2009). The other half showed resistance to use of electronic-teaching tools within their courses.

Anyway, awareness of electronic-teaching and learning has expanded among the staff from year to year. The more experienced lecturers in e-learning are constantly encouraging colleagues towards the new method of working. The application of different activities within e-learning are presented every year at the "*Slovenian Chemical Days, Conference*" which takes place at the FCCE in Maribor every autumn. The Computer Centre of the UM, Department for e-learning, prepares learning workshops three times a year. Recently, in December 2010, a Workshop on the electronic-teaching environment Moodle's usage was held at FCCE in Maribor. The Workshop was led by a lecturer of the Faculty who has many years experiences in e-learning. The participation of the teaching staff was very low. Only six lecturers and assistants were interested in Moodle application during the pedagogical process. At the end of the Workshop, participants filled-in an electronic questionnaire which included six questions concerning Moodle's application. On the question »*How often do you use Moodle?*« one answered several times a year, two of them replied never, and three of them said once a week. Their knowledge of Moodle was estimated at a 1,7 grade on a five point scale (1-insufficient, 2-sufficient, 3-well, 4-very good, 5-excellent). They said, they used Moodle:

- for informing and sending exam grades,
- for the publication of study materials,
- for questionnaires,
- for displaying a list of students.

On the question »*Do you mean that Moodle facilitates the implementation of work and saves time?*« three of them agreed, one said it does not save time but facilitates the implementation of the pedagogic process, two of them could not agree or disagree with the statement as they had not used Moodle yet. Four participants of the Workshop knew that UM organises educational workshops on Moodle application three times a year but they had not participated in any of them yet. Two participants knew and already participated to them. The answers on the question »*Why don't you use Moodle more often?*« were similar i.e. they did not have enough time for additional education and they did not know enough about the Moodle application.

3.3 Multimedia e-text-books (e-material)

Because at e-learning, students' educations are largely left to them, text-books should be prepared in appropriate forms. Beside electronic learning environments and its tools and activities, which could be used within the learning process, multimedia electronic text-books are useful tools, which additionally implement the education process. A lot of sources and modules can be inserted into such text-books such as: video, animations, internet links, short quizzes with different type of questions etc. In general, learning with multimedia e-materials is more motivated and successful compared with live lessons or other media (video, simulation, and a combination of graph and audio presentations), which enable easier learning. Such material adapts students to various learning styles and facilitates a constructive and enquiry-based approach to learning (Clark & Feldon, 2005; Krnel & Bajd, 2009). When students use multimedia e-text-books, they can better prepare themselves for examinations. Usually, they easily pass e-tests, oral, and written exams and colloquiums.

A quality multimedia e-text-book may only be prepared by the lecturer who teaches the subject. The preparation of an e-text-book is a great challenge, but interesting and responsible work, which takes a lot of time and effort. The lecturer often asks himself/herself what information should be included in e-material. He/she needs to be aware that the content should be clear and concise. Because multimedia e-material may contain animations, quizzes, online links etc., the lecturer should know where and how to enter these tools. His/her skills and knowledge of using them should be comprehensive.

An example of a multimedia e-chapter has already been created for the Process Synthesis Course at the FCCE in Maribor. The chapter is entitled Reaction-path Synthesis and it is an electronic version of the chapter, which is included in the classic text-book, and is usually available to students. The lecturer wanted to know how students will accept this version and what the study results will be achieved. Different types of electronic modules are included within the e-material as: cloze activities, multi-choice type questions, external web-sites, true-false questions, wiki articles, and reading activities. The eXe-learning XHTML editor was used for creating the multimedia e-chapter (New Zealand Government Tertiary Education Commission et al., 2011).

During the academic years 2008/2009, 2009/2010 and 2010/2011, a group of students who had the possibility of using the multimedia e-chapter on the Process Synthesis Course, gave feedback about its usage to the lecturer on the basis of a questionnaire. It consisted of 8 questions, 5 of which were multiple-choice questions, and 3 essay-type questions. The questionnaire was filled-in by 53 students. Among these were also those who had not used the e-chapter. The main reason why they had not used it was that they did not know that such a kind of chapter even existed, because they had not followed the news and instructions on Moodle, regularly.

The results showed that students mainly used both possibilities for learning i.e. the chapter in classical text-book, which is available, and the multimedia electronic chapter (72 %). Of those students who used the multimedia e-chapter, 77 % thought that such a kind of chapter was more appropriate for learning than the classical chapter because it consists of modules for dynamic learning, and 88 % said that they needed less time for studying the chapter material with the e-chapter in comparison with the classical one. More theory was retained in the memory. The same number of students realised that the multimedia e-chapter usage was a good preparation for the electronic-assessment of knowledge.

On the question as to why they did or did not use the multimedia e-chapter, students gave different answers.

One student said: »*The content in the multimedia e-chapter is more transparent and regulated. Learning is more friendly.*«

Another replied: »*It is great because you can check your knowledge.*«

One student thought: »*I prefer the classic way of learning from my notes where I can underline the important things, and annotate the notes.*«

Another replied: »*I like the colour-coded words in the e-chapter.*«

The answer of one student was interesting: »*Such learning is tiring for the eyes. You have to look at the screen continuously.*«

4. Conclusion

Undergraduate-study reforms have placed the student at the centre of the education process. The curricula have been mainly reduced, so that students themselves undertake more responsibilities for better study results. For this reason, the traditional methods of teaching and learning should now be supplemented by non-traditional methods and technologies. These include active and cooperative learning, project work, and e-learning, which help students achieve better results. Students at the FCCE in Maribor, Slovenia now have significant experience with non-traditional learning methods, especially with e-learning. They use electronic-learning environments and e-materials, which enable communication between lecturer-student and the assessment of knowledge. Different kinds of e-tools enable the students to obtain good study results. Since the Chapter focuses on the experiences of e-learning usage from both the students' and pedagogic staffs' points of view, the electronic environments, and their functionalities were not presented in detail. They have already been described in other sources (Krajnc, 2006; Krajnc, 2009).

Students' feedback on the multimedia electronic-chapter of the text-book showed that such a kind of e-material contributes to a better understanding of the subject's content and can better prepare them for electronic and classical examinations. Students who choose the electronic manner for learning usually finish their course obligations within the course time-frame or within one or two weeks after finishing the lectures. For this reason, more time is left for other courses.

Good study results were obtained with on-going electronic-assessment of knowledge, especially at Bologna Courses within the first and second semesters of a study year, when a lot of students are enrolled. It is important that students are not forced into new ways of working because this can lead to stress, but rather allow them to always choose between the traditional way of learning with the text-books.

The pedagogic staff at the FCCE in Maribor already have seven years of experience in e-learning. The results show that the incorporation of electronic-learning environments into education process improves lectures and the quality and efficiency of the study. E-learning leads to a heavier workload for the lecturer at the start, but this reduces over time.

Electronic-learning environments offer a lot of modules and activities that require the continuous enhancement of lecturers' knowledge. Pedagogic staff at the FCCE have the opportunity to enhance their skills through various workshops organised by the UM or the Faculty.

There are challenges for the future. The lecturers who already successfully use e-learning during their courses should encourage other colleagues to use new methods of learning. Sceptic lecturers should know about e-learning implemented lectures to make them more dynamic. The great challenge is to convince lecturers that pedagogic work is also research work like other scientific research. It is recommended that pedagogic staff focus their efforts and time on multimedia e-material production. The faster tempo of life namely shows that, it will be necessary to optimise study time, so the use of quality multimedia e-text-books will be inevitable in the future.

5. References

Clark, R. E. & Feldon, D. F. (2005). Five Common but Questionable Principles of Multimedia Learning, In: *The Cambridge Handbook of Multimedia Learning*, Mayer, R. E. (Ed.), pp. 97-116, Cambridge University Press, ISBN 0-521-83873-8, ISBN 0-521-54751-2, New York.

Dongil, S., Yoon, E. S., Park, S. J. & Lee, E. S. (2000). Web-based interactive virtual laboratory system for unit operations and process system engineering education, *Computers and Chemical Engineering*, Vol. 24, No. 2-7, pp. 1381-1385, ISSN: 0098-1354.

Dougiamas, M. (1999). Moodle (Modular Object-Oriented Dynamic Learning Environment), In: *online*, July 2011, *https://estudij.uni-mb.si*

Excell, P. S. (2000). Experiments in the use of multiple-choice examinations for electromagnetics-related topics, *IEEE Trans. Education*, Vol. 43, No. 3, pp. 250-256, ISSN: 0018-9359.

Felder, R., Woods, D. R., Stice, J. E. & Rugarcia, A. (2000). The future of Engineering Education, Part 2. Teaching Methods that work, *Chem. Engr. Education*, Vol. 34, No. 1, pp. 26-39. ISSN: 0009-2479.

Floyed Smith, T., Baah, D., Bradley, J., Sidler, M., Hall, R., Daughtrey, T. & Curtis, C. (2000). A Synchronous Distance Education Course for Non-Scientists Coordinated Among Three Universities, *Chem. Engr. Education*, Vol. 44, No. 1, pp. 30-34. ISSN: 0009-2479.

Granda, J. C., Uria, C., Suarez, F. J. & Garcia, D. F. (2010). Supporting Technologies for Synchronous E-learning, In: *E-learning Experiences and Future*, Soomro, S. (ed.), pp. 111-128, InTech, ISBN 978-953-307-092-6.

Hadley, K. R. & Debelak, K. A. (2009). Wiki Technology as a design tool for a Capstone Design Course, *Chem. Engr. Education*, Vol. 43, No. 3, pp. 194 – 200. ISSN: 0009-2479.

Hussmann, S., Covic, G. & Patel N. (2004). Effective Teaching and Learning in Engineering Education using a Novel Web-based Tutorial and Assessment Tool for Advanced Electronics, *Int. J. Eng. Ed.*, Vol. 20, No. 2, pp. 161-169. ISSN: 0949-149X.

Krajnc, M. (2006). Incorporating e-learning into educational process, *Proceedings of CHISA 2006* on CD-ROM, Prague, August 2006. ISBN 80-86059-45-6.

Krajnc, M. (2008). Electronic assessment of knowledge in chemical engineering courses, *Proceeding of CHISA 2008* on CD-ROM, Prague, August 2008. ISBN 978-80-02-02047-9.

Krajnc, M. (2009). E-learning Environment Integration in the Chemical Engineering Education Process, *Int. J. Eng. Ed.*, Vol. 25, No. 2, pp. 349-357. ISSN: 0949-149X.

Krnel, D. & Bajd, B. (2009). Learning and e-materials, *Acta Didactica Napocensia*, Vol. 2, No. 1, pp. 97-107. ISSN 2065-1430.

Lau, H. Y. K. & Mak, K. L. (2005). A Configurable E-learning System for Industrial Engineering, *Int. J. Eng. Ed.*, Vol. 21, No. 2, pp. 262-276. ISSN: 0949-149X.

Le Roux, G. A. C., Reis, G. B., de Jesus, C. D. F., Giordano, R. C., Cruz, A. J. G., Moreira Jr., P. F., Nascimento, C. A. O. & Loureiro, L. V. (2010). Cooperative Weblab: A Tool for Cooperative Learning in Chemical Engineering in a Global Environment, *Chem. Engr. Education*, Vol. 44, No. 1, pp. 9-12. ISSN: 0009-2479.

Maurice, S. A. & Lissel, S. (2006). Evaluating Online Testing Technology, *Int. J. Eng. Ed.*, Vol. 22, No. 4, pp. 839-848. ISSN: 0949-149X.

New Zealand Government Tertiary Education Commission, The Auckland University, The Auckland University and Technology, Tairawhiti Polytechnic. (2001). eXe-the learning XHTML editor. In: *online*. July 2011, Available from: *http://exelearning.org/wiki*

Paik, W., Lee, J. Y. & McMahon, E. (2004). Facilitating Collaborative Learning in Virtual (and Sometimes Mobile) Environments, *Proceedings of WISE 2004 International Workshops*, Brisbane, Australia, November 2004.

Peat, M. (2000). Towards first year biology online: a virtual learning environment. *Educational Technology & Society*, Vol. 3, No. 3, pp. 203-207. ISSN 1436-4522.

Pei-Chen, S., Tsai, R. J., Finger, G., Yueh-Yang, C. & Yeh, D. (2008). What drives a succeeful e-Learning? An empirical investigation of the critical factors influencing learner satisfaction. *Computers & Education* , Vol. 50, No. 4, pp. 1183-1202. ISSN: 0360-1315.

Richardson, W. (2006). *Blogs, Wikis, Podcasts, and other Powerful Web Tools for Classrooms* (2nd Ed.), Corwin Press, ISBN 1-4129-2767-6, Thousand Oaks, CA.

Rodríguez, F., Berenguel, M. & Guzmán, J. L. (2006). A Virtual Course on Automation of Agricultural Systems, *Int. J. Eng. Ed.*, Vol. 22, No. 6, pp. 1197-1210. ISSN: 0949-149X.

Rossiter, D., Petrulis, R. & Biggs, C. A. (2010). A Blended Approach to Problem-Based Learning in the Freshman Year, *Chem. Engr. Education*, Vol. 44, No. 1, pp. 23-29. ISSN: 0009-2479.

Schaad, D. E., Franzoni, L. P., Paul, C., Bauer, A. & Morgan, K. (2008). A Perfect Storm: Examining Natural Disasters by Combining Traditional Teaching Methods with Service-Learning and InnovativeTechnology, *Int. J. Eng. Ed.*, Vol. 24, No. 3, pp. 450 – 465. ISSN: 0949-149X.

Selmer, A., Kraft, M., Moros, R. & Colton C. K. (2007). Weblabs in Chemical Engineering Education, Trans IchemE, part D, *Education for Chemical Engineers*, Vol. 2, No. 1, (January 2007), pp. 38-45. ISSN: 1749-7728.

8

E-Learning in Mechatronic Systems Supported by Virtual Experimentation

Viliam Fedák, František Ďurovský and Peter Keusch
Technical University of Košice
Slovakia

1. Introduction

Due to its origin, Mechatronics, consisting of symbiosis of Mechanical Engineering and Electrical Engineering, presents a complex science. Synergistic effects in mechatronic systems and mutual interactions among subsystems of various nature cause considerable difficulties at their teaching and learning. There are plenty of mechatronic systems of various kind, size and complexity which the specialist has to deal at their design with – starting from miniature ones up to large industrial mechatronic systems presented e.g. by continuous production lines.

In every system, regardless its nature, we are interesting in its performance and behavior – whether it is linear or non-linear, oscillating or non-oscillating, which are its time constants, time response, frequency response, placement of system poles and zeros in the plane, how to control the system, which control method to apply, and finally, how to realize control algorithm and its debugging. When designing control algorithms for a complex mechatronic system, students should know and verify behavior of individual subsystems, i.e. they should possess satisfactory knowledge from mechanical, electrical and control engineering.

Like in other fields, also in mechatronic engineering education, the concepts taught through lectures should be completed by practical laboratory experimentation (Cheng & Chiu, 2010). Here the students observe phenomena that are rather difficult to explain by written material. The students are interested in experiments with real models. During experimentation they get practical experience, skills and also a self-confidence that are necessary to solve real problems. But experimentation on real industrial systems usually is out of question. A lot of effort was made in searching new methods – how to create enough space for students' better acknowledgement with the systems and how to train them for practical problems solutions. One way how to fully substitute a physical system consists in system dynamics emulation, as shown in (Potkonjak et al., 2010), but this method requires an ample equipment. Another way consists in sharing expensive equipment by more institutions and creating distance experiments. Well elaborated description of distance experimentation in power electronics is shown in (Bauer, 2008, 1) or a more general approach to a set of distance experiments in several fields of electrical engineering is presented in (Bauer, 2008, 2). Although such distance laboratory satisfies needs for training of students, its development is enough time-consuming and labor-intensive. It requires special equipment connected to internet, good organization of booking system, maintenance of the server, and usually, after several years with changing the staff, the distance laboratory interrupts its activity.

These are reasons why in the first step very often we confide in the simulation resources where the mathematical model in form of differential equations is applied to calculate dynamics and by simulation provides the data that would otherwise be measured on a real system. This approach is rather sophisticated, knowledge demanding, and also time consuming. It requires analytical approach - a good knowledge of the system to be analyzed, mathematical background, and skills programming the simulation model, solving the equations, and finally – visualization of results.

A way to save time and burden at maintenance consists in development of virtual models. They can create an intermediate stage prior accessing students to experimentation on laboratory models, without any special knowledge about their background, mathematical and simulation model development. Numerous projects are running there that are focused to development of virtual models and laboratories and many examples are available nowadays. A general approach to virtual laboratories is described by (Babich & Mavrommatis, 2004) and specially, to virtual laboratory in mechatronics by (Cheng & Chiu, 2010; Pipan et al, 2008). Most effort was done for robotics (Bianchi, 1999; Potkonjak, 2010; Faculty of Electrical Engineering in Belgrade, n.d.) but also many others could be mentioned. In the electrical and control engineering some successful solutions are known, e.g. (Saadat; Petropol-Serb, 2007, Educational Matlab GUIs). Such virtual models are undamageable and their screen can be designed so that they look like apparatus. They can also serve for staff training in system control. The virtual models are accessible via internet and thus, the student can utilize all the features of e-learning - self study, regardless the place and time.

To be effective in design of virtual models there is need for a simple development process of the virtual purpose–oriented model that can run online, directly on the student's computer, and gives enough graphical and numerical information the student requires. The requirements in our case are met by developed virtual models that are based on Graphic User Interface (GUI) MATALB. This is a powerful data-processing tool allowing simulation of dynamic systems in a simple way having user friendly graphic environment.

The organization of the contribution is as follows: after general description of design methodology for virtual models in GUI MATLAB (chapter 2) in the third chapter we describe development of several typical models of simple mechatronic subsystems starting from kinematic diagram, showing briefly their mathematical and simulation models. Emphasis is put on development of the virtual model itself and description of its features. Finally in the fourth chapter we share some experiences from training of students by virtual models and in conclusion we present ideas for our future work.

2. Methodology at design of virtual models

2.1 Procedure at designing GUI MATLAB

The developed virtual models are based on GUI MATLAB. Their development starts from a kinematic scheme of the system and its description by mathematical equations. Manipulating them the mathematical and simulation model are derived. Its dynamics is verified by simulation in Simulink. The GUI MATLAB itself is developed in Graphic User Development Environment (GUIDE), which practically presents a graphic editor. GUIDE contains a set of tools (objects) for user environment design. The development procedure is depicted in Fig. 1.

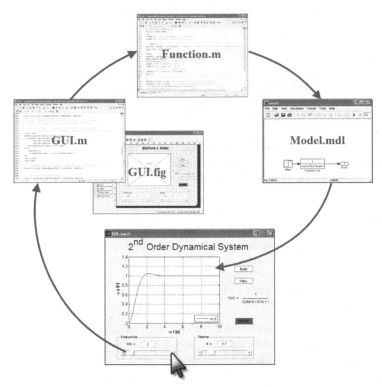

Fig. 1. Procedure of activities in development of virtual model (here based on example of the 2nd order dynamical system)

The editor enables the user to interact directly with elements presented on the screen. These elements (called objects) replace the keyed entry of commands and menus. Users typically select screen objects and actions by using a mouse. The objects navigate the screen and execute commands by using menu bars, buttons, sliders, pull-down menus and editing windows that enable to input characters (incl. numbers). MATLAB automatically generates a relative M-file (GUI.m) containing callbacks interconnected with the objects in the adjoining file GUI.fig. The program written into the callbacks is realized immediately after the object activation (by pressing a button, shifting a slider, inserting a value into editing window, etc.). In the background of GUI a function (Function.m in Fig. 1) collects variable parameters from the GUI screen and sends them into the system model that is built-up in the Simulink environment (Model.mdl). The obtained time response is displayed on a graph placed in a frame on the GUI screen. Similarly, using suitable MATLAB commands it is possible to obtain frequency characteristics, system poles placement and many other features that can be programmed in MATLAB.

2.2 Principles of Imaging and Ergonomics of the Virtual Model GUI Control Screen

The GUI providing human-computer interaction is one of the most important parts in the functional virtual model. To make learning easier, the learner should interact with the computer easy, intuitively, without any learning a complex control of the virtual model and he should get required information in a transparent, well-arranged form.

The GUI for a virtual model has two components:

- *Input*, where the user inputs system parameters, chooses mode of calculation and displays the figures (pictures like kinematic scheme, sketch/photo of device/ mechanism etc., block diagram, mathematical model – equations, etc.) and chooses number and form of required outputs – alphanumerical values and/or graphs. They are usually controlled by buttons/radio buttons, sliders, and alphanumerical editing windows.
- *Output*, where the information is displayed in usable form: in the graphic one (in our case time responses, frequency responses, zero-pole map but also figures as mentioned above) or in an alphanumeric form (values of transfer function coefficients, values of system poles and system zeros, tables, etc.).

To develop a suitable GUI screen for the mechatronic system virtual model, whose visual appearance could be enough complex, the designer must understand principles of good interface and screen design. Generally, the rules are described in (Galitz, 2007). Based on the general rules we adapt and extend them for design of virtual model GUI MATLAB screen. Some rules can be kept intuitively but for proper design, the designer should know all features and possibilities. The most important principles, when designing the placement objects on GUI screen, are:

- *Legibility* — information should be noticeable and distinguishable.
- *Readability* — information is identifiable and interpretable.
- *Coloring display features* — in order to attract and call attention to different screen elements.
- *Guiding the eye* by placement and grouping command objects by visual lines.

Further the designer should deal with the user considerations, as follows:

- Visually pleasing (user friendly) *composition of the screen*.
- *Organizing screen elements*.
- *Screen navigation* and flow.
- Choice of implicitly *pre-setting the system parameters* and their range (so that virtual models can be generally used in large ranges of parameter changes).
- *Changing the system parameters* by sliders, inputting numerical values into text editing windows.

Finally, the designer has to maintain a top-to-bottom, left-to-right flow through the screen. Visually pleasing composition of objects on the screen should keep the following qualities (where it is advantageous and meaningful):

- *Balance* – the design elements have an equal weight, left to right, top to bottom. Balance is most often informal or asymmetrical, with elements of different colors, sizes and shapes being positioned to strike the proper relationships.

- *Symmetry* – duplication across horizontal or vertical axes occurs.
- *Regularity* - uniformity of elements based on some principle or plan which is achieved by establishing standard and consistently spaced columns and rows starting points for screen elements, but it is also achieved by using elements similar in size, shape, color, and spacing.
  The opposite of regularity, *irregularity*, exists, when no such plan or principle is apparent. A critical element on a screen will stand out better, however, if it is not regularized.
- *Sequentiality* is a plan of presentation to guide the eye through the screen in a logical order, with the most important information significantly placed. It can be achieved by alignment, spacing, and grouping.
- *Unity* and *uniformity* - using similar sizes, shapes, or colors for related information.
- *Proportion* of the graphs (time responses, frequency characteristics, zero-pole placement in the plane) using the following ration of sides: square (1:1), square root of two (1:1,414), golden rectangle (1:1,618), square root of three (1:1,732), double square (1:2).
- *Simplicity* consists in combination of elements that result in ease of comprehending and well-arranged objects (inputs, outputs, control) on the screen.
- *Alignment* – in sense of horizontal or columnar alignment of the objects on the screen.
- *Functional groupings* of associated elements - grouping screen element aids in establishing structure, meaningful relationships, and meaningful form.
- Proper *screen-based controls*. From view of ergonomics, the controlling elements should be placed in bottom or on the right side of the screen (avoiding to cross the screen by the mouse pointer when changing the input parameters or mode of the output).
- Provide effective *internationalization* so that people speaking different languages may use the developed virtual models.

3. Virtual models of mechatronic systems

As already mentioned in the Introduction, the mechatronic systems are of complex nature, and consist basically of mechanical, electrical and control subsystems (but also those of other nature, e.g. hydraulic and pneumatic systems are not excluded). Perfect understanding of mechanical subsystems behavior at various combinations of mechanical and technological parameters presents a presumption for further correct design of the control strategy. Thus, there exists a variety of subsystems the learner should learn to be able to understand their behavior and mutual effects.

In this subchapter we are going to present a set of virtual models and describe the screens that were designed applying the principles shown in the precedent subchapter. Some screens of virtual models are more-or less sophisticated but their use and control of modes are intuitive. After presenting system and its virtual model, more examples and variations of applications are presented there.

3.1 Multi-mass rotating systems with elastic connection

In the first phase we have developed virtual models of simple mechanical systems, starting from mechanical multi-mass oscillating systems (in our case 2- and 3-mass rotating and translation ones), which occurs often in industry, like:

- in flexible joints of robots and manipulators,
- in case of drive systems connected with the load by a long flexible shaft,
- in multi-motor drive systems with flexible connection through processed strip,
- at cranes and lifts with elastic rope, etc.

A system with two rotating masses connected by an elastic coupling element presents a very schematic and visual example of an elastic connection (Fig. 2).

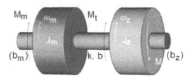

Fig. 2. Kinematic diagram of a rotating system with elastic connecting shaft

The left side consist of a mass disk of the driving motor (moment of inertia J_m and the driving torque M_m) and the load side disk on the right side with the load moment of inertia J_z is loaded by a load torque M_z. The connecting torsional shaft is characterized by its torsional elasticity k and torsional damping b. Similarly, mechanical losses on the driving side are characterized by damping b_m and on the load side by damping b_z).

The system dynamics is described easily by three differential equations:

Motion equation on the motor side: $M_m - M_t = J_m \dfrac{d\omega_m}{dt} + b_m.\omega_m$ (1)

Motion equation on the load side: $M_t - M_z = J_z \dfrac{d\omega_z}{dt} + b_z.\omega_z$ (2)

Torsional torque: $M_t = k(\phi_m - \phi_z) + b.(\omega_m - \omega_z)$ (3)

where the angles are: $\phi_m = \int \omega_m \, dt$ and $\phi_m = \int \omega_m \, dt$ (4)

The corresponding block diagram is shown in Fig. 3. This creates basis for Simulink scheme and core for the virtual model.

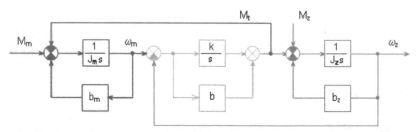

Fig. 3. Block diagram of two-mass rotating system with elastic connection

The GUI screen of the virtual model is shown in Fig. 4. The virtual model response starts immediately after any parameter change. The GUI screen (Fig. 4) consists of several parts:

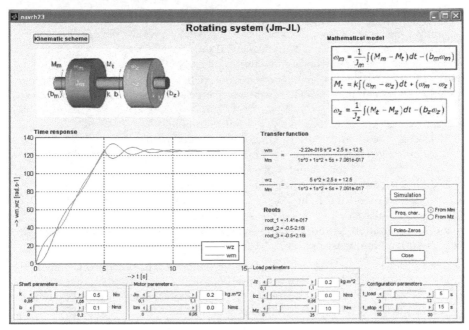

Fig. 4. GUI screen of the virtual model of two-mass rotating system with elastic connection

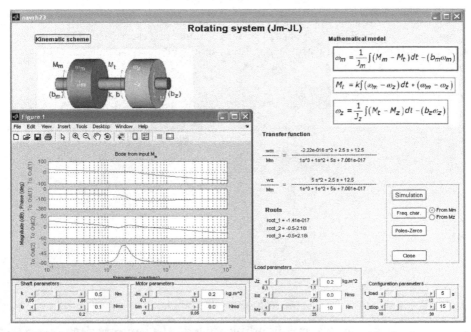

Fig. 5. GUI screen of the virtual model of two-mass rotating system with elastic connection, in the new window there is the frequency characteristic

- *System description* in the upper third of the screen:
  – panels Kinematic scheme/Block diagram - a switch above the picture.
  – panel *Mathematical description* (mathematical model).
- *Inputs*, i.e. system parameters ergonomically placed in the bottom part
- *Outputs*: time responses, frequency characteristics (Fig. 5), transfer functions and position of system poles. Value of parameters are set by a slider or inserted into editing boxes:
  – *Shaft parameters*: k – shaft elasticity, b – shaft damping,
  – *Motor (mechanical) parameters*: J_m – motor moment of inertia,
  b_m – damping corresponding to friction in the motor bearings,
  – *Load parameters*: J_z – load moment of inertia,
  b_Z damping corresponding to friction in the load bearings.
- Controls, placed on the right side: Simulation, Frequency characteristics and Poles-Zeros (a map of system poles and zeros position being drawn in a new window). In the panel Configuration parameters there are: t_stop – simulation time and t_load – time, in which the load torque is applied.

Finally, the button $\boxed{\text{Close}}$ closes the virtual model window. The described virtual model is relatively simple. It enables to observe system dynamical analysis in time and frequency domains at varying mechanical parameters and thus the student learns influence of the system parameters to time response, frequency characteristics and position of system poles.

3.2 Variations of mechanical systems with elastic connections

Based on previous example variations of virtual models of multi-mass elastic joints were developed. As a practical example of such system a model of a car axle suspension is shown here (Fig. 6) that consists of a wheel (a simplified model of a car - so called one-quarter car model), its passive suspension and driver seat.

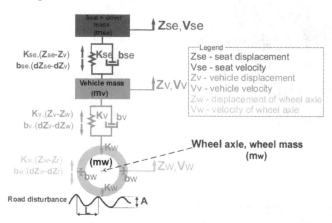

Fig. 6. Kinematic diagram of a car suspension simplified model

As the input variable to the system a disturbance in form of a harmonic signal occurs there that presents a cart-track. The output variables are: vertical position and speed of oscillating masses – of the seat with driver, chassis and wheel itself. Fig. 7 shows a block diagram. The simplified model of the car suspension presents a highly oscillating linear system of the 6th order.

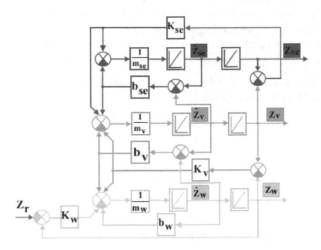

Fig. 7. Block diagram of a car suspension simplified model

Finally, Fig. 8 shows the virtual model. Here the students can tune the parameters of the springs and dampers (for prescribed masses and character of the road surface) and to observe position oscillation of the seat with driver.

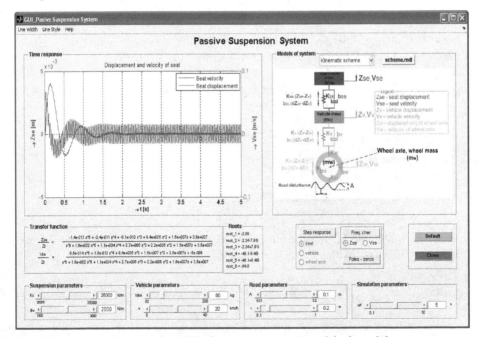

Fig. 8. GUI screen of the virtual model of car suspension simplified model

3.3 Single mathematical pendulum

In many institutions, a mathematical pendulum presents one of basic mechanical subsystems for verification of properties of advanced control structures. There are several modifications of the mechanical system – simple pendulum, double pendulum, single pendulum on the chart, single pendulum on the chart with a tension spring, reverse pendulum and many other arrangements that make the mechanical subsystems more complex.

Let's present briefly its mathematical model, and based on this, the properties of its virtual model. The kinematic scheme is shown in Fig. 9.

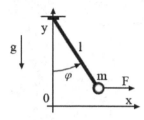

Fig. 9. Kinematic scheme of a simple mathematical pendulum

From the geometry of the pendulum there are easily derived basic equations for position of the simple pendulum:

$$x = l.\sin\phi,\tag{5}$$

$$y = l.(1 - \cos\phi)\tag{6}$$

The mathematical model is derived using the 2nd order Lagrange equation. Firstly, the equations for the kinetic T and potential V energy of the system are derived:

$$T = \frac{1}{2}m.\dot{x}^2 = \frac{1}{2}m.(l.\dot{\phi})^2 = \frac{1}{2}m.l^2.\dot{\phi}^2\tag{7}$$

$$V = mgy = mgl(1 - \cos\phi)\tag{8}$$

The 2nd order Lagrange equation is in the form

$$\frac{d}{dt}\left(\frac{\partial T}{\partial \dot{q}_j}\right) - \frac{\partial T}{\partial q_j} = -\frac{\partial V}{\partial q_j} - \frac{\partial D}{\partial \dot{q}_j} + Q_j\tag{9}$$

After a sort calculation and manipulation of equations we get the final differential equation describing pendulum oscillations, incl. its damping:

$$\ddot{\phi} = \frac{F - b.\dot{\phi} - m.g.l.}{m.l^2}\phi\tag{10}$$

From this equation it is easy to get the value of the angle ϕ. After completing it by the equations (4), (5) describing the system kinematics we can get the block diagram (Fig. 10).

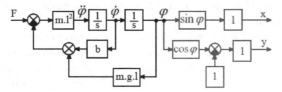

Fig. 10. Block diagram of the simple mathematical pendulum

It creates a base for the virtual model. From control point of view, it is a nonlinear 2nd order system. The corresponding Simulink scheme is shown in Fig. 11.

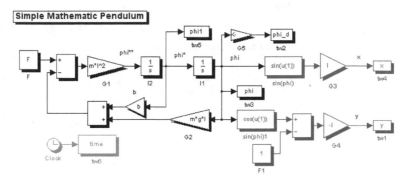

Fig. 11. Simulink block diagram of a simple mathematical pendulum

Based on the Simulink file, the GUI is designed. Its screen is shown in Fig. 12.

Here, the screen consists of 5 parts. Let's describe their functionality in detail:

- *Mechanical model of system*. In this section there occur pictures describing mechanical system model. In the left part there is a block diagram (compare with that in Fig. 6). In the right part the button *Equation/Kinematic scheme* it is possible to switch between the equations describing the mechanical system and kinematic scheme of the system (Fig. 9). The button ⟨Mdl File⟩ serves to show Simulink program scheme (Fig. 11) - by opening the proper mdl file.
- *Output characteristics*. Here are two sub-screens to display output characteristics. *Graph A: Time responses* serves to show time responses, in this case the variables x, y and φ. *Graph B: Functions* serves to show functions - $y = f(x)$ a $\varphi = f(\dot{\varphi})$. To draw a course in some of the graphs, one has to start simulation by pushing a button in the section Simulation.
- *Simulation*. The section serves to control the simulation. The buttons trigger the graphs. It consists of two subsections, namely *Graph A* and *Graph B*.
- The subsection *Graph A* contains the buttons ⟨x⟩, ⟨phi⟩, ⟨y⟩ and ⟨x y⟩, that triggers the time courses in the graph *Graph A: Time responses* in the section *Characteristics*.Each button triggers the time course of the depicted variable, i.e. the button buttons ⟨x⟩ triggers the time course of the variable x, *etc.* Similarly there works the buttons ⟨y = f (x)⟩ and ⟨$\varphi=f(\dot{\varphi})$⟩ in the subsection *Graph B*, but with the distinction, there are not displayed any time responses but the functions depicted on the button that are draw in the *Graph*

B: Functions. It should be noted that prior simulation the actual input parameters are read and after this the simulation starts.

- *Control Panel.* In this section there are only two buttons to control the whole screen. The first one button Default serves to reading pre-set values of the mechanical system parameters and their immediate writing into the section *Input parameters* (pre-setting the position of sliders and numerical values in the editing screens). The button Close finishes the work and closes the GUI screen.

- Input parameters. The section serves to system parameters entry. Each variable has a starting value and a limited range (the limits are set separately), that can be re-activated by pushing the button Default . The value can be changed either by a slider or inserting numeric value into the editing.

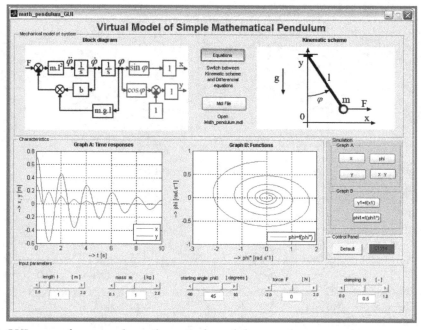

Fig. 12. GUI screen for a simple mathematical pendulum

3.3.1 variations of pendulum model

To get a more complicated system (in order to verify a more complex control algorithms) there were developed some modifications of the basic pendulum model.

Pendulum on the Cart

The pendulum is coupled to a moving cart. This is a principle of a crane trolley and the subsystems serves do develop a control algorithm preventing oscillation of the arm with a load at moving the trolley. The kinematic scheme is shown in Fig. 13.

In comparison with the previous subsystem the simple mathematical pendulum on a cart presents the 4th order non-linear system. In comparison with the previous model the virtual model contains more parameters to be set. Its functionality is similar to that of a simple pendulum; the model only contains more parameter to be set.

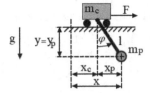

Fig. 13. Kinematic scheme of a simple mathematical pendulum on a cart

Double Mathematical Pendulum

This mechanical subsystem consists of two pendulums where the second one is connected to end of the first one. The kinematic scheme is shown in Fig. 14.

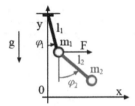

Fig. 14. Kinematic scheme of a double mathematical pendulum

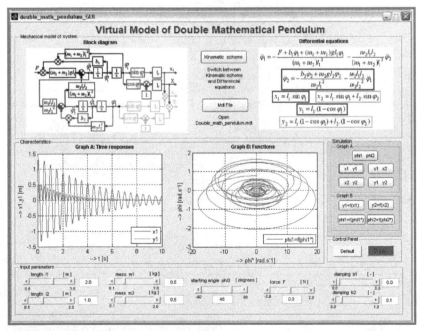

Fig. 15. Virtual model of a double pendulum

It is the 4th order non-linear system but more complex that the previous one. The complexity of the system follows up also from the virtual model screen (Fig. 15).

3.4 Control of a direct current drive in frequency domain

Let's start to develop a virtual model in GUI MATLAB for a speed controlled direct current (DC) motor supplied by DC converter and two control loops: current and speed ones. The design is performed in the frequency domain. Although this is a simple and generally known example, we shall show some features of virtual model construction and enhance model features. The principal scheme of connection the motor (in linear region without a limiter serving for calculation of controllers only) is shown in Fig. 16 and principal connection of the speed controlled DC drive is in Fig. 17.

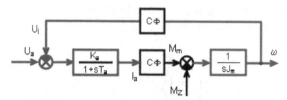

Fig. 16. Block diagram of a DC motor

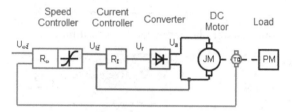

Fig. 17. Principal diagram of connection of speed controlled DC drive

Fig. 18 shows appropriate block diagram of the DC drive and its corresponding Simulink scheme is depicted in Fig. 19.

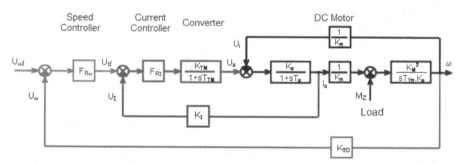

Fig. 18. Block diagram of speed controlled DC drive

The current controller of the PI type is calculated on basis of the Optimum Modulus Criterion from the drive system parameters. General form of its transfer function is:

$$F_{RI} = K_{RI} + \frac{1}{sT_{il}} \tag{11}$$

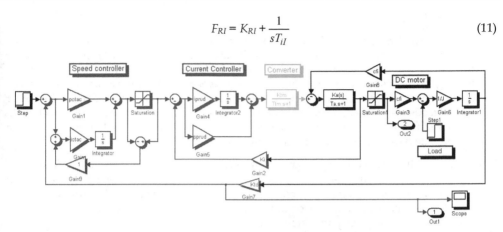

Fig. 19. Interconnection of blocks in the Simulink program

After calculation of current controller parameters and simplification of the current control loop, the speed controller is calculated based on the Symmetrical Optimum Criterion, again of PI type, having the transfer function:

$$F_{R\omega} = K_{R\omega} + \frac{1}{sT_{i\omega}} \tag{12}$$

Fig. 20. shows the basic view on the virtual GUI model of speed controlled DC drive.

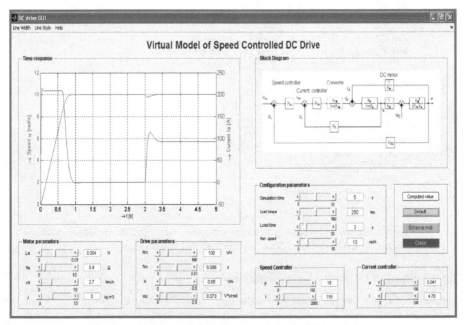

Fig. 20. GUI screen for the virtual model of the speed controlled DC drive

Virtual model features:

- *Time response* (the graph on the left side) – here the graph with time courses of the motor current and speed are shown. Immediately after any change of a system parameter (motor -, drive -, or controller parameters) by a slider or inserting a numeric value into editing box the simulation starts and new time responses are drawn, like in a real drive.
- *Block diagram* (the picture on the right side) displays the system block diagram. In other virtual models here can be switched between kinematic diagram, mathematical model, etc.).
- *Change of the system parameters* by sliders or numerical value in the bottom part of the screen. The details of these panels are shown in Fig. 21.

Before starting the model, implicit parameters are set up and they can be changed later. After pushing the button | Computed value | the parameters of controllers are calculated from the set values of parameters. There simultaneously appears a small window with the question if the calculated values of controller parameters are acceptable or not. If not, the learner can set up the own parameters and can try to tune them according to the time responses of the drive. To be returned to starting values, the learner pushes the button | Default | (similar to the system restart). The advantage of the virtual model consists in the fact that the learner does not need to know the mathematical model running in background and he can concentrate himself to analysis of properties of the drive – to observe influence of a parameter on the system behavior. As shown, the learner can set up his own parameters of the controller (to tune the controllers) or used the pre-calculated parameters based on the pre-set criteria.

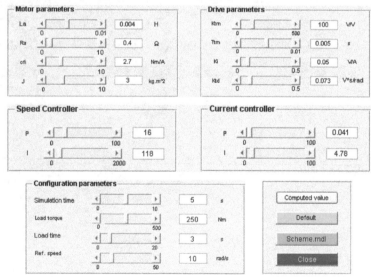

Fig. 21. Panels with sliders to change system parameters, configuration parameters (parameters of simulation and motor load), and mode of the output

3.5 State control of DC motor (in time domain)

This task is dual to the previous one when the system has state-space controllers. Again it is a more complex GUI involving synthesis of the state-space controllers giving the possibility to change parameters of the calculated controllers and thus to tune the controllers based o time responses. The computing algorithm is different from the previous one and belongs to more complex one. The computation starts from the state-space model of the DC motor having the block diagram in Fig. 16 that is in the form of the state equation (13) and the output equation (14).

$$u_i = A.x + b.u + e.z = \begin{bmatrix} 0 & \dfrac{K_m}{T_m.K_a} \\ -\dfrac{K_a}{K_m.T_a} & -\dfrac{1}{T_a} \end{bmatrix} x + \begin{bmatrix} 0 \\ \dfrac{K_T.K_a}{T_a} \end{bmatrix} u + \begin{bmatrix} -\dfrac{K_m^2}{T_m.K_a} \\ 0 \end{bmatrix} z \qquad (13)$$

$$y = c^T x = \begin{bmatrix} 1 & 0 \end{bmatrix} x \qquad (14)$$

where A is system matrix, x – state vector, b – input vector, c^T - output vector e- disturbance vector, u – input variable, y - output vector. The motor parameters correspond to the Fig. 16. The control structure with the feedback through the state controller - vector r^T is shown in Fig. 22 (the integrator at the input serves to reject constant or slowly changing disturbances what is a common case).

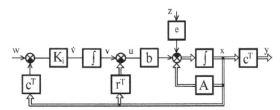

Fig. 22. Control structure with the state-space controller

The control structure is described in the state-space by the known state equation:

$$\begin{bmatrix} \dot{x} \\ \dot{v} \end{bmatrix} = \begin{bmatrix} A - br^T & b \\ -K_i.c^T & 0 \end{bmatrix} \begin{bmatrix} x \\ v \end{bmatrix} + \begin{bmatrix} 0 \\ K_i \end{bmatrix} w + \begin{bmatrix} e \\ 0 \end{bmatrix} z \qquad (15)$$

The core of the virtual model consists in numerical calculation of the parameters K_i, r_1, r_2 by the pole placement method: for a prescribed position of poles (usually a triple negative root giving the fastest system response on the aperiodicity boundary) the required polynomial is compared with the system polynomial and missing parameters of the controller are calculated from a set of linear algebraic equations.

The control structure in Simulink to simulate time responses is shown in (Fig. 23).

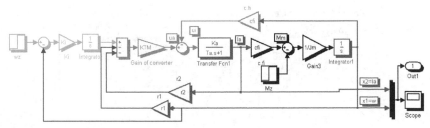

Fig. 23. Simulink model of the state-space control of DC drive

Fig. 24 shows the virtual model that enables to calculate state-space controller parameters and visualize time responses of the current and speed.

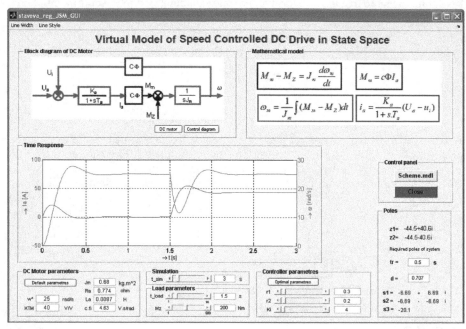

Fig. 24. Virtual model of state-space controlled DC drive

The panel *Controller parameters* (Fig. 25a) serves to setting parameters of the state controller – by tuning or selecting the button Optimal parameters to calculate poles position placement. Here:

r_1 – feedback from state variable x_1 (motor speed),
r_2 – feedback from state variable x_2 (motor current),
K_i – gain of the integrator (to reject steady-state disturbances).

The state controller parameters are calculated automatically (Fig. 25b) on basis of required values of control time and damping (panel *Poles*, the item *Required course*). In the upper part of the panel Poles real positions of poles are shown.

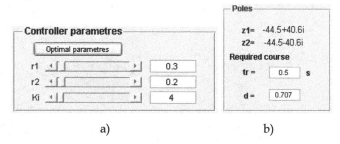

a)   b)

Fig. 25. Panels: a) to set up controller parameters, b) to see position of real and required poles

4. Experiences with virtual models

Except of presented virtual models a series of further ones was developed to suit institutional needs in mechatronic systems teaching. The virtual modules are collected in the Virtual Laboratory of Mechatronic Systems that is available on the website (KEM TU Kosice, 2010).

A set of tens virtual models from all fields of mechatronics are used by the departmental staff as e-learning support in teaching of various subjects (just list several of them: Mechatronic Systems Modeling, Control Theory, Electrical Actuators and Drives, Servodrives, Motion Control, Control of Robots, Mechatronics of Production Systems, and others).

In order the students would get more skills and practical experiences we have divided the student laboratory work into three phases:

1. *Design and simulation* – for a given plant the student has:
   – to derive the mathematical model,
   – to compose the block diagram,
   – to design control,
   – to verify system behavior by simulation.
2. *Verification and analysis* – for a designed control algorithm the student has:
   – to verify the design using a virtual reference model and
   – to perform system analysis (small experiments round a working point) in order to get the system responses (in time and frequency domains) and to investigate system behavior at various values of system parameters and in various working points.
3. *Final verification* of the design on the laboratory model (by programming the embedded control system).

The first two phases are performed outside of the laboratory. The student has to his/her disposal guidelines and reference virtual models that are available through internet for 24/7 hours. Within the institution network they run online (due to limited SW licenses) and outside of the institution the student has to download them and run on own computer (having installed MATLAB).

The reference virtual models also facilitate the teacher review of the student projects – the teacher does not need to check in details the simulating diagrams and search for eventual errors. On other side, the student has a model (i.e. a template) to verify whether he derived and designed a proper solution (e.g. proper parameters of controllers).

Let's note that the third phase of his projects is usually done in the laboratory on the laboratory model under teacher's supervision - for complex systems we prefer the presence of the students in the lab and consultations with the teacher.

The virtual models are also used in lectures to describe and explain principles of complex system behavior at various values of parameters.

5. Conclusion

The chapter describes principles of virtual models development of electromechanical systems that support eLearning in field of mechatronics. The developed virtual models enable to perform analysis of the real system in various working points and to observe influence of the parameters changes to system behavior. The shown virtual models are of various complexity – the simpler ones enable virtual analysis of system and complex virtual models deals also with synthesis of system controllers. Using them, the students can compare and verify their own design performed on basis of design rules application.

Development procedure and features of the virtual models are presented on several typical examples. Here, MATLAB/Simulink software was chosen as one of the best and widespread programming tools for development of virtual models that enables relatively simply programming of even complex systems. Based on the procedure a whole series of virtual models (more than 30) designed in GUI MATLAB was developed at the author's institution in recent years. They are accessible trough internet – through the website of the Virtual Laboratory for Control of Mechatronic Systems (KEM TU Kosice, 2010).

A big advantage of developed virtual models consists in the fact the students do not need to know the complexity of dynamical system which simulation scheme is working in the background of; they change only system parameters on the screen – e.g. mechanical parameters in case of mechanical subsystems (moments of inertia, constants of the elasticity and damping of the flexible joints), parameters of electrical systems (resistance, capacitance, inductance, gains, …), etc., select form and input signals (shape and amplitude of forcing and load signals) and select mode of calculation and outputs (graphs displaying). The parameters of virtual models can be changed by a slider or inputting numerical values into editable boxes.

A shortcoming of developed models consists in the fact they run on computers having installed the MATLAB program. To overcome this difficulty our future work will be concentrated to application of the browser plugins, which are necessary to run MATLAB application on computers not having installed the MATLAB program, e.g. by using VCLab plugin (Ruhr-Universität Bochum, 2011). It must be noted that this application enables to run MATLAB operation without simulation (i.e. without a Simulink scheme), without 3D virtual reality views and without animation, so the advantage on one side will complicate development of the virtual modules by application more mathematical subroutines. But this restriction does not make any serious problem and can be easily solved by application several subroutines.

The developed virtual models are in intensive use and they complete basic e-learning support in various subjects from field of mechatronics. They also serve at lecturing basic subjects from fields of modeling mechanical subsystems, electrical drive systems, system control, and various electrical systems up to mechatronic ones.

6. Acknowledgement

This work was supported by Slovak Cultural and Educational Agency of the Ministry of Education of Slovak Republic under the contract KEGA 103-039 TUKE-4/2010 "Students' Skills Development for Mechatronic Systems Control".

7. References

Bauer, P.; Fedák, V. & Rompelman O. (2008). PEMCWebLab - Distance and Virtual Laboratories in Electrical Engineering – Development and Trends, *Proceedings of*

Power Electronics and Motion Control International Conference, EPE-PEMC 2008, ISBN 978-1-4244-1742-1, Poznaň, September 1-3, 2008

Bauer P.; Fedák V.; Hájek V. & Lampropoulos, I. (2008). Survey of Distance Laboratories in Power Electronics, Proceedings of IEEE 39th Annual Power Electronics Specialists Conference, ISBN 978-1-4244-1667-7, Rhodes, Greece June 15-19, 2008

Babich A. & Mavrommatis K. (2004). Virtual Laboratory Concept for Engineering Education, Proceedings of International Conference on Engineering Education and Research "Progress Through Partnership", ISSN 1562-3580, VSB-TUO, Ostrava, 2004

Bianchi R. A. C. & La Neve, A. (1999). Distance Learning through a Robotic Virtual Lab, Date of access: July 31, 2011, Available from <http://fei.edu.br/~rbianchi/publications/icee1999-robot.pdf>

Cheng, K. W. E.; Chan, C. L.; Cheung, N. C. & Sutanto, D. (2004). Virtual laboratory development for teaching power electronics, Proceedings of Power Electronics and Motion Control International Conference, EPE-PEMC 2004, ISBN 9984-32-010-3, Riga, Latvia. September 2-4, 2004.

Cheng, M. H. M. & Chiu G. T. C. (2010). A mechatronic approach to a virtual laboratory service on internet, International Journal of Virtual Technology and Multimedia, Vol. 1, No. 2, 2010, pp. 140 – 154, ISSN 1741-1874

Coito F.; Gomes L. & Costa A. (2007). Simulation, Emulation and Remote Experiments, Proceedings of the Workshop on using VR in Education, pp. 99-110, ISBN 978-989-20-0715-1, Lisboa, March 2007,

Ďurovský, F. & Fedák, V. (2010). Integrated Mechatronic Systems Laboratory, Proceedings of the 14th Power Electronics and Motion Control International Conference, EPE-EPMC 2010, ISBN 978-1-4244-7854-5, Ohrid, Macedonia. September 6-8, 2010.

Ernest, E.; Sztylka, R.; Ufnalski, B. & Koczara W. (2006). Methods in Teaching Modern AC Drives: Inverter-fed Motor System with Internet-based Remote Control Panel, 12th International Power Electronics and Motion Control Conference, EPE-PEMC 2006, pp. 2130 – 2133, ISBN 1-4244-0121-6, Portorož, August 30 – September 1, 2006

Faculty of Electrical Engineering in Belgrade (n.d.). Virtual Laboratory for Distance Learning in Robotics and Mechatronics. The idea of distance learning. (n.d.). Date of access: July 31, 2011, Available from <http://robot.etf.rs/ index.php/researchprojects/virtual-laboratory-for-distance-learning-in-robotics-and-mechatronics/>

Fedák, V.; Fetyko, J. & Repiščák, M. (2005). Computer Supported Education for Industrial Mechatronic Systems, Proceedings of Computer Based Learning in Science International Conference, CBLIS 2005, pp. 19-27, ISBN 9963-607-63-2, Žilina, July 2-6, 2005

Fedák, V.; Balogh, T.; Bauer, P. & Jusko S. (2008). Virtual and Remote Experimentation in Motion Control, Proceedings of the 11th International Conference on Mechatronics, ISBN 978-80-8075-305-4, AD University of Trencin, Trenčianske Teplice, June 4-6, 2008

Fedák, V.; Hric, M. & Ďurovský, F. (2010). Laboratory Model of Continuous Line with Multi-Motor Drive, Proceedings of the XXIV. Int. Scientific Conference microCAD 2010,

Section K: Electrotechnics and Electronics, ISBN 978-963-661-925-1, University of Miskolc, March 18-20, 2010

Galitz, W. O. (2007). *The Essential Guide to User Interface Design. An Introduction to GUI Design Principles and Techniques*, Wiley Publishing, Inc., ISBN 978-0-470-05342-3, Indianapolis, Indiana

Georgia Institute of Technology (n.d.), *Educational Matlab GUIs*, Date of access: July 31, 2011, Available from <http://users.ece.gatech.edu/mcclella/ matlabGUIs/>

Hercog, R. D.; Jezernik, K. (2007). Advanced control course with teleoperation in the mechatronics study, *Proceedings of 16th Int. Conf. on Electrical Drives and Power Electronics*, EDPE 2007, The High Tatras, September 24-26, 2007

KEM TU Kosice (2010). Virtual Laboratory of Mechatronic Systems Control, In: *web site of the project KEGA, No 3/4203/06*, Date of access: July 31, 2011, Available from < http://andromeda.fei.tuke.sk/> (in Slovak)

MeRLab (n.d.). Innovative Remote Laboratory in the Etraining of Mechatronics, Date of access: July 31, 2011, Available from <www.merlab.eu>

Pipan, M.; Arh, T.; Blažič, B. J. (2008). Innovative Remote Laboratory in the Enhanced E-training of Mechatronics, *Proceedings of the 7th WSEAS International Conference on Circuits, Systems, Electronics, Control and Signal Processing* (CSECS'08), Puerto De La Cruz, Canary Islands, Spain, December 15-17, 2008

Petropol-Serb, G.D.; Petropol-Serb, I.; Campeanu, A. & Petrisor, A. (2007). Using GUI of Matlab to create a virtual laboratory to study an induction machine. EUROCON, 2007. *The International Conference on Computer as a Tool*, ISBN 978-1-4244-0813-9, Warsaw, September 9-12, 2007

Potkonjak, V.; Vukobratović, M.; Jovanović, K. & Medenica, M. (2010). Virtual Mechatronic/Robotic laboratory - A step further in distance learning, *Computers & Education archive*, Vol. 55 , Issue 2 (Sept. 2010), pp. 465-475, ISSN 0360-1315

Ruhr-Universität Bochum (2011), Lehrstuhl für Automatisierungstechnik und Prozessinformatik. Virtual Control Lab 3.1 MATLAB Plugin. Date of access: October 31, 2011, Available from <http://www.atp.ruhr-uni-bochum.de/VCLab/ software/MatlabPlugin/MatlabPlugin.html/>

Saadat, H. (n.d.). MATLAB Graphical User Interface for EE Students. Date of access: July 31, 2011, Available from <http://people.msoe.edu/ ~saadat/matlabgui.htm>

Technical University of Kosice (n.d.). Students' Skills Development for Mechatronic Systems Control. In: *Project KEGA 103-039TUKE-4/2010*

Wong, H.; Kapila, V. & Tzes A. (2001). Mechatronics/Process Control Remote Laboratory. *Proceedings of the 2001 American Society for Engineering Education, Annual Conference & Exposition*, Albuquerque, NM, 2001.

9

Medical Education for YouTube Generation

Jarmila Potomkova, Vladimir Mihal and Daniel Schwarz
Palacky University Olomouc, Masaryk University Brno
Czech Republic

1. Introduction

There have been great changes in medical education environment during the 20th century due to advances in biological sciences, increasing demands from health services (Bleakley et al., 2011; Cooke et al., 2006), and in the past two decades dynamic development of information and communication technologies (ICT) (Masic et al., 2011). They have increased the efficiency of learning and promoted the implementation of evidence-based practice (Howick, 2011; Tilson et al., 2011). For the first time in the history of mankind electronic repositories of medical knowledge started to be available in the public domain (Cullen, 2006; Taylor, 2006; Westwood, 2001). At the end of a century of evolution and changes the scope of medical education had grown enormously (Platt et al., 1999; Koschmann, 1995). At present, most of medical students belong to the generation grown up with modern information and communication technologies, referred to as YouTube generation, Generation Y, Millennials, Generation Next, Net Generation (Borges et al., 2006; Farnan et al., 2008). Internet-based technologies have become part of our daily lives and dramatically changed the interaction between physicians-in-training, educators and the world of knowledge, thus offering new challenges and opportunities (Shamji & Law, 2011; Ruiz et al., 2006). At the global level, there are some attempts to propose a concept of global health education with key indicators to evaluate and monitor educational interventions (Bozorgmehr et al., 2011). Watching the phenomenon of globalization, one has to admit that healthcare services and medical education cannot escape its impact. A new concept of a global profession of medicine has been in the limelight for the past decade with an urgent need to specify a set of core competences for doctors, regardless of where they had been trained (Schwarz, 2001; Celletti et al., 2011).

This chapter is structured in sections covering three main issues. Section 2 reviews current trends in web-based medical teaching & learning with the emphasis on their efficiency, configurations and instructional methods. Web 2.0 is discussed separately in Section 3, demonstrating potential implementation of wikis and podcasting to make theoretical and pre-clinical subjects more attractive, but also pointing at controversies and pitfalls of this new technology in medical and healthcare contexts. In Section 4 the authors describe methods and procedures used to re-design a paediatric undergraduate curriculum in a European country (Czech Republic). The innovation of educational interventions was based on three cornerstones, ie. case-based reasoning, evidence-based medicine, and blended learning. The authors demonstrate all current arguments and opportunities to view medical education not as a sum of knowledge, but as a practical know-how. This approach should be supported by information and communication technologies, eg. development of e-learning portals. We are presenting the educational portal Mefanet as a unique solution. The outcomes of the project including student feedback are presented as figures, graphs and verbatims. The section ends with a brief proposal for developers of case-based learning environment in medicine.

The methods used to compile this chapter included brain-storming, literature review, deduction, curriculum re-design, web-portal development, qualitative analysis of attitudes, and statistical analysis.

2. Online learning in medical education

Medicine is a sophisticated mix of knowledge, skills, behaviour and attitudes. Learning goals can be achieved by different modalities from face-to-face lecturing, bedside teaching & learning, mentoring, small-group learning, self-study, self-assessment etc. Since 1990, the rapid spread of internet-based technologies has been leading to the breath-taking metamorphosis of medical curricula, particularly due to e-learning. E-learning solutions can be implemented in most areas of undergraduate and continuing medical education, in particular knowledge acquisition, skills training, attitudes development, formative and summative assessment (Genn, 2001; Dent & Harden, 2009a, b).

Even though the core patient requirements and expectations of doctors remain more or less the same as they have been across the centuries, nowadays future doctors must get ready for changing conditions of healthcare services delivery with a patient as an important partner in the decision-making process (Dent & Harden, 2009b). A new profile of healthcare professionals is posing demands on educators and modes of knowledge delivery. It should be taken into consideration that future doctors need informed professional educators, not merely amateur tutors.

The newly developed, innovated, revised, and/or re-designed curricula are characterized by a decrease in volume of factual knowledge presented face-to-face, emphasis on adult learning styles, self-directed learning, problem-solving, critical thinking, shift from passive to active learning and performance (Choules, 2007). Their milestones include cultivation of communication skills, thorough and responsible preparation for professional life, efficient teamwork and readiness for implementation of evidence-based practice.

In 1998, Towle (Towle, 1998) formulated a set of future challenges in the process of both undergraduate and continuing medical education to make conditions to teach and learn traditional professional skills in information society era. In particular, he emphasized the following activities: teaching scientific behaviour, promoting use of information technology, respecting new doctor-patient relationships, enhancing educational competences of medical teachers, extending learning delivery modalities in medical curricula, and ensuring guided participation of students in clinical situations.

2.1 Efficiency of online learning

The implementation of online (internet-based, web-based) learning styles in medical education is relatively well-documented by plethora of articles. The first reports date back to the early 1990s describing new experience, outcomes, students' perceptions, advantages as well as controversies of this emerging trend in medical education.

In 2008 Cook and colleagues (Cook et al., 2008) published one of the first meta-analyses with the intention to analyze the existing studies and demonstrate educational outcomes of online instruction as compared to other teaching & learning modalities. They included practicing and student physicians, nurses, pharmacists, dentists and other healthcare professionals as target groups. The analysis of a total of 201 eligible studies clearly demonstrated that from the global point of view internet-based medical instruction had large positive effects compared with non-Internet or no interventions across medical disciplines irrespective of types of learners and concrete outcomes. It may be concluded that further research should be oriented on 2 key areas: (1) effective implementation of internet-based courses, and (2) definition of suitable learning contexts and objectives.

Wong and his team (Wong et al., 2010) used a "realist review" (qualitative systematic review) to identify and elucidate the relationship between context, mechanism and outcomes of internet-based courses for doctors and medical students. They focused on theoretical models how the Internet could support learning. This realist review included a total of 249 primary studies and brought about 3 key findings: (1) Internet courses must engage their target group of learners to use technology that should be perceived as "useful" (promote learning and save time) and "easy-to-use"; (2) Interactivity is highly valued by learners, ie. entering into a dialogue with the course tutor, fellow students and/or virtual tutorial to get feedback on their understanding and performance; (3) Course design is an important factor that has to interact properly with its content, didactic features, and types of learners.

The authors formulated suggestions for authors of internet-based courses to increase the educational outcome in the context of two basic issues, namely technology acceptance and interactive dialogue. Technology acceptance comprises such parameters as perceived usefulness, ease-of-use, suitable format, learners' habits and expectations. Interactive dialogue deals with human-human interactions and human-technical interactions. Both of the modes of interaction include feedback and knowledge assessment.

2.2 Configurations and instructional methods

Cook and his team (Cook et al., 2010) performed another systematic review based on their previous experience about attitudes of medical educators towards internet-based courses. Most of them considered web-based learning as a set of similar activities with more or less homogenous effects, and obviously their studies did not properly describe the interventions used. This systematic review aimed at filling this gap and studied various configurations, instructional methods and presentation elements of web-based learning to help teachers define their instructional interventions. They identified 266 articles including 78 randomized controlled trials comparing web-based learning with no intervention or another educational intervention. The most frequent participants were medical students and postgraduate trainees.

The analysis produced enough data to make a list of most frequently used web-based learning configurations: at least some written text (89 %); multimedia (55 %); online communication via e-mail, threaded discussion, chat, videoconferencing (32 %); synchronous components (9 %).

It was interesting to see that up to about 60 % of the courses used a blended web-based learning method and non-computer-based instruction (eg. face-to-face lectures, small group activities), 32 % assigned reading, and 23 % clinical experience (ie. bedside teaching).

As far as instructional methods are concerned, it was fascinating to reveal that 77 % of the courses used specific methods different from the text with most common being patient cases (real, hypothetical), self-assessment questions and feedback; 30 % of the online instruction was characterized by a high level of interactivity. Other methods included eg. practice exercises and spacing of learning.

These findings are of practical importance for online course developers, because they offer a vast diversity of approaches to reach the educational goals, respecting learners' needs and learning contexts.

3. Web 2.0 applications

In the new millennium we have been witnessing outbreak and spread of new Internet technologies simply defined as the read/write web which is referred to as Web 2.0. The „early" web (Web 1.0) may be characterized by a strong capability to connect people, search for materials, documents etc., whilst web 2.0 makes it easier to create and publish new content by the users. Moreover, social web is about discussion, interpersonal networking, personalization of learning activities, openness to new experience, sharing knowledge and ideas. It is people-centered web (Boulos & Wheeler, 2007).

Its popularity is spreading very fast, partly due to the fact that it is free and requires few technological skills. It encompasses blogs, podcasts, wikis, multimedia sharing, social bookmarking, instant messaging, really simple syndication (RSS), social networking etc. Users are no longer mere consumers, but they may edit, comment, create and share content with the others. Even though most of the activities are social, Web 2.0 is capable enough to substantially influence future online teaching and learning „anytime - any place". Its exploitation for medical consultation, education and publication purposes is definitely increasing (Sandars & Schroter, 2007; Lemley & Burnham, 2009) even if at low speed.

Schreiber & Giustini (2009) published an overview of efficient implementations of Web 2.0 features to improve qualitative parameters of the existing popular medical sites (eg. Health Education Assets Library, MedEdPortal), prestigious medical journals with high impact factors (Archives of Internal Medicine, British Medical Journal, Cochrane Database of Systematic Reviews, Lancet, New England Journal of Medicine, Southern Medical Journal), or introduce new Web 2.0-based products (eg. Clinical Cases and Images Blog, Science Roll Blog, AskDrWiki and others).

3.1 Web 2.0 applications in medical education

An increasing number of authors have been reporting possible usage of web 2.0 applications in medical education (Boulos et al., 2006; Jham et al, 2008; Jalali et al., 2009; Wilson et al, 2009; Alikhan et al., 2010; Chretien et al., 2010; Logan et al., 2010; Vejrazka et al., 2010; Saarinen et al., 2011). On the condition that they are used effectively, wikis, blogs and podcasts could help students, clinician teachers and also patients enhance their learning performance, increase their engagement and improve collaborationware. Social media have sufficient capacity to change academic medicine and attract not only trainees, but also educators irrespective of their will and readiness. Naturally, the faculty must accept their responsibility in preparing future doctors to use social media to communicate with their colleagues and patients.

Some authors (Saarinen et al., 2011) point out that learning course developers cannot integrate Web 2.0 technology without having surveyed students' familiarity with the applications and/or barriers to them. There may be barriers in overall perception of social media with their openness to share and exchange knowledge and ideas. The best way how to overcome controversies on the side of educators and learners is to start with small projects and integrate web 2.0 applications into the existing educational portals to enhance sharing documents, multimedia, distribute news, one-to-many communication, collaborative learning, synchronous and asynchronous discussion. Last but no least it requires a teacher committment to take up a deal of responsibility for the quality of the content posted and distributed via Web 2.0 applications to show learners they can trust the learning materials (Vejrazka et al., 2010).

Further research should be conducted to define the best ways to integrate these tools into current undergraduate and continuing medical education e-learning courses. Web 2.0 can be regarded as a linking element for different forms of web-based learning activities.

Among Web 2.0 applications, podcasting and wiki are particularly suitable for undergraduate and continuing medical education, partly due to the fact that their content can be quality-controlled by professionals.

3.1.1 Podcasting

Podcasting is an example of mobile educational resources and its principle is the creation of audio and/or video for the target audience to access the information "where – when – how" they want (Jham et al., 2008). The advantages of distributing lectures, journal contents, presentations and procedures have been described in dental education, nursing and especially in clinical medicine (Boulos et al., 2006; Clauson & Vidal, 2008; Alikhan et al., 2010). There is much space for prestigious journals, conference organizers and large institutions to become more involved in developing informative, evidence-based podcasts at regular intervals and ensure access to archive collections.

3.1.2 Wiki

Wikipedia has acquired great popularity over the years and few users think about such attributes as quality, trustworthiness, reliability etc. Logan et al. (2010) claimed that it would need more scientists and educators to edit its contents regularly. They have proposed ten rules for anyone who is planning to add new facts, in particular: register an account – know your audience – do not infringe copyright – cite, cite, cite – share your expertise, but do not argue from authority – write neutrally and with due weight – ask for help.

Medical wikis should be controlled by qualified registered contributors, because many are open to modifications by anybody who can post incorrect content, copyrighted materials without citing the original, edit the content to produce erroneous document or even delete a good piece of information.

Some authors (Jalali et al., 2009) are calling for critical appraisal of information disseminated through wikis in situations when wikis are developed, edited and maintained by students themselves. If managed reasonably, integrated into the existing websites and containing knowledge targeted to faculty learning objectives, they can represent an invaluable learning tool (Vejrazka et al., 2010).

3.1.3 Controversies

In spite of enormous popularity of Web 2.0 applications among millennials and new challenges for medical professionals, legitimate concerns have been arising about integrity of these technologies for medical students. However, the complete depth of the problem has not yet been recognized.

A US survey (Chretien et al., 2009) revealed that out of 78 medical schools under study (ie. 60 %) reported incidents due to students' posting unprofessional content online, eg. violation of patient confidentiality, use of profanity, discriminatory language, sexually suggestive materials, communication about medical profession and patients in a negative tone, photos of drug use etc. In spite of its positive aspect, ie. user-generated content for healthcare and medical education, web 2.0 risks broadcasting unprofessional content online that can show medical profession in a negative light. Tradition and social contract between medicine and society are based not only on physicians´ knowledge and skills, but also on their attitudes including behaviour, empathy, altruism and trustworthiness. It would be unforgivable to stand idly and watch erosion of these old values. Therefore, medical school administrators and teachers have to keep pace with advances in information technology and develop policies and procedures regarding professional use of Web 2.0 by medical students. It should be taken into consideration that students may not be aware of all the nets, traps and dangers of online posting of unprofessional information in terms of their future careers (Ferdig et al., 2008;

Other authors (Farnan et al., 2008; Garner & O'Sullivan, 2010) are even calling for protection of medical students by their educators who should familiarize themselves with possible pitfalls of the new technology, such as misrepresentation and misjudgement. The students must be well-aware of different ways of online behaviour that could spoil their future reputation of physicians, eg. unauthorized videos showing people in an uncomplimentary light, unprofessional personal contributions, patient stories violating patient confidentiality, communication about medical profession and patients in a negative way etc. Medical schools mission is now not only professional fitness of their future graduates but also professional behaviour in social media environment.

Santoro (2007) has revealed another important issue concerning the openness and ease of use of the Web 2.0 tools, namely reliability of the contents. The nature of these tools enables anybody to alter the document and re-post it without peer-review. In such a way the educational materials may become unreliable which poses a risk for medical education as a whole. Large-scale studies are needed to evaluate limits and benefits of Web 2.0 tools and look for practical solutions.

4. Transition to web-supported evidence based paediatric curriculum

In the beginning of each innovative educational process should be a vision followed by never-ending efforts to motivate and encourage both trainers and trainees to apply new methods, features and tools. Palacky University Olomouc (Czech Republic) paediatricians undertook a project to implement an evidence-based healthcare approach around real-life scenarios, and develop a sound methodology including web-based learning materials.

4.1 Objectives

The cornerstone of the paediatric curriculum redesign was the intention to implement real case scenarios (Bell et al., 2009) and motivate students to make the cases evidence-based (Kiessling et al., 2011). The clinical education was supplemented with librarian-guided search skills training and information retrieval (Parkhill et al., 2011), selection and interpretation of papers to help students make correct clinical decisions with the assistance of their preceptors. The success of the curriculum re-engineering was dependent on the condition that the amount of contact hours remains unchanged; this was incentives to develop hypermedia learning environment and sets of instructional e-materials to substitute for traditional teaching methods. When developing online supports, priority was given to educational principles and included: relevance, reliability, validity of content, clarity of delivery, effective use of time and appropriate assessment.

4.2 Educational interventions

In accordance with the published experience three educational strategies were chosen to re-design the paediatric curriculum, namely case-based reasoning & learning, evidence-based medicine, and blended learning.

4.2.1 Case-based reasoning & learning

Learning through experience is an important approach employed by humans to comprehend new problems. Medical practice management is facing a challenge of knowledge discovery from the growing volume of information. Recently, there has been a hot debate about the role of casuistry in the context of evidence-based decision-making. Case-based reasoning (CBR) matches the natural reasoning model similar to that used by physicians (Marcus et al., 2004; Holt et al., 2005).

In 1996, R. Schank (Schank, 1996), one of the influential contributors to artificial intelligence and cognitive psychology, wrote: „Learning from experiences is the fundamental process of case-based reasoning. Taking case-based reasoning seriously as a cognitive model implies that experiences play a fundamental role in human learning as well. This has important effects on what and how to teach. Learning by doing works because it teaches implicitly rather than explicitly. Things that are learned implicitly need only be experienced in the proper way at the proper time. In order to make classrooms into learning-by-doing experiences we need to allow students to be in situations that are germane to their interests."

A decade later, deMantaras and colleagues (deMantaras et al., 2005) confirmed that CBR was a procedure encompassing the significance of prior experience during future problem solving. New problems can be tackled by reusing, and if possible, *modifying* the solutions to similar problems that had been solved in the past. It became applicable in a wide range of disciplines and domains, including medicine. Case-based reasoning gave rise to case-based teaching that is generally considered a superior instructional methodology contrary to lectures, because it motivates learners' critical thinking skills. Even though much is known about the role played by facilitators in case-based teaching, there are still numerous controversies on the impact of the format and structure of cases on teaching and learning (Kim et al., 2006).

This educational strategy offers medical students new efficient opportunities to improve their understanding of the theories and to develop necessary skills in clinical problem solving. From the practical point of view it seems obvious that case based learning promotes deeper attitudes to instruction and reduces reliance on surface approaches (Marcus et al., 2004; Nunn, 2011).

4.2.2 Evidence-based medicine

In early 1990s a team of experts named as Evidence Based Medicine Working Group defined a new trend in medical education and practice as follows: "Evidence-based medicine de-emphasizes intuition, unsystematic clinical experience, and pathophysiologic rationale as sufficient grounds for clinical decision making and stresses the examination of evidence from clinical research. Evidence-based medicine requires new skills of the physician, including efficient literature searching and the application of formal rules of evidence evaluating the clinical literature"(Evidence Based Medicine Working Group, 1992). Since then, it has been regarded as an approach to teaching practice of medicine (Ismach, 2004; Shuval et al., 2007; Swanwick, 2010). It was a lucky coincidence that the trend of evidence-based medicine started to develop at the same time period as the Internet. The skill of "efficient literature searching" thus appeared in the new light and circumstances due to the increasing availability of electronic databases. At present, with two decades of the existence of the Internet it might seem that efficient medical literature searching is part of information literacy, but actually it is not. As reported by some authors (Hadley et al., 2007; Ilic et al. 2011), a skill to efficiently retrieve best evidence still remains a crucial step in achieving competency in evidence-based practice. The integration of search skills training into evidence-based clinical curricula is a powerful tool to demonstrate students the importance and practical use of evidence-based medicine principles.

In this context, Tonelli (Tonelli, 2006) provoked a hot debate about integrating "real" evidence into practice as a substitute for standard evidence-based approaches. He introduced other kinds of medical knowledge, such as (a) empirical evidence, (b) experiential evidence, (c) pathophysiologic rationale, (d) patient goals and values, and (e) system features. He emphasized that none of the topics had a priority over others, and the relative importance of a topic would depend upon the circumstances of the particular case. The skilled clinician must weigh these potentially conflicting evidentiary and non-evidentiary aspects for action to employ both practical and theoretical reasoning and to make the best choice for a respective patient. His paper was followed by numerous thought-provoking comments (Buetow, 2006; Djulbegovic, 2006; Gupta, 2006; Lipman, 2006; Loughlin, 2006; Miettinen, 2006; Porta, 2006; SáCouto, 2006; Tanenbaum, 2006; Upshur, 2006) that are worth reading and considering for integrated evidence-based medicine curricula development.

4.2.3 Blended learning

In the beginning of the new millennium when evidence based medicine and Internet were firmly anchored in medical education and practice, new concepts were appearing for integrated evidence based medicine curricula (Green, 2000). Some authors (Hmelo-Silver et al., 2000; Marcus et al., 2004) reported that traditional case-based instructional models could be re-designed to comply with evidence-based medicine principles exploiting most of the advantages of online technologies, but not in the pure format. This method is referred to as blended/hybrid learning, and it has been defined as the combination of face-to-face and online learning opportunities, while reducing classroom contact hours (Dziuban et al., 2004). At present (Donnelly, 2010; Kitchenham, 2011), blended learning represents a mainstream for universities and is seen as a leader in medical education. Learners can be flexible in their education, not constrained by time and distance and satisfied with information technology usage. In parallel, there are numerous advantages for the teachers (eg. better time management, cost savings), and particularly control over the main features of medical education, including dehumanization of medicine (Graham 2004; Harding et al. 2005; De Silva et al., 2010; Aronoff et al., 2010).

Other authors described advantages of blended learning as follows:

"Inherent in blended learning is a fundamental redesign of the instructional model, shifting from lecture to student-centred instruction, increasing all forms of interaction and incorporating formative and summative assessment"(Twigg, 2003; Dziuban et al., 2004).

„Blended learning is a combined and integrated use of e-Learning and face-to-face (F2F) learning activities to develop a community of learning"(Schaffer & Small, 2004).

„Blended learning complements face-to-face classes with eLearning modules" (Voos, 2003).

„It is possible to bring the advantages of face-to-face classes and online courses together".

"It supports a wide range of learning models, such as situated, associative, systemic, simulative and constructivist learning which help to improve the quality of medical education" (Sharpe et al. 2006).

„Clinical education that uses blended learning for communication and reflection may provide flexibility to address clinical placement logistics and may enhance student learning" (Gray & Tobin, 2010).

4.3 Process and outcomes

The process of redesigning the existing undergraduate paediatric curriculum of Palacky University Olomouc (Czech Republic) started as a pilot project in 2007 with the goal to introduce basic principles of evidence based medicine to the 5th-year students of general medicine.

The main change can be characterized as transition from the disease-oriented education (DOE) to patient-oriented evidence that matters (POEM). Besides traditional lectures, seminars, outpatient and bedside teaching the students take a real case scenario exercise. What does that mean? In pairs, the trainees get an actual patient, ask a clinical question, transform it into a PICO (patient-intervention-comparison-outcome) format and make a relevant PubMed search. Under careful teacher guidance and supervision they complete the patient file, and analyze at least one research paper to answer the assigned clinical question.

To follow the four basic steps of evidence-based medicine (1-ask a question, 2-acquire information, 3-appraise information, 4-apply evidence), clinical education is supplemented with various formats of librarian-facilitated   search skills training, ie. mandatory non-interactive online demonstration of PubMed search, elective small-group hands-on training, and web-based tutorial. Online learning materials are available through the Czech and Slovak educational network of medical faculties MEFANET (http://www.mefanet.cz). During case scenario exercise students get as much mentoring as necessary, both face-to-face and web-based, inluding the asynchronous communication service run by the university for registered users.

In the end students present their case reports at a mini-conference and their performance is evaluated according to a set of pre-defined criteria by an assessment committee nominated by the head of the Paediatric Department. The redesigned curriculum was approved by Palacky University Medical Faculty management and officially introduced since academic year 2008/2009. The portfolio of the main innovative educational features contains patient-oriented approach, evidence-based medicine workshop, evidence-based bedside teaching & learning, blended learning, technology-driven information gathering, library-facilitated interactive search skills training, real case scenario exercise, web-based information skills tutorial, e-mentoring, e-portal with a collection of medical education materials MEFANET - http://mefanet.upol.cz

4.4 Student feedback

The pilot version of the innovated paediatric curriculum was assessed by a cohort of 106 medical students during academic year 2007/2008. The questionnaire survey showed that up to 85 % of the respondents had expressed positive attitudes to the re-engineered curriculum, whilst 8 % had critical remarks and 7 % negative impressions (Fig. 1). Some of the student feedback issues were used by the curriculum developers to make minor changes and improvements.

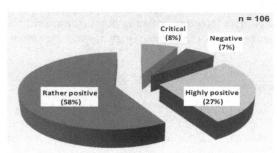

Fig. 1. Pilot version of redesigned paediatric curriculum : student feedback in academic year 2007/2008.

In the next two consecutive academic years 2008/2009 and 2009/2010 a total of 226 medical students who had completed the paediatric clerkship were surveyed by a questionnaire consisting of structured questions (1-to-5 rating + open-ended). The trainees expressed their opinion about perceived values of the curricular features, in particular value of practical training (Fig. 2), teachers' willingness (Fig. 3), and impact of instruction on increased interest in the discipline (Fig. 4). The results demonstrate the following best scored instructional features : teachers' willingness (score 1 by 72% respondents), quality of practical training (score 1 by 44% respondents), and increasing interest in the specialty (score 1 by 32% respondents).

Fig. 2. Perceived value of practical training quality in the newly implemented paediatric curriculum in academic years 2008/2009 and 2009/2010.

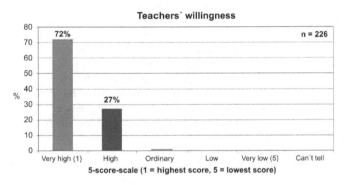

Fig. 3. Perceived value of teachers' willingness in the newly implemented paediatriac curriculum in academic years 2008/2009 and 2009/2010.

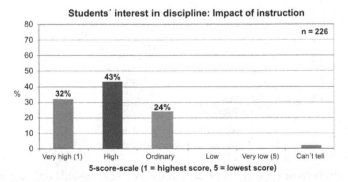

Fig. 4. Perceived value of increasing interest in the discipline due to the newly implemented paediatric curriculum in academic years 2008/2009 and 2009/2010.

Open-ended questions produced some thought-provoking verbatims:

„I found this learning activity refreshing, illustrative, enriching, BUT extremely time consuming..."

"For me, it was a waste of time, not a very efficient educational tool...I prefer textbooks."

„In the beginning, I was hopeless, because I had no idea what it was going to be about. Later on I understood that searching databases should be always inevitable to find the best treatment option for my patients. Having completed the clerkship, I decided to become a paediatrician..."

„I was especially fond of the EBM workshop, including demonstration how and why to search for relevant literature."

"I am very happy that I had an opportunity to be trained how to search PubMed, even if the beginnings were not very easy. Now I feel competent enough to find what I need."

There was a separate questionnaire survey among the same cohort of the students (n = 226) focused on their perceptions of 3 modes of information skills training that included mandatory non-interactive demonstration of a PubMed search, elective interactive small-group hands-on classes and online tutorial with animations, fulltext examples of various study designs, templates for study design interpretation etc. There were 4 structured questions to reply. Up to 70 % of the students self-reported their post-training level of search skills as average, but satisfactory to accomplish the task, 82 % of the respondents were fully satisfied with the hybrid instruction package consisting of a non-interactive PubMed search demonstration supplemented with the web-based search skills tutorial, whilst 14% did not find this package sufficient without subsequent interactive hands-on sessions. In this context, the survey data showed that nearly 62 % of the respondents regarded subsequent hands-on training as important, whilst a total of 45 % did attend the sessions. Fisher's exact test confirmed the statistically significant correlation (p<0.0001) between these two perceived values: 89 % of the hands-on session participants agreed on its efficiency, as well as up to 39 % of those who had not actually attended the interactive classes (Fig. 5).

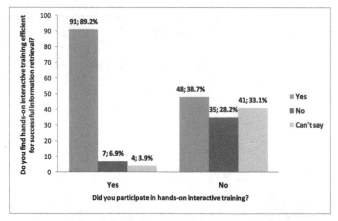

Fig. 5. Correlation between perceived value of hands-on search skills training and attendance in the training sessions (Fisher's exact test) among a cohort of medical students (n = 226) in academic years 2008/2009 and 2009/2010.

4.5 MEFANET portal platform

As already mentioned, all of the multimedia online materials with various configurations (text, images, audio, video, PowerPoint presentations, databases, asynchronous discussion facilities) promoting implementation of a blended learning method for evidence-based paediatric clinical instruction are available from one peer-reviewed portal MEFANET (http://www.mefanet.cz)

In 2007, the MEFANET project (MEdical FAculties NETwork) initiated an international, effective and open cooperation among 11 medical faculties in the Czech Republic and Slovakia. One of the elementary goals of this educational network has been to advance medical teaching with the use of modern information and communication technologies. As an instrument, the MEFANET team decided to develop an original and uniform solution to publish and share digital educational content. There are 3 fundamental principles across the portal platform: (1) medical disciplines linker, (2) federative framework for user authentication, (3) four-dimensional quality assessment (Schwarz et al., 2011).

Authors of online instructional materials have the right to manage user access privileges. The access can be either free or requires authentication.

The main gateway contains a collection of hundreds of digital learning materials developed by educators from different universities relevant to a total of 48 medical specialties. Currently, the network provides services to about 4,000 teachers and almost 22,000 medical and health sciences students.

4.6 A proposal for developers of case-based learning environment in medicine

a. Select attractive, authentic clinical problems to place students *in medias res* and motivate them to take responsibility for learning through decision-making;
b. Encourage learners to solve the clinical problem in a way consistent with professional practice and methodologies (eg. include search skills training and journal clubs as educational interventions);
c. Offer students as much support and guidance as possible; apply mentorship, but promote creative approaches, such as critical thinking, and keep them far from fragmented solutions and memorizing mere facts.

5. Conclusion

Two decades have been enough for the Internet to become an integral part of our daily activities. Current students, often called YouTube generation, Millennials, Generation Y, Net Generation, are unlikely to be satisfied with traditional teaching and learning methods. Medical students often prefer more visual and hands-on methods of information and knowledge acquisition (Ashraf, 2009).

Based on our experience, we can argue that innovative clinical curricula should be a mixture of tradition, modern medicine, technology, and humanity. In such a way they have the power to increase students' interest in the specialty if integrated with evidence-based practice, information literacy training, and supported by online learning materials (Fieschi et al., 2010; Trukhacheva et al., 2011; Motteram & Sharma, 2009).

Case-based learning belongs to the traditional educational interventions in medicine (Williams, 2005). We are in concert with the published opinions that a revival of case method, in particular with real patients and evidence-based, offers an effective alternative of interactive learning (Tarnvik, 2007). Medical students can get the authentic experience how best evidence is implemented at the point of care, including published research (Harden, 2001). These aspects contribute to better motivation for their future jobs. In parallel, clinical teachers become more involved in evidence-based practice, their knowledgebase is improving and the usage of fee-based institutional information resources is more efficient. It is urgently needed that schools incorporate learner-centered teaching and medical educators implement innovative techniques engaging students and delivering them learning content in a time- and resource-efficient manner.

The blended learning approach has been proven practical for medical instruction and opens new horizons for introducing Web 2.0 technologies in a reliable manner to support medical professionalism of future doctors. In our setting, we have had little experience with Web 2.0 apps, so far limited to podcasting lectures (audio synched with PowerPoint). According to other authors, students appreciate online media as review of lectures or a substitute to attending a class (Brittain et al., 2006).

Online learning & teaching requires a reliable ICT support, either to assist teachers, or enable e-publishing of the courses. E-publishing of medical learning materials is a specific issue due to teacher-student-patient relationships including ethical and law aspects. Our 5-year- experience with MEFANET has confirmed the benefits of the centralized ICT support provided across academic networks. Our solution is applicable to other networks, both at national and international levels.

Evidence-based medicine has been acknowledged as a dominant competency in modern health care services delivery. The capability to retrieve and critically appraise the published research has now an irreplaceable position in the portfolio of clinical skills. These information skills must be taught at the undergraduate level. Large-scale studies are needed to compare curricula with evidence-based instruction during pre-clinical and clinical years in terms of practical applicability and sustainability of the acquired skills (Khader et al., 2011).

In spite of technological advances in the digital era (Web 1.0, Web 2.0 apps), medical education should and hopefully will retain its traditional humanistic feature through case-based teaching/learning and peer-guided format, guaranteeing affective, pedagogic, and organizational support. While students find, filter, and focus, their teachers must be ready to act as guides, facilitators and mentors (Schichtel, 2010).

The authors of this chapter had no ambition to encompass all aspects of Web 1.0 and Web 2.0 apps in medical education worldwide. However, the recent WHO report emphasizes necessary multi-sectoral reforms in low- and middle-income countries to improve alignment between educational institutions and health services delivery (Celletti et al., 2011). Used in proper time, online teaching and learning will definitely be of the same value as in other regions.

General visions to shape Generation Y medical education comprise above all (1) progress towards competency-based curriculum, (2) reduced fragmentation in clinical clerkships, (3) case-based and patient-oriented learning with implementation of evidence-based medicine principles, (4) reasonable use of online learning strategies combined with face-to-face instruction, (5) regular monitoring, update and innovation of the web-based learning materials.

6. Acknowledgement

This publication was supported by project CZ.1.07/2.4.00/12.0050. The authors express their thanks Ms. K. Langova and Ms. Z. Michalikova for technical assistance.

7. References

Alikhan, A., Kaur, R. R. & Feldman, S. R. (2010). Podcasting in dermatology education, *Journal of Dermatological Treatment* Vol. 21(No. 2): 73-79.

Aronoff, S. C., Evans, B., Fleece, D., Lyons, P., Kaplan, L. & Rojas, R. (2010). Integrating evidence based medicine into undergraduate medical education: combining online instruction with clinical clerkship, *Teaching and Learning in Medicine* Vol. 22(No. 3): 219-223.

Ashraf, B. (2009). Teaching the Google-eyed YouTube generation, *Education and Training* Vol. 51(No. 5/6): 343-352.

Bell, K., Boshuizen, H. P. A., Scherpbier, A. & Dornan, T. (2009). When only the real thing will do: junior medical students' learning from real patients, *Medical Education* Vol. 43(No. 11): 1036-1043.

Bleakley, A., Bligh, J. & Browne, J. *Medical education for the future: identity, power and location.* Springer, ISBN 9789048196913, Dordrecht.

Borges, N. J., Manuel, S., Elam, C. L. & Jones, B. J. (2006). Comparing millennial and generation X medical students at one medical school, *Academic Medicine* Vol. 81: 571-576.

Boulos, M. N. K., Maramba, I. & Wheeler, S. (2006). Wikis, blogs and podcasts: a new generation of web-based tools for virtual collaborative clinical practice and education, *BMC Medical Education* Vol. 6: 41.

Bozorgmehr, K., Saint, V. A. & Tinnemann, P. (2011). The ´global health´ education framework: a conceptual guide for monitoring, evaluation and practice, *Globalization and Health Health* Vol. 7(No. 1): 8. doi 10.1186/1744-8603-7-8.

Boulos, M. N. K. & Wheeler, S. (2007). The emerging Web 2.0 software: an enabling suite of sociable technologies in health and health care education, *Health Information & Library Journal* Vol. 24(No. 1): 2-23.

Buetow, S. (2006). Opportunities to elaborate on casuistry in clinical decision making. Commentary on Tonelli (2006). Integrating evidence into clinical practice: an alternative to evidence-based approaches, *Journal of Evaluation in Clinical Practice* Vol. 12(No. 4): 427-432.

Brittain, S., Glowacki, P., Van Ittersum, J. & Johnson, L. (2006) Podcasting lectures, *Educause Quarterly* (No. 3): 24-31.

Celletti, F., Reynolds, T. A., Wright, A., Stoertz, A. & Dayrit, M. (2011). Educating a new generation of doctors to improve the health of populations in low- and middle-income countries, *PloS Medicine* Vol. 8(No. 10): e1001108.

Choules, A. P. (2007). The use of e-learning in medical education: a review of the current situation, *Postgraduate Medical Journal* Vol. 83(No. 978): 212-216.

Chretien, K. C., Greysen, S. R., Chretien, J.-P. & Kind, T. (2009). Online posting of unprofessional content by medical students, *JAMA* Vol. 302(No. 12): 1309-1315.

Chretien, K. C., Goldman, E. F., Beckman, L. & Kind, T. (2010). It's your own risk: medical students' perspectives on online professionalism, *Academic Medicine* Vol. 85(No. 10 Suppl.): S68-S71.

Clauson, K. A. &Vidal, D. M. (2008). Overview of biomedical journal podcasts, *American Journal of Health-System Pharmacy* Vol. 65(No. 22): 2155-2158.

Cook, D. A., Levinson, A. J., Garside, S., Dupras, D. M., Erwin, P. J. & Montori, V. M. (2008). Internet-based learning in the health professions: a meta-analysis, *JAMA* Vol. 300(No. 10): 1181-1196.

Cook, D. A., Garside, S., Levinson, A. J., Dupras, D. M. & Montori, V. M. (2010). What do we mean by web-based learning? A systematic review of the variability of interventions, *Medical Education* Vol. 44(No. 8): 765-774.

Cooke, M., Irby, D. M., Sullivan, W. & Ludmerer, K. M. (2006). American medical education 100 years after the Flexner report, *New England Journal of Medicine* Vol. 355: 1339-1344.

Cullen, R. (2006). Health information on the internet: a study of providers, quality, and users, Praeger, ISBN 9780865693227, Westport, Conn.

De Mantaras, L. R., McSherry, D., Bridge, D., Leake, D., Smyth, B., Craw, S., Faltings, B., Maher, M. L., Cox, M. T., Forbus, K., Keane, M., Aamodt, A. & Watson, I. (2005). Retrieval, reuse, revision and retention in case-based reasoning, *The Knowledge Engineering Review* Vol. 20(No. 3): 215-240.

De Silva, N. K., Dietrich, J. E. & Young, A. E. (2010). Pediatric and adolescent gynecology learned via a web-based computerized case series, *Journal of Pediatric and Adolescent Gynecology* Vol. 23: 115-115.

Dent, J. A. & Harden, R. M. (2009a). *A Practical Guide for Medical Teachers* (3rd. ed.), Churchill Livingstone/Elsevier Health Sciences, Edinburgh/New York.

Dent, J. A. & Harden, R. M. (2009b). New horizons in medical education, In: *A Practical Guide for Medical Teachers* (3rd ed.), J.A. Dent & R.M. Harden (Ed.), pp. 3-9, Churchill Livingstone/Elsevier Health Sciences, ISBN 9780702031236, Edinburgh/New York.

Djulbegovic, B. (2006). Evidence and decision making. Commentary on M. R. Tonelli (2006), Integrating evidence into clinical practice: an alternative approach to evidence-based approaches. Journal of Evaluation in Clinical Practice 12, 248-256, *Journal of Evaluation in Clinical Practice* Vol. 12(No. 3): 257-259.

Donnelly, R. (2010). Harmonizing technology with interaction in blended problem-based learning, *Computers & Education* Vol. 54: 350-359.

Dziuban C. D., Hartman, J. L. & Moskal, P. D. (2004). Blended learning, *Educause Learning B ulletin* Vol. 7: 2-12.

Evidence-based Medicine Working Group. (1992). Evidence-based medicine: a new approach to the teaching of medicine, *JAMA* Vol. 268(No. 17): 2420-2425.

Farnan, J. M., Paro, J. A., Higa, J., Edelson, J. & Arora, V. M. (2008). The YouTube generation: implications for medical professionalism, *Perspectives in Biology and Medicine* Vol. 51(No. 4): 517-524.

Ferdig, R. E., Dawson, K., Black, E. W., Black, N. M. P. & Thompson, L. A. (2008). Medical students' and residents' use of online social networking tools: Implications for teaching professionalism in medical education, *First Monday* Vol. 13(No. 9), URL: http://pear.accc.uic.edu/htbin/cgiwrap/bin/ojs/index.php/fm/article/view/21 61/2026

Fieschi, M., Soula, H., Giorgi, R., GouvernetJ., Fieschi, D., Votti, G., Volot, T. & Berland, Y. (2002). Experomenting with new paradigms for medical education and the emergence of distance learning degree using the Internet: teaching evidence-based medicine, *Medical Informatics & the Internet in Medicine* Vol. 27(No. 1): 1-11.

Garner, J. & O'Sullivan, H. (2010). Facebook and the professional behaviours of undergraduate medical students, *The Clinical Teacher* Vol. 7: 112-115.

Genn, J. M. (2001). AMEE Medical Education Guide No. 23 (Part 1): Curriculum, environment, climate, quality and change in medical education - a unifying perspective, *Medical Teacher* Vol. 23(No. 4): 337-344.

Graham, C. R. (2004). Blended learning systems: Definition, current trends, and future directions. In:*The Handbook of Blended Learning: Global Perspectives,Local Designs*, C. J. Bonk & C. R. Graham (Ed.), pp. 3–21, Pfeiffer: Zurich.

Gray, K. &Tobin, J. (2010). Introducing an online community into a clinical education setting: a pilot study of student and staff engagement and outcomes using blended learning, *BMC Medical Education* Vol. 10: 6.

Green, M. L. (2000). Evidence-based medicine training in graduate medical education: past, present and future, *Journal of Evaluation in Clinical Practice* Vol. 3(No. 2): 121-138.

Gupta, M. (2006). Beyond 'evidence'. Commentary on Tonelli (2006), Integrating evidence into clinical practice: an alternative to evidence-based approaches. Journal of Evaluation in Clinical Practice 12, 248-256, *Journal of Evaluation in Clinical Practice* Vol. 12(No. 3): 296-298.

Hadley, J., Wall, D. & Khan, K. (2007). Learning needs analysis to guide teaching evidence-based medicine: knowledge and beliefs amongst trainers from various specialities, *BMC Medical Education* Vol. 7: 11.

Harden, R. M. (2001). AMEE guide No. 21: Curriculum mapping: a tool for transparent and authentic teaching and learning, *Medical Teacher* Vol. 23(No. 2): 123-137.

Harding, A., Kaczynski, D. & Wood, L. (2005). Evaluation of blended learning: Analysis of qualitative data, *Proceedings of the Blended Learning in Science Teaching and Learning*, ISBN 1864877448, September 2005, University of Sydney, pp. 56–61.

Hmelo-Silver, C. E., Nagarajan, A. & Day, R. S. (2000). „It´s harder than we thought it would be": a comparative case study of expert-novice experimentation strategies, *Science and Education* Vol. 86: 219-243.

Holt, A., Bichindaritz, I., Schmidt, R. & Perner, P. (2005). Medical applications in case-based reasoning, *The Knowledge Engineering Review* Vol. 20(No. 3): 289-292.

Howick, J. (2011). *The philosophy of evidence-based medicine*, Wiley-Blackwell/BMJ Books, ISBN 9781405196673, Chichester, West Sussex.

Ilic, D., Tepper, K. & Misso, M. (2011). Teaching evidence based medicine literature searching skills to medical students during the clinical years – a protocol for a randomized controlled trial, *BMC Medical Education* Vol. 11: 48.

Ismach, R. B. (2004). Teaching evidence-based medicine to medical students, *Academic Emergency Medicine* Vol. 11(No. 12): e6-10.

Jalali, A., Mioduszewski, M., Gauthier, M. & Varpio, L. (2009). Wiki use and challenges in undergraduate medical education, *Medical Education* Vol. 43(No. 11): 1117.

Jham, B. C., Duraes, G. V., Strassler, H. E. & Sensi, L. G. (2008). Joining the podcast revolution, *Journal of Dental Education* Vol. 72(No. 3): 278-281.

Khader, Y. S., Batayaha, W. & Al-Omari, M. The effect of evidence-based medicine (EBM) training seminars on the knowledge and attitudes of medical students towards EBM, *Journal of Evaluation in Clinical Practice* Vol. 17(No. 4): 640-643.

Kiessling, A., Lewitt, M. & Henriksson, P. (2011). Case-based training of evidence-based clinical practice in primary care and decreased mortality in patients with coronary heart disease, *Annals of Family Medicine* Vol. 9(No. 3): 211-218.

Kim, S., Phillips, W. R., Pinsky, L., Brock, D., Phillips, K. & Keary, J. (2006). A conceptual framework for developing teaching cases: a review and synthesis of the literature across disciplines, *Medical Education* Vol. 40(No. 9): 867-876.

Kitchenham, A. (2011). *Blended Learning across Disciplines: Models for Implementation*, IGI Global, ISBN 9781609604790, Hershey (PA), USA.

Koschmann, T. (1995). Medical education and computer literacy: learning about, through, and with computers, *Academic Medicine* Vol. 70(No. 9): 818-821.

Lemley, T. & Burnham, J. (2009). Web 2.0 tools in medical and nursing curricula, *Journal of Medical Library Association* Vol. 97(No. 1): 50-52.

Lipman, T. (2006). Evidence and casuistry. Commentary on Tonelli (2006), Integrating evidence into clinical practice: an alternative to evidence-based approaches. Journal of Evaluation in Clinical Practice 12, 248-256, *Journal of Evaluation in Clinical Practice* Vol. 12(No. 3): 269-272.

Logan, D. W., Sandal, M., Gardber, P. P., Manske, M. & Bateman, A. (2010). Ten simple rules for editing Wikipedia, *PloS Computational Biology* Vol. 6(No. 9): e1000947.

Loughlin, M. (2006). The future for medical epistemology? Commentary on Tonelli (2006), Integrating evidence into clinical practice: an alternative to evidence-based approaches. Journal of Evaluation in Clinical Practice 12, 248-256, *Journal of Evaluation in Clinical Practice* Vol. 12(No. 3): 289-291.

Marcus, G., Taylor, R. & Ellis, R. A. (2004). Implications for the design of online case based learning activities based on the student blended learning experience, *Proceedings of the 21st ASCILITE Conference*, Perth, December 2004, pp. 577-586.

Masic, I., Pandza, H., Toromanovic, S., Masic, F., Sivic, S., Zunic, L. & Masic, Z. (2011). Information technologies (ITs) in medical education, *Acta Informatica Medica* Vol. 19(No. 3): 68-78.

Miettinen, O. S. (2006). Evidence-based medicine, case-based medicine; scientific medicine, quasi-scientific medicine. Commentary on Tonelli (2006), Integrating evidence into clinical practice: an alternative to evidence-based approaches. Journal of Evaluation in Clinical Practice 12, 248-256, *Journal of Evaluation in Clinical Practice* Vol. 12(No. 3): 260-264.

Motteram, G. & Sharma, P. (2009). Blended learning in a Web 2.0 world, *International Journal of Emerging Technologies & Society* Vol. 7(No. 2): 83-96.

Nunn, R. (2011). Mere anecdotes: evidence and stories in medicine, *Journal of Evaluation in Clinical Practice* Vol. 17: doi: 10.1111/j.1365-2753.2011.01727.

Parkhill, A. F., Clavisi, O., Pattuwage, L., Chau, M., Turner, T., Bragge, P. & Gruen, R. (2011). Searches for evidence mapping: effective, shorter, cheaper, *Journal of Medical Library Association* Vol. 99(No. 2): 157-160.

Platt, M. W., Anderson, W. & Obenshain, S. S. (1999). Use of student-centered, computer-mediated communication to enhance the medical school curriculum, *Medical Education* Vol. 33: 757-761.

Porta, M. (2006). Five warrants for medical decision making: some considerations and a proposal to better integrated evidence-based medicine into everyday practice. Commentary on Tonelli (2006), Integrating evidence into clinical practice: an alternative to evidence-based approcahes. Journal of Evaluation in Clinical Practice 12, 248-256, *Journal of Evaluation in Clinical Practice* Vol. 12(No. 3): 265-268.

Rajabi, F., Majdzadeh, R. & Ziaee, S. A. M. (2011). Trends in medical education: an example From a developing country, *Archives of Iranian Medicine* Vol. 14(2): 132-138.

Ruiz, J. G., Mintzer, M. J. & Leipzig, R. M. (2006). The impact of E-learning in medical education, *Academic Medicine* Vol. 81: 207-212.

Sá Couto, J. (2006) Can we forget how to treat patients? Commentary on Tonelli (2006),Integrating evidence into clinical practice: an alternative to evidence-based approaches. Journal of Evaluation in Clinical Practice 12, 248-256, *Journal of Evaluation in Clinical Practice* Vol. 12(No. 3):277-280.

Saarinen, C., Arora, V., Fergusen, B & Chretien, C. (2011). Incorporating social media into medical education, *Academic Internal Medicine Insight* Vol. 9(No. 1): 12-19.

Sandars, J. & Schroter, S. (2007). Web 2.0 technologies for undergraduate and postgraduate medical education: an online survey, *Postgraduate Medical Journal* Vol. 83: 759-762.

Santoro, E. (2007). Podcast, wiki e blog: il web 2.0 al servizio della formazione e dell'aggiornamento del medico, *Recenti Progressi in Medicina* Vol. 98 (No. 10): 484-494.

Sawyer, T., Stein, A., Olson, H. & Mahnke, C. B. (2011). Development of the competency-based objective resident education using virtual patients system, *Medical Education Development* Vol. 1: e5.

Schank, R. C. (1996). Goal-based scenarios: case-based reasoning meets learning by doing, In: *Case-based reasoning: experiences, lessons & future directions*, D. Leake (Ed.), pp. 295-347, AAAI Press/The MIT Press, URL: http://cogprints.org/635/1/CBRMeetsLBD_for_Leake.html

Schichtel, M. (2010). Core-competence skills in e-mentoring for medical educators: a conceptual exploration, *Medical Teacher* Vol. 32: e248-e262.

Schreiber, W. E. & Giustini, D. (2009). Pathology in the era of Web 2.0, *American Journal of Clinical Pathology* Vol. 132: 824-828.

Schwarz, M. R. (2001). Globalization and medical education, *Medical Teacher* Vol. 23(No. 6): 533-534.

Schwarz, D., Komenda, M., Majernik, J., Mihal, V., Stipek, S. & Dusek, L. (2011). Mefanet after four years of progressing: standardization of educational web platform among medical faculties, In: *MEFANET report 04: Efficient multimedia teaching tools in medical education*, D. Schwarz et al. (Ed.), pp. 119-124, Masaryk University Brno, ISBN 9788021055391, Brno.

Shaffer, K. & Small, J. E. (2004). Blended learning in medical education: use of an integrated approach with web-based small group modules and didactic instruction for teaching radiologic anatomy, *Academic Radiology* Vol. 11(No. 9): 1059-1070.

Shamji, A. I. & Law, M. (2011). The role of technology in medical education: lessons from the University of Toronto, *UTMJ* Vol. 88(No. 3): 150-153.

Sharpe, R., Benfield, G., Roberts, G. & Francis, R. (October 2006). The undergraduate experience of blended learning: a review of UK literature and research. In: *The Higher Education Academy*, 12.01.2011, URL: http://www.heacademy.ac.uk/4884.htm

Shuval, K., Berkovits, E., Netzer, D., Hekselman, I., Linn, S., Brezis, M. & Reis, S. (2007). Evaluating the impact of an evidence-based medicine educational intervention on primary care doctors' attitudes, knowledge and clinical behaviour: a controlled trial and before and after study, *Journal of Evaluation in Clinical Practice* Vol. 13(No. 4):581-598.

Swanwick,T. (2010). *Understanding medical education: evidence, theory and practice,*Wiley-Blackwell, ISBN 9781405196802, Chichester, West Sussex.

Tanenbaum, S. J. (2006). Evidence by any other name. Commentary on Tonelli (2006), Integrating evidence into clinical practice: an alternative to evidence-based approaches. *Journal of Evaluation in Clinical Practice* Vol. 12(No. 3): 273-276.

Tarnvik, A. (2007). Revival of the case method: a way to retain student-centered learning in a post-PBL era, *Medical Teacher* Vol. 29(No. 1): e32-36.

Taylor, P. (2006). *From patient data to medical knowledge: zhe principles and practice of health informatics,* John Wiley &Sons, ISBN 9780727917731, Malden, Mass.

Tilson, J. K., Kaplan, S. R., Harris, J. L., Hutchinson, A., Ilic, D., Niederman, R., Potomkova, J. & Zwolsman, S. E. (2011). Sicily statement on classification and development of of evidence-based practice learning assessment tools. *BMC Medical Education* Vol. 11: 78.

Tonelli, M. R. (2006). Integrating evidence into clinical practice: an alternative to evidence-based approaches, *Journal of Evaluation in Clinical Practice* Vol. 12(3): 248-256.

Towle, A. (1998). Continuing medical education. Changes in health care and continuing medical education for the 21st century, *BMJ* Vol. 316(No. 7127): 301-304.

Trukhacheva, N., Tchernysheva, S. & Krjaklina, T. (2011). The impact of e-learning on medical education in Russia, *E-learning and Digital Media* Vol. 8(No. 1): 31-35.

Twigg, C. A. (2003). Improving learning and reducing costs: new models for online learning. *Educause Review* Vol. 38(No. 5), 28.

Upshur, R. E. (2006). The complex, the exhausted and the personal: reflections on the relationship between evidence-based medicine and casuistry. Commentary on Tonelli 2006) Integrating evidence into clinical practice: an alternative to evidence-based approaches. Journal of Evaluation in Clinical Practice (2006), 12, 248-256, *Journal of Evaluation in Clinical Practice* Vol. 12(No. 3): 281-288.

Vejrazka, M., Stuka, C. & Stipek, S. (2010). Wikilectures – an instrument of Mefanet network based on technologies of Web 2.0, In: *Mefanet Report 02: Medical Teaching with the Use of Advanced Technology,* D. Schwarz et al. *(Ed.),* pp. 121-125, Masaryk University, ISBN 978802105302, Brno.

Voos, R. (2003). Blended learning - what is it and where might it take us?, *Sloan-C View: Perspectives in Quality Online Education* Vol. 2(No. 1): 3–5.

Westwood, J. D. (2001). *Medicine meets virtual reality 2001: outer space, inner space, virtual space,* IOS Press, ISBN 9781586031435, Amsterdam/Washington D.C.

Williams, B. (2005). Case based learning – a review of the literature: is there scope for this educational paradigm in prehospital education?, *Emergency Medicine Journal* Vol. 22: 577-581.

Wilson, P., Petticrew, Y. & Booth, A. (2009). After the Gold rush? A systematic and critical review of general medical podcasts, *Journal of the Royal Society of Medicine* Vol. 102(No. 2): 69-74.

Wong, G., Greenhalgh, T. & Pawson, R. (2010). Internet-based medical education: a realist review of what works, for whom and in what circumstances, *BMC Medical Education* 10: 12.

10

Interactive WhiteBoard:
Effective Interactive Teaching Strategy
Designs for Biology Teaching

Kai-Ti Yang[1] and Tzu-Hua Wang[2,*]
[1]National Taiwan Normal University
[2]National HsinChu University of Education
Taiwan (R.O.C.)

1. Introduction

The goal of this chapter is to design interactive teaching strategies with Interactive WhiteBoard (IWB) and investigate their effectiveness on Biology teaching. In recent years, with the rapid development of Information Communication Technology (ICT), integrating multimedia presentation tools to perform better teaching has become easier in today's classroom. Among many ICT systems, the innovation and introduction of IWB has not only changed the traditional classroom but symbolizes a key revolution in the history of whiteboard development. Researchers have identified a number of advantages of using IWB in teaching and learning: flexibility and versatility, multimedia/multimodal presentation, improving teaching efficiency, supporting planning and the development of resources, improving students' skills of using ICT technology, interactivity and participation during course, improving students' learning motivation, and improving students' understanding (BECTA, 2007; Glover, Miller, Averis, & Door, 2005; Holmes, 2009; Northcote, Mildenhall, Marshall, & Swan,2010;Slay, Sieborger, & Hadgkinson-Williams, 2008; Smith, Higgins, Wall, & Miller, 2005; Wall, Higgins, Smith, 2005). The IWB realizes interactive operations between the whiteboard and the computer. It has become a new interface to consolidate all teaching resources in a traditional classroom. Many countries, such as the United Kingdom, Japan, Singapore, Malaysia, China, and Russia, have invested heavily in the IWB and attempted to implement it in schools of all levels. In Taiwan, the government also invests a large amount of money to introduce IWB into classrooms. Since 2006, the Taiwan's Ministry of Education officially announced that more than $50 million NTD (roughly $15 million USD) would be invested in promoting the preliminary integration of IWB into instruction. Following the trend of integrating IWB into teaching, this research tries to understand how to make good use of the advantages of IWB to make students have better learning effectiveness on junior high school Biology.

Among the topics of junior high school Biology, cell division, photosynthesis, cell respiration, food chain, food web and evolution are the topics difficult to teach and learn. Both teachers

---

*Corresponding Author

and students believe that cell division is most difficult to learn of all topics (Oztap, Ozay, & Oztap, 2003). Many related studies have shown that students of different ages and in different grades all have a poor understanding of cell division (Lewis, Leach, Wood-Roinson, 2000a, b; Lewis & Wood-Roinson, 2000; Smith, 1991). Lewis et al. (2000a, b) pointed out that students had a poor understanding of cell division because they are not clear about the basic structures of genetics and therefore easily become confused about the terminology. Lewis et al. argued that students will be able to develop a better understanding if these basic structures are clearly presented. Brown (1995) and Oztap et al. (2003) noted that teaching needs to emphasize the dynamic nature of the cell division using a variety of teaching aids such as photographs, film and videos, particularly time-lapse phase contrast microscopy, to demonstrate the change of the chromosomes at different stages of cell division and build chromosome models so that it will be easier for students to overcome learning difficulties.

The major advantages of IWB indicated in the literature and their potential in Biology teaching are explained as follows (BECTA, 2007; Glover et al., 2005; Holmes, 2009; Northcote et al., 2010; Slay et al., 2008; Smith et al., 2005; Wall et al., 2005) :

Advantage 1: Flexibility and versatility

The IWB can be used in teaching students of different ages and for different topics. Its functions, including making notes, flipping back and forth to review material, saving the drawings and texts, and moving the intended objects and focusing on them. It can improve flexibility and versatility of teaching. Therefore, IWB is suitable for teaching high school Biology courses. In addition, IWB can focus on specified content and enlarge multimedia objects based on teacher and student needs. Notes can also be made on the content through the IWB screen. Moreover, teachers can record the teaching process (including the notes) and interactions with students for later review.

Advantage 2: Multimedia/Multimodal presentation

The IWB is a new interface integrating all teaching resources. Its built-in teaching software and dynamic multimedia presentation can attract students' attention and help them understand abstract concepts. In Biology teaching, the visual nature of IWB presentations can improve student learning by delivering micro or dynamic representations of abstract concepts such as the process of cell division or the structures and functions inside bodies such as blood circulation. IWB also supports multimedia and multimodal presentation. Multiple representations can be simultaneously shown on the screen to satisfy needs of students with different learning styles.

Advantage 3: Improving teaching efficiency

Teachers can present many multimedia resources on the IWB to improve teaching efficiency. For example, the structures of chromosomes can be presented using images, videos or 3D models to help students build chromosome models. In addition, students can use the IWB to improve and facilitate their learning process. Teachers can design teaching activities for the IWB, which may help students actively think and operate the IWB. For example, teachers can provide unfinished flow charts about the process of cell division for students to complete through discussion. Teachers can also provide students pictures about chromosomes' changes in each stage of cell division and make them arrange the pictures in right order and explain how the quantity of DNA and chromosome changes.

Advantage 4: Supporting planning and the development of resources

The IWB has a large teaching material resource database where teachers can access various animations and music for different subjects, such as frog anatomy, and use them to develop digital materials for teaching activities.

Advantage 5: Improving students' skills of using ICT technology

Teachers can use the IWB to help students better engage in the learning environment. Students can improve their skills in using ICT by discussing with peers or observing teachers' and peers' operation.

Advantage 6: Interactivity and participation during course

The interactivity enabled by IWB can improve interaction in classroom and make students and teachers feel closer to each other. They can have more eye-contact than using laptops and teachers are therefore more able to control the classroom. Moreover, the IWB is more beneficial to the teaching of subjects involving many inquiry activities and requiring extensive participation of students, such as science subjects.

Advantage 7: Improving students' learning motivation

The IWB's ability to dynamically integrate audio and visual presentation can make teaching activities more lively and realistic. Compared with common 2D presentations and textbooks, IWB can better attract students' attention and enhance their learning motivation.

Advantage 8: Improving students' understanding

The IWB is characterized by visual nature and supports multiple representations, which not only attracts students' attention but improves their understanding of the topics. For example, an IWB can simultaneously show on its large screen the 2D pictures of chromosome structures and a 3D video demonstrating the relation between chromosomes, genes and genetic information. This can not only improve understanding of students with different learning styles but enhance their ability to interpret the relationship between the 2D pictures and the 3D video by combining the information they deliver.

The abovementioned advantages of integrating IWB into the teaching of junior high school Biology courses show that introducing IWB into the classroom will be able to provide teachers with a way to present the dynamic nature of cell division, and the relationships between cells, chromosomes, genes and genetic information with multimedia and multimodal representation. Students can in turn develop a thorough concept structure. Moreover, IWB's high interactivity facilitates student participation in learning and promotes their learning motivation. With this in mind, in this research we design digital teaching materials and activities that use the IWB to teach cell division, in order to investigate the viability and effectiveness of integrating IWB into the teaching of cell division. This research adopts a quasi-experimental design to investigate the effectiveness of IWB-integrated instruction and traditional ICT-integrated instruction on junior high school Biology teaching.

2. Methodology

This section introduces the participants, instruments, research design, and data collection and analysis of this research.

2.1 Participants

Fifty-four junior high school seventh graders participated in this study. Adopting a quasi-experimental design, this study divided the participating students into two groups, the IWB group (n=27) and the T group (n=27). The T group received traditional ICT-integrated instruction, which means the teacher lectured by projecting Microsoft PowerPoint slides onto the projection screen. The IWB group received IWB-integrated instruction.

2.2 Instruments

2.2.1 Interactive Whiteboard (IWB) - SmartBoard™

The IWB used in this study is the SmartBoard™ made by a Canadian company, SMART™ Technologies, using analog resistive technology. The whiteboard is connected to a notebook or a computer through the USB cable, and then the notebook or computer is connected to the projector. Signals of the projector are projected onto the IWB. By adjusting the IWB, teachers can operate the computer by touching the IWB, as shown in Figure 1. The IWB can immediately save the written texts, drawings and other messages on the IWB panel to the connected computer.

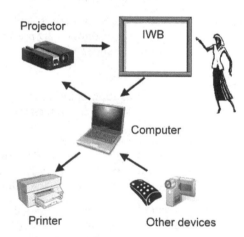

Fig. 1. Interactive Whiteboard system structure and operation

2.2.2 Digital teaching materials and teaching method

Teaching materials used in this study focus on the 'Cell Division' topic of junior high school Biology course in Taiwan. Teaching contents cover three sub-topics: 'Chromosome and Its Importance,' 'The Role of Mitosis' and 'Meiosis and Sexual Life Cycle.' Teaching materials for 'Chromosome and Its Importance' focus on the following concepts: chromosomes are located in nucleus; chromosomes contain heredity substances – genes to determine individual's traits; chromosome number varies with species; homologous chromosomes. 'The Role of Mitosis' and 'Meiosis and Sexual Life Cycle' primarily aim to enable students to understand when mitosis and meiosis happen and the significance of the two kinds of cell division.

The digital teaching materials designed in this study are mainly images, pictures and Adobe Flash animations. Materials used by the two groups included the same concepts, and both groups were lectured by the same teacher. The main difference is that in the IWB group, the digital teaching materials can be used on the NoteBook™ software, which is provided by SMART™ Technologies. Further, the teacher can interact with the students through the IWB screen. In the T group, the digital teaching materials are presented for teaching in the traditional way of using a projector to project PowerPoint slides onto the screen, and interaction between the teacher and students is limited to verbal communication. The teaching methods of the IWB and the T group are explained below.

2.2.2.1 Teaching method of IWB group

Prior to teaching, students have prior knowledge about cells. They know that the nucleus is related to heredity but are not clear about its contents. Lewis et al. (2000a, b) pointed out that junior high school students are not clear about the relationship between the cell, chromosomes and genetic information. If students would like to develop a coherent conceptual framework for a better understanding of genetics and inheritance, they first must have a clear understanding if the relationship between the basic structures – cell, nucleus, chromosome and gene. Therefore, in 'Chromosome and Its Importance,' the teacher enables the students understand the relationship between the cell, the nucleus, chromatins, chromosomes, genes and genetic information through the images from microscopes and 2D pictures. Moreover, to enhance student understanding of the relationship between the cell, the nucleus, chromosomes and genes, the teacher designs activities that call for the students to answer questions and touch the IWB to collaboratively match the genetic structures. This section also includes the interpretation and application of DNA fingerprint. The teacher also designs an activity to make students work together to identify the blood relationship between a child and his parents through the knowledge about DNA fingerprint and explain the reasons for peers (Figure 2). Moreover, to resolve student misconceptions about sex

Fig. 2. Students are learning in IWB group

chromosomes (X , Y chromosome) and autosomes identified by Lewis et al.(2000a), students are made to directly compare the karyotypes of male and female, circle the differences on the IWB themselves, and count the number of chromosomes. In addition, students are allowed to touch the species on the Adobe Flash animation whose chromosome number they would like to know. After comparison, they can come out with the conclusion that different species have different chromosome numbers and that the chromosome number does not imply a hierarchy of species (Figure 3). Finally, the concepts about homologous chromosomes, ploidy and alleles are introduced through human karyotypes. By dragging and making the separated homologous chromosomes together through the IWB, students will acquire a better understanding of the concept. In order to enable students to clearly identify concepts about alleles, this information is presented using cartoon pictures— In addition, the concept of ploidy is presented by having students compare the karyotypes of human somatic cells and germ cells.

In 'The Role of Mitosis,' the Q and A teaching activities are used to help students understand the significance and process of mitosis. The IWB screen is divided into two parts. The left part presents the significance of mitosis, the process by which a cell is divided into two identical cells. On the right, the IWB displays the process of mitosis but does not show how the chromosomes change in the nucleus (see step1 in Figure 4). Instead, to enable students to think actively about the chromosome change in mitosis, the teacher adopts Q and A teaching activities that compel the students to answer the questions about chromosome changes in each stage (see step2 and step3 in Figures 4). Moreover, to clear students' confusion about the terminology, students are made to match the terminology, including 'chromosome duplication,' 'chromosomes convene on the metaphase plate,'

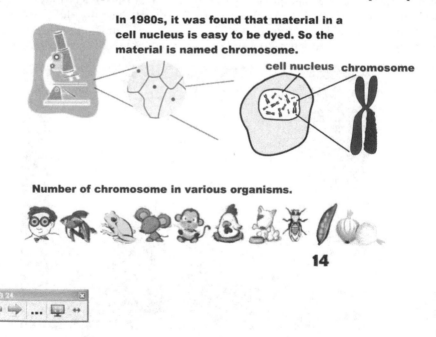

Fig. 3. Screenshot of the teaching materials (Yang, Wang, & Chiu, 2011)

'separation of sister chromatids' and 'one cell divides into two identical cells,' with their corresponding stages (see step4 in Figures 4). Then, to make students have a deeper impression and understanding of the changes in ploidy, DNA quantity and chromosome number, pictures of each stage of mitosis are projected on the IWB screen for students to work together in assigning them to the mitosis process on the correct stages(see 1-5 in Figure 5), explaining the reason for their operation, assigning the descriptions(see part A in Figure 5) on the correct arrows (see part B in Figure 5), and then drawing diagrams about the changes in ploidy, DNA quantity and chromosome number (see part C in Figure 5).

In 'Meiosis and Sexual Life Cycle,' the teacher also adopts Q and A teaching activities to enable the students to understand the significance of meiosis and when and where it happens. Human karyotypes are also used to help students understand that if meiosis does not occur in gametes before fertilization, the problem of tetraploidy may happen. Then students learn about meiosis using similar methods stated above. They are first guided to answer the chromosome change of meiosis stage by stage and then compare the differences between meiosis and mitosis. Students need to identity the following concepts about meiosis: 'chromosomes replicate once but divide twice,' 'there are four daughter cells,' 'homologs separate during anaphase I' and 'sister chromatids separate during anaphase II.' They make notes on the IWB screen and understand the concept that meiosis is the main cause of genetic variation in the sexual life cycle. Moreover, by competing to answer questions

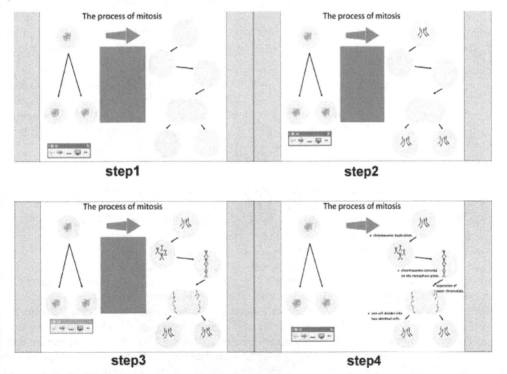

Fig. 4. The four steps of teaching the concept of mitosis in IWB group. The big rectangles in this figure are the masks for the correct answers.

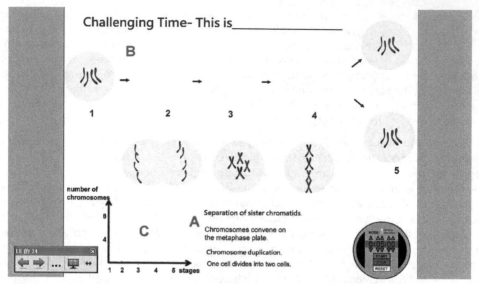

Fig. 5. Screenshot of the teaching materials for the concept of mitosis in IWB group

and working together to complete the meiosis process, using similar methods stated above, students can familiarize themselves with the process of meiosis again. They are also required to draw the changes in the number of chromosome sets, chromosome numbers and the DNA quantity.

Finally, to enable students to clearly distinguish mitosis from meiosis, the teacher makes two tables comparing the two kinds of cell division, sexual reproduction and asexual reproduction on IWB screen, and then has the students complete the tables collaboratively. Their commonalities and differences are presented explicitly, as suggested by Lewis et al. (2000a).

2.2.2.2 Teaching method of T group

The digital teaching materials used by the IWB group and the T group cover the same concepts and are presented by the same teacher. The main difference is that in the IWB group, the digital teaching materials can be used for teaching on the IWB, while in the T group, these digital teaching materials are presented in the traditional way of using a projector to project MicroSoft PowerPoint slides (PPT slides) onto the screen, and interaction between the teacher and students is limited to verbal communication. In other words, the IWB and T groups present the same teaching materials in the same order. The only difference is that in the IWB group, students are allowed to operate the IWB collaboratively during teaching activities. In the T group, students only answer questions verbally during Q & A teaching activities, and the teacher presents teaching materials with PPT slides one by one. Therefore, in the sub-topic of 'Chromosome and Its Importance,' teaching materials are all designed to enable students in the T group to learn the basic structures through pictures. However, in the IWB group, students compete to answer questions and do the matching about relationship between basic structures on the IWB. In the T group, after the teacher raises questions, students compete to answer and then the teacher uses simple animations embedded in the PPT slides to present the relationship between basic structures. In addition, there is also a Q & A teaching activity after the teacher explains how to interpret and apply DNA fingerprint. After students compete to answer questions, the teacher shows the correct answers with the animations embedded in the PPT slides. Moreover, the teacher directly demonstrates the Adobe Flash animation illustrating that the location and contents of chromosomes and the chromosome number varies with species.

In the sub-topic of 'The Role of Mitosis,' the Q & A teaching activities are used to help students understand the significance of mitosis. The screen of the PPT slide is divided into two parts. The left side of the screen shows the significance of cell division – a single cell is divided into two identical cells. The right side of the screen shows the diagram the process of mitosis but not the changes of chromosomes in the nucleus. After conducting Q & A teaching activities with students, the teacher displays the animation embedded in the PPT slides to show how the chromosomes change in each stage and the terminology of each stage during the mitosis process (Figure 6). To give the students a deeper understanding of the changes in the number of chromosome sets, chromosome number, and quantity of DNA, the teacher also presents the PPT slides and displays the animation embedded in the PPT slides to present the process of mitosis and changes of DNA and chromosomes after having Q & A teaching activities with students. The teacher teaches the sub-topic of 'Meiosis and Sexual Life Cycle' in the same way as the sub-topic of 'The Role of Mitosis.' The table is also shown in the animations built into the PPT slides after the teacher finish the Q & A teaching activity interaction with her students.

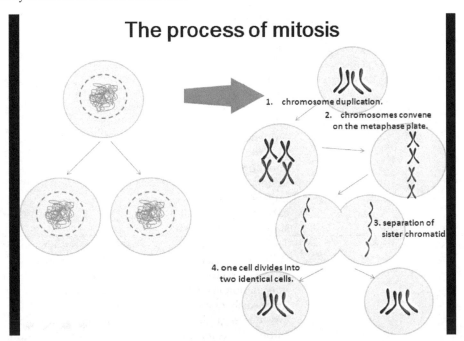

Fig. 6. Screenshot of the teaching materials for the concept of mitosis in T group

2.2.3 Comparison of IWB and Traditional technology-integrated teaching method

Differences between the teaching methods of the IWB and the T group are listed in the Table 1:

Teaching sub-topics	IWB group	T group
Chromosome and Its Importance	• In addition to using pictures to present the basic structures, students also match pictures of the basic genetic structures by competing to answer questions, touching the IWB or coloring and circling with colored pens so that their understanding and impression of the concepts and terminology can be enhanced. • Karyotypes of male and female are simultaneously shown on the large screen of the IWB, which is used to help students understand the concepts of sex chromosomes and autosomes. • Students can actively play the Adobe Flash animations so that their understanding and impression of the concepts and their ICT skills can be improved.	• Although PPT slides can present many pictures and animations, the animations embedded in the PPT slides are displayed linearly after Q & A teaching activities. • Teacher's interaction with students is limited to verbal communication; all software operation is done by the teacher.
The Role of Mitosis	• The large screen of the IWB is divided into two parts so that information can be more easily shown together to guide students to think about and complete each stage of mitosis and	• Animations embedded in the PPT slides are displayed linearly after Q & A teaching activities. • Teacher's interaction with students is limited to verbal communication; all

	enable them to clearly learn the related terminology. • To improve students' understanding, activities are designed to make students compete to answer questions, work together operating the IWB to complete the process of mitosis and draw the changes in the chromosome number, quantity of DNA and chromosome sets.	software operation is done by the teacher.
Meiosis and Sexual Life Cycle	• The teaching method is the same as that used to teach mitosis, but the IWB can provide rapid cross-page comparison and it is convenient to make notes on the IWB screen to enable the students to clearly understand the difference between the two kinds of cell division. • Students are allowed to write on the IWB and compare mitosis with meiosis and sexual reproduction with asexual reproduction so that their understanding of the relationship can be improved.	• Animations embedded in the PPT slides are displayed linearly after Q & A teaching activities. • Teacher's interaction with students is limited to verbal communication; all software operation is done by the teacher.

Table 1. Comparison of the teaching activities in IWB and T groups

2.2.4 Summative assessment

The summative assessment in this research is used to understand student learning effectiveness. The design of the 25 summative assessment items are based on the teaching materials and a Two-Way Chart is used to ensure a reasonable distribution of the items. The summative assessment was also reviewed by two experts in assessment and course design and one experienced junior high school Biology teacher. The Cronbach α of the summative assessment is 0.860. The average difficulty is 0.564.

2.3 Research design

To understand how the integration of the IWB into teaching influences the learning effectiveness of seventh graders in a junior high school in Taiwan, this research uses the quasi-experimental design to divide the participants into the experimental group (IWB group) and the control group (T group). IWB group learns in the teaching environment integrated with IWB while the T group learns in an environment using traditional ICT, The where teaching is done by projecting Microsoft PowerPoint slides onto a traditional projection screen through a projector. However, the two groups are lectured by the same teacher. Before teaching, to understand the student's entry behavior of learning, students were asked to take the pre-test of the summative assessment. Then students received five classes in which the information technology was integrated into the instruction. After the five classes, students took the post-test of the summative assessment.

2.4 Data collection and analysis

The data collected are all quantitative data, including the pre-test and post-test scores of the summative assessment. To investigate how integrating an IWB into teaching of junior high school cell division influences student learning effectiveness, this study uses two different kinds of data analysis techniques. First, to investigate the effectiveness of two different types of teaching method, ANCOVA was conducted on the scores of the summative assessment. The pre-test scores of the summative assessment are taken as covariate, the two different types of teaching method as a fixed factor and the post-test scores of the summative assessment as the dependent variable. This analysis aims to understand how the two different types of teaching method influence the learning effectiveness of junior high school students. This study further adopts effect size analysis (Cohen, 1988) to investigate how the two different types of teaching methods influence student learning effectiveness on the three different sub-topics. According to the definition of Cohen (1988), Cohen's d less than 0.2 means 'small' effect size, between 0.2 and 0.5 means 'small to middle' effect size, between 0.5 and 0.8 means 'middle to large' effect size, while larger than 0.8 means 'large' effect size.

3. Results

To investigate the effectiveness of IWB-integrated instruction and traditional ICT-integrated instruction on junior high school Biology teaching, this research adopts ANCOVA and effect size analysis to perform data analysis.

3.1 Effectiveness of two different types of teaching method

To understand the influences on junior high school student learning effectiveness of the two different types of teaching method (TTM), this study compares the student learning effectiveness of the IWB group and the T group using ANCOVA. The TTM is taken as the fixed factor, the pre-test scores of the summative assessment are taken as the covariate, and the post-test scores of the summative assessment are taken as the dependent variable. Before ANCOVA, the homogeneity of variance assumption was tested. The Levene's test for equality of variances was not significant (F =1.314, p > 0.05). In addition, the assumption of homogeneity of regression coefficients was also tested (F =1.349, p > 0.05). The results indicate that neither homogeneity assumption was violated. The results of the ANCOVA analysis are shown in Table 2.

Sources	SS	df	MS	F	Post Hoc
Pre-test	3212.755	1	3212.755	11.684**	
TTM	5986.231	1	5986.231	21.771**	IWB>T
Error	14023.393	51	274.968		
Total	191440.000	54			
Corrected Total	26104.000	53			

** p<.01
TTM: Two different types of teaching method
IWB: Interactive Whiteboard group
T: Traditional ICT-integrated group

Table 2. ANCOVA summary table (n=54)

Table 2 shows that the pre-test scores have a significant influence on the post-test scores (F=11.684, p<0.01). Further, the TTM also has a significant influence on the scores of post-test (F=21.771, p<0.01). The result means that student learning in instructional environments using the two different types of teaching method has significantly different learning effectiveness. Moreover, after conducting the LSD PostHoc analysis, it is found that students in the IWB group have significantly better learning effectiveness than those in the T group.

3.2 Effect size analysis on the effectiveness of two different types of teaching method in facilitating student learning

This study uses the effect size to investigate the effectiveness of the two different types of teaching method in facilitating student learning. In Table 3, the results show that the effect size of student learning effectiveness in the IWB group is 2.214, while the effect size of student learning effectiveness in the T group is 0.888. Based on the above, it is known that students in the IWB group have better learning effectiveness than students in the T group. This study further investigates the effectiveness of the two different types of teaching method in facilitating students to learn the three different sub-topics. In Table 3, the results show that students in the IWB group have better learning effectiveness than those in the T group across all three sub-topics. The effect sizes of IWB group student effectiveness in learning the three sub-topics all belong to 'large' effect size (Chromosome and Its Significance: Cohen's d=1.646; The Role of Mitosis: Cohen's d=1.041; Meiosis and Sexual Life Cycle: Cohen's d=0.957). However, in the T group, the effect size of student effectiveness in learning the sub-topic of 'Chromosome and Its Significance' belongs to 'large' effect size (Cohen's d=1.278). The effect size of student effectiveness in learning the sub-topics of 'The Role of Mitosis' (Cohen's d=0.627) and 'Meiosis and Sexual Life Cycle' (Cohen's d=0.269) belong to ' middle to large' effect size and 'small to middle' effect size. These results show that integrating an IWB into teaching can lead to better learning effectiveness for the cell division topic. Moreover, compared with the T group, student learning effectiveness for the two sub-topics, 'The Role of Mitosis' and 'Meiosis and Sexual Life Cycle,' is especially effective in the IWB group.

Teaching sub-topics	IWB group (n=27)			T group (n=27)		
	Pre-test (%)	Post-test (%)	Cohen's d	Pre-test (%)	Post-test (%)	Cohen's d
Chromosome and Its Importance (n=7)	31.6 (SD=19.2)	63.4 (SD=19.5)	1.646	27.5 (SD=15.0)	54.5 (SD=25.8)	1.278
The Role of Mitosis (n=7)	26.0 (SD=22.1)	52.0 (SD=27.6)	1.041	25.4 (SD=15.2)	39.6 (SD=28.3)	0.627
Meiosis and Sexual Life Cycle (n=11)	35.6 (SD=17.3)	50.5 (SD=13.7)	0.957	32.3 (SD=13.2)	36.7 (SD=18.9)	0.269
Total	35.2 (SD=14.7)	68.1 (SD=16.2)	2.214	29.0 (SD=9.2)	42.5 (SD=19.4)	0.888

Pre-test: The average correct answering rate of items about three different learning topics in the pre-test of the summative assessment.

Post-test: The average correct answering rate of items about three different learning topics in the post-test of the summative assessment.

Table 3. Effect size analysis on students' learning effectiveness about three different sub-topics

4. Concluding remarks

Cell division has always been one of the topics both students and teachers find difficult for students to learn, and meiosis is the most difficult part (Brown, 1995; Oztap et al., 2003). Brown (1995) and Oztap et al. (2003) argued that the teaching method is one of the reasons student have difficulty in learning cell division. Brown suggested that to help students learn, the dynamic nature of cell division should be emphasized and teachers should properly use 2D and 3D pictures to help students build chromosome models. The findings of this study show that compared to traditional ICT-integrated instruction, IWB is more effective in improving student learning in cell division. Among all sub-topics of cell division, IWB is especially effective in assisting students in learning 'The Role of Mitosis' and 'Meiosis and Sexual Life Cycle.' Traditional ICT-integrated instruction can only improve student learning effectiveness for the sub-topic of 'Chromosome and Its Significance'. This may be because compared with the traditional ICT-integrated instruction, IWB can better consolidate multimodal representations, combining the key concepts, such as genes, chromosomes, and genetic information, more closely together with the terminology and more clearly presenting their relationships. Students can therefore develop a more coherent conceptual framework to serve as basis of their learning of cell division. This may resolve the learning difficulties caused by the basic concepts – cell, nucleus, gene and genetic information and the relationships between them which are implied separately in different teaching topics (Lewis et al., 2000b).

The interactive nature of IWB improves interaction between the teacher and students and peers. In teaching of the two sub-topics, 'The Role of Mitosis' and 'Meiosis and Sexual Life Cycle,' this study tries to make the interactive nature of IWB more closely integrated into teaching activities. Students work together to complete the tasks of answering questions about the processes of the two kinds of cell division and thinking about the difference between mitosis and meiosis by comparison of the chromosome duplication, number of divisions, number of daughter cells and genetic composition. This may explain why students have better learning effectiveness. According to several researchers (Levy, 2002; Torff & Tirotta, 2010; Wall, Higgins, & Smith, 2005), students think that when they are allowed to use IWB, their learning can be greatly improved and their learning process can be better facilitated. In traditional ICT-integrated instruction, the interaction between the teacher and students is limited to verbal communication and the messages are delivered by PPT slides in a more linear way. By comparison, an IWB can better integrate multimedia presentations. This may be the reason that students have lower learning effectiveness when traditional ICT-integrated instruction is adopted.

5. Educational implications

Based on research findings, this study argues that the teaching methods are the reason cell division is thought to be the topic most difficult to learn by junior high school students, following Brown (1995) and Lewis et al. (2000b). Oztap et al.(2003) showed that students do not have a coherent conceptual framework and often feel confused about genetic terminology. If the relationship between basic structures such as cell, nucleus, chromosomes and genes can be clearly presented and students can be assisted in building chromosome models, they will be able to overcome learning difficulties. Brown (1995) also stated that during teaching activities, both 2D pictures and 3D pictures were suggested to be provided to help students build chromosome models. According to Brown, this study suggests that during teaching activities, teachers can try to integrate multimedia into the teaching of the 'Chromosome and Its Significance.' For example, pictures of a dyed cell under microscope can be used to demonstrate the relationship between cell, nucleus and chromosomes, 2D and 3D pictures can be used to show the structure of chromosome, and dynamic videos or animations can be used to present the chromatin packing in a eukaryotic chromosome. After students have a clear understanding of basic genetic concepts and develop a more coherent conceptual framework, they will find it easier to learn more about cell division.

Currently, the traditional ICT-integrated instruction always uses Microsoft PowerPoint slides (PPT slides) to enrich classroom teaching. Although PPT slides allow teachers to integrate multimedia presentation, the slides do not support Adobe-Flash-animation-based interactive media. They can only be presented in a linear and page-by-page way when used in teaching activities, which makes the teaching possibilities more restricted. However, this study integrates an IWB into teaching. IWB can integrate both multimedia and Adobe-Flash-animation-based interactive media presentation to help teachers perform multimedia and multimodal teaching. Moreover, IWB supports rapid cross-page comparison and zoned page presentation. The differences between the two kinds of cell division can be clearly shown, enabling better understanding. The key characteristic of IWB, high interactivity, allows teachers to have more eye-contact and interaction with students, in addition to verbal communication. It is also easier for teachers to design activities facilitating interaction and cooperation between students. Teachers and students feel closer to each other, as Wood (2002) argued, and students are more motivated to concentrate on and participate in teaching activities (Homles, 2009; Northcote et al., 2010; Slay et al., 2008; Smith et al., 2005; Wall et al., 2005). These advantages largely overcome the limitations of PPT slides in teaching and student learning effectiveness. Based on the findings of this study, building chromosome models is vital to the learning of cell division. The dynamic process of cell division and the micro-view of chromosome changes are also keys to overcome student learning difficulties in understanding cell division. If ICT and multimedia and multimodal presentation can be properly used, student learning will be more effective when studying cell division.

6. Note

- It is herein stated that all the trademarks and product names referred to in this research are the property of their respective owners. In addition, all the figures adopted in this research are the property of their respective owners.
- Some objects used in the Figure 2, Figure 3, Figure 4, and Figure 5 are adopted from the NoteBook™ software. The Figure 3, Figure 4, Figure 5 and Figure 6 are screenshots of the e-Learning materials in this research. The e-Learning materials are constructed by the NoteBook™ software. For more information about the NoteBook™ software, you can visit http://smarttech.com/

7. Acknowledgement

The authors deeply appreciate the National Science Council in Taiwan for the financial support and encouragement under Grant No. 97-2511-S-134-006-MY2 and 99-2511-S-134-002-MY3.

8. References

British Educational Communications and Technology (BECTA) (2007). Harnessing Technology schools survey 2007. In: *BECTA*, 23.07.2011, Available from http://dera.ioe.ac.uk/1554/1/becta_2007_htssfindings_report.pdf

Brown, C. R. (1995).*The effective teaching of biology*. Longman publishing, ISBN 0582095050, New York, USA.

Cohen, J. (1988). *Statistical power analysis for the behavioral sciences*, Erlbaum, ISBN 0805802835, Hillsdale, NJ.

Glover, D., Miller, D., Averis, D., & Door, V. (2005). The interactive whiteboard: a literature survey, *Technology, Pedagogy and Education*, Vol.14, No.2, pp.155-170, ISSN 1475-939X.

Holmes, K. (2009). Planning to teach with digital tools: Introducing the interactive whiteboard to pre-service secondary mathematics teachers, *Australasian Journal of Educational Technology*, Vol.25, No.3, pp.351-365, ISSN 1449-3098.

Levy, P. (2002). *Interactive whiteboards in learning and teaching in two Sheffield schools: A developmental study*. In: *The University of Sheffield*. 23.07.2011, Available from http://dis.shef.ac.uk/eirg/projects/wboards.htm

Lewis, J., & Wood-Roinson, C. (2000). Genes, chromosomes, cell devision and inheritance – do students see any relationship? *International Journal of Science Education*, Vol.22, No.2, pp.177-197, ISSN 0950-0693.

Lewis, J, Leach, J, & Wood-Roinson, C. (2000a). What's in a cell? – young people's understanding of the genetic relationship between cells, within an individual, *International Journal of Biological Education*, Vol.34, No.3, pp.129-132, ISSN 0021-9266.

Lewis, J, Leach, J, & Wood-Roinson, C. (2000b). Chromosomes: The missing link – young people's understanding of mitosis, meiosis, and fertilization, *International Journal of Biological Education*, Vol.34, No.4, pp.189-199, ISSN 0021-9266.

Northcote, M., Mildenhall, P., Marshall, L., & Swan, P. (2010). Interactive whiteboards: Interactive or just whiteboards? *Australasian Journal of Educational Technology*, Vol. 26, No.4, pp.494-510, ISSN 1449-3098.

Oztap, H., Ozay, E., & Oztap, F. (2003). Teaching cell division to secondary school students: An investigation of difficulties experienced by Turkish teachers, *International Journal of Biological Education*, Vol. 38, No.1, pp.13-15, ISSN 0021-9266.

Slay, H., Sieborger, I., & Hodgkinson-Williams, C. (2008). Interactive whiteboard: Real beauty or just lipstick? *Computers & Education*, Vol. 51, No. 3, pp. 1321-1341, ISSN 0360-1315.

Smith, H. J., Higgins, S., Wall, K., & Miller, J. (2005). Interactive whiteboards: boon or bandwagon? A critical review of the literature, *Journal of Computer Assisted Learning*, Vol.21, No.2, pp.91- 101, ISSN 0266-4909.

Smith, M. U. (1991). Teaching cell division: Students' difficulties and teaching recommendations, *Journal of College Science Teaching*, Vol. 21, No. 1, pp.28-33, ISSN 0047-231X.

Torff, B. & Tirotta, R. (2010). Interactive whiteboards produce small gains in elementary students' self-reported motivation in mathematics, *Computers & Education*, Vol.54, No.2, pp.379-383, ISSN 0360-1315.

Wall, K., Higgins, S., & Smith, H. J. (2005). "The visual helps me understand the complicated things": Pupil views of teaching and learning with interactive whiteboards, *British Journal of Education Technology*, Vol.36, No.5, pp. 851-867, ISSN 0007-1013.

Wood, C. (2002). Interactive whiteboards – a luxury too far? In: *The Association for ICT in Education*, 07.23.2011, Available from http://acitt.digitalbrain.com/acitt/web/resources/pubs/Journal%2002/whiteboards.htm

Yang, K. T., Wang, T. H., & Chiu, M. H. (2011). Implementation of Interactive Whiteboard in improving the learning effectiveness of junior high school students with different cognitive styles—A case study of 'Cell Division'course, *Curriculum & Instruction Quarterly*, Vol.14, No.4, pp. 187-208, ISSN 1560-1277.

Part 3

New Approaches

11

A New Scientific Formulation of Tajweed Rules for E-Learning of Quran Phonological Rules

Yahya O. Mohamed Elhadj[1], Mohamed Aoun-Allah[2],
Imad A. Alsughaiyer[2] and Abdallah Alansari[3]
[1]*Information Technology Deanship,*
[2]*College of Computer & Information Sciences,*
[3]*College of Arabic Language,*
Al-Imam Muhammad Ibn Saud Islamic University, Riyadh,
Kingdom of Saudi Arabia

1. Introduction

Recitation of the Holy Quran is governed by a variety of rules called "Tajweed rules" (Correct pronunciation of the Holy Quran). Reciting the Holy Quran in the appropriate way is very important for all Muslims and is indispensable in Islamic worshiping such as prayers. So, teaching how to recite it correctly was transmitted, since its revelation to the prophet (PBUH), orally from teachers to learners throughout generations. Such a method has been considered as the only way to learn it until the twentieth century, where technology produced recording systems and electronic devices that are able to keep both text and sound of the Quran with tajweed rules. Since then, it becomes possible to listen Quranic recitations recorded from authentic reciters. Many computer-programs have been then appeared to assist novice learners by listening while following corresponding text on the screen. However, efforts spent by the computer scientists in general for the sake of the noble Quran are still limited and have been concentrated only on the direct application of the Information Technology techniques, such as storing, listening, searching, etc, without using more elaborated techniques in the domain.

This work is a part of a project aiming to build a computerized-environment for learning the Holy Quran and its sciences (Computerized teaching of the Holy Quran "CTHQ") (Elhadj et al., 2010a). Our objective in the CTHQ project was to improve computerization of the Holy Quran by introducing advanced techniques and methodologies. Four main tracks have been designed to carry out this project. In the first track, an environment for teaching how to memorize the Holy Quran in a manner similar to the usual way followed in the Quranic inculcation schools was proposed (Alsughayeir & Elhadj, 2006; Elhadj, 2010). In the second track, automatic speech recognition technologies have been used to teach how to recite the Holy Quran correctly (Alghamdi et al., 2007; Elhadj et al., 2012, 2010b, 2009; Elhadj, 2009a, 2009b). In the third track, techniques for determining the similarity (tashaboh) between verses (ayahs) of the noble Quran were investigated (Alsughayeir & Ohali, 2007). Computer-tools have been developed for analyzing the text of the noble Quran based on complete words and their stems in order to link similar verses (Alsughayeir et al., 2009; Elhadj et al.,

2009c, 2009d). In the fourth track, our focus was on the automatic processing of tajweed rules by proposing a mathematical formulation of these rules that can be easily processed by a machine (Elhadj & Aoun-Allah, 2011; Elhadj et al., 2009e). In this chapter, we discuss how this kind of formulation was proposed, its advantages and benefits, and how it was programmed in an efficient plug-in engine. The development of an e-learning system for tajweed rules that uses this engine will also be presented. A general integrated environment for self-learning of the holy Quran and its sciences including Tajweed will be also briefly introduced.

This chapter proceeds as follows. Sections 2, 3, and 4 deal with Tajweed where the first one presents an introduction. Section 3 surveys previous efforts to computerization of Tajweed whereas Section 4 concentrates on our new formulation. We discuss in Section 5 a prerequisite to our engine of automatic processing of Tajweed rules, which is detailed in Section 6. Our Tajweed Learning System (ETaj) will be presented in the Section 7 and a couple of its important interfaces will be given in Section 8. Finally, before concluding this chapter, we shortly present a global learning environment for Quran and its sciences composed of several subsystems including Tajweed teaching system.

2. Overview of Tajweed rules

Reading of the Holy Quran is quite different from the reading of a normal Arabic text due to the pronunciation rules that have to be respected during the recitation. As an example, consider the duration of vowels that may vary from 2 to 6 times that of a single consonant depending on the context. Indeed, there are two kinds of vowels in the Arabic language, short vowels which are keystrokes placed either above or below the preceding consonant and long vowels which denotes a certain repetition of short vowels. There are also other tajweed rules related to:

a.   types of nasalization (called "ghunnah غنة"),
b.   heaviness and lightness (called respectively "tafkheem تفخيم" and "tarqeeq ترقيق"), which means making some sounds emphatic or non-emphatic,
c.   types of stops which means making a voiceless break at a Quranic word for a brief moment (called "waqf وقف"),
d.   degrees of vibrations or unrest (called "qalqalah قلقلة") which means producing the voiced stop consonants with a schwa-like sound at the end,
e.   etc.

To preserve the Holy Quran from any alteration in its pronunciation and then to guarantee its perfect reading, early Muslim scholars described Quranic recitation methods very accurately by textual rules as well as sound ones. These descriptions are classified into categories depending on some sound properties or features. These categories are often summarized as follows:

a.   category "Noon sakinah" & "Tanween" (باب النون الساكنة والتنوين)
b.   category "Meem sakinah" (باب الميم الساكنة)
c.   category "Qalqalah" (باب القلقلة)
d.   category "Tafkheem" & "Tarqeeq" (باب التفخيم والترقيق)
e.   category "Al Mad" (lengthening باب المد)
f.   etc.

Each category has a set of rules governing the pronunciation of underlying sounds. More details regarding the classification of Tajweed rules can be obtained from the official site of King Fahd Complex for the Printing of Holy Quran at this link: www.qurancomplex.org.

3. Previous efforts related to computerization of Tajweed

Teaching how to apply Tajweed rules during Quranic recitation has been done through teachers who pronounce the Quranic sounds accurately. With the era of computers, it becomes possible to computerize the learning process of Tajweed, but this need an appropriate description of its rules. To the best of our knowledge, there was no attempt to describe them by a scientific algorithm, which could be processed automatically by a machine. This was a conclusion from a large survey we conducted on the Quranic software currently available on the market, which was published in (Alsughayeir & Elhadj, 2006). The methodology employed to conduct this study consisted of collecting a maximum number of Quranic applications, either for desktop, web-based or hand-held applications. Each application was separately studied and evaluated in order to know the characteristics and services it offers.

It appeared that softwares developed for the sake of the Holy Quran are still very limited either in their objectives or in the term of availability and relevance of features. Regarding the Tajweed by itself, it was only given as a small part of the surveyed programs. It is offered, at almost all programs, in a classical manner as textual lessons with some graphical explanation of sound production. No dynamic interaction was proposed to allow, neither efficient learning nor any kinds of intelligent processing.

4. New formulation of Tajweed rules

In order to find a scientific formulation of tajweed rules, we studied them thoroughly with the assistance of an expert in the domain and finally we came out with the conclusion that almost all Tajweed rules described textually by scholars could be written in a scientific manner and consequently automatically treated by a computer.

Our study concluded that to extract the tajweed rule for any letter the maximum number of words concerned by the rule is two; i.e. either the previous or the following word. And in terms of letters, there are at most 6 letters concerned by the rule which are either preceding or following the letter itself. Moreover, many rules are applicable only to a letter at the end of a word which is easily detectable by comparing the next letter to a space character.

For instance, in the category of "Noon Sakinah" & "Tanween" if any letter "Noon Sakinah" or diacritic "Tanween" appears at the end of a word followed by any of these characters "ي ر م ل و ن" in the following word then the 2 letters should be assimilated. Moreover, this category is subdivided into two sections where the assimilation could be with "Ghunnah" (a sound effect) or without when the letter is followed respectively by "ن و م ي" or "ل ر". We proposed a whole scientific formulation of such textual description of rules into machine readable rules as indicated in the example in Table 1 taking in consideration the following notations:

a.   "C" means the character treated and "S" its diacritic
b.   "C+1" or "C-1" represent respectively the character (or characters separated by a comma) immediately following (rep. preceding) the character treated.

c. And in the same way we define "C+2", "C+3",... or "C-2", "C-3",... according to the extent of the rule.
d. "*" is used as a wildcard character to replace any letter or diacritic.
e. "Space" represents a space character (between two words).
f. "Text" is human comprehensible message to be displayed to the user if needed.
g. And finally, the "Ruling" of the rule which denotes its name.

C = * ; S = ًٌٍ ; C+1 = Space; S = * ; C+2 = ي،و،م،ن ; S = * ; Text = يُدغم التنوين بغنة في حروف (ي،و،م،ن) Ruling = IdghamGhunnah (Table 1.A)	C = ن ; S = ْ ; C+1 = Space; S = * ; C+2 = ي،و،م،ن ; S= * ; Text = تدغم النون الساكنة بغنة في حروف (ي،و،م،ن) Ruling = IdghamGhunnah (Table 1.B)
C = م ; S = ْ ; C+1 = Space ; S = * ; C+2 = م ; S = * ; Text = تُدغم الميم في الميم إدغامًا شفويا بغنة Ruling = IdghamGhunnah (Table 1.C)	C-1 = * ; S = ْ ; C = ا ى ; S = * ; C+1 = Space ; S = * ; C+2 = ي،و،م،ن ; S = * ; Text = يُدغم التنوين بغنة في حروف(ي،و،م،ن) Ruling = IdghamGhunnah (Table 1.D)

Table 1. Rules describing a couple of cases of assimilation with Ghunnah

Table 1.A (resp. Table 1.B) describes a rule stating that if any character with a "tanween" diacritic (resp. a "Noon" character with "Sakn" diacritic) at the end of a word followed by a word starting by any of "ن و م ي" letters, then there is assimilation with Ghunnah. Table 1.D describes a special case of the rule in Table 1.B where "tanween" is followed by a "lenghthening" at the end of the word. Finally, Table 1.C deals with a "Meem" character with "Sakin" diacritic as last letter in a word followed by "Meem" character with any diacritic as first letter in the next word and where the ruling is the same as previously.

Using this technique of writing "tajweed" rules, we finished describing those of 5 most important categories (or chapters): "Al Mad" (lengthening), "qalqala" (unrest), "Noon Sakinah" & "Tanween", "Meem Sakinah", and "Tafkheem" & "Tarqeeq". This results in a total number of almost 200 rules. Moreover, any advanced tajweed rule could be easily added by writing it as described earlier in the rules text file.

Notice that we faced many difficulties in writing our rule set as described above. The most important difficulty was the overlap of rules. This situation happens when more than one rule could be triggered for one letter. For instance, in the word "السماء" we have a lengthening of obligatory 4 cycles but when it is the last word in a verse it changes to optionally 2, 4 or 6 cycles. To overcome this overlap, we added to each rule a priority in order to avoid the conflict between triggered rules and by choosing only the rule with the highest priority.

5. Need of a textual version of the Holy Quran with full diacritics

The Holy Quran is generally written in a special font which could not be edited in text editor software. Consequently, a text editable version of the Holy Quran that contains no missing diacritic was necessary to get our automatic processing works correctly. However, this textual editable version as we need it was almost inexistent. Therefore, we looked for the most agreed version to which we manually added full diacritics and then it was given to scholars for revision and validation.

6. Automatic processing of Tajweed rules: Taj Engine (TajE)

The Tajweed rule set described in section 4 is interpreted by an inference engine (TajE) able to deal with our rulings formulation and that can be used alone (See Figure 1) or integrated with other components for both identification and verification of Tajweed rules in any Quranic verse (or even any Arabic diacritized text).

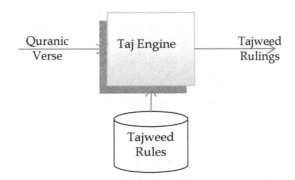

Fig. 1. Structure of the Taj Engine

This inference engine works like an expert system inference engine in forward chaining and one level inference. In other words, for each character of the treated text, our engine tests all rules once to find the rule or those rules that could be triggered. Conflicting rules are treated by the rule priority explained in Section 4.

As presented earlier, TajE engine could be used either for identification or for verification of Tajweed rulings. The first option (identification) aims to extract Tajweed rulings from Quranic verses. It is very helpful in different situation, especially to assist a student during his memorization of the Holy Quran.

The second option (verification) of the TajE engine is to ensure if a Tajweed ruling really occurred in a specific place in the Quranic verse (See Figure 2). This is also a very important property as it can be used in an interactive manner for teaching and correcting Tajweed exercises. A detailed typical exercise scenario is described in the following section.

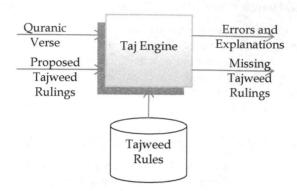

Fig. 2. Taj Engine used for verification

7. Tajweed learning system: ETaj

Our main objective is to design an easy to use e-learning system for Tajweed using our developed TajE engine. It is intended to be used by students to help them learning, verifying their knowledge, and to train them on Tajweed for the noble intention of correctly reciting the Holy Quran.

The proposed system has been designed to include the following features:

a. **General Rules of Recitation and its Ethics:** these are stored guidelines about general rules of recitation like position of stops and their rulings. Reading ethics like "Estiatha الإستعاذة" and "Basmalah البسملة", etc. are also included.
b. **Tajweed Rulings:** this option offers to the student rich text lessons about Tajweed rulings along with examples in text and audio formats. The student could interact with by pausing, stopping or replaying the audio files.
c. **Exercises:** they cover all Tajweed categories and are taken by student using TajE engine described in the previous section. A typical scenario is given below. Another option for examination is offered to students to pass examinations in a manner very similar to exercises but in a less helpful way and by assigning a final mark to the learner.

Exercises and examination options of ETaj system are implemented as follows:

a. A student starts by choosing the Tajweed category he wants to practice or be tested on.
b. According to his choice, all rulings under the category will be displayed with a specific color associated to each ruling.
c. Besides, a verse or a couple of verses chosen randomly will be displayed too. We notice here that the selection of verses is totally random among all Quran verses and having a fixed minimum number of the selected category rulings. This property offers to our system a great dynamic aspect. The selection process is either done on the fly by searching the Holy Quran using first option of the TajE engine to extract verses with the minimum number of rules, or by selecting them from a database of ruling occurrences already filled using our TajE engine beforehand. Obviously, the first technique is slower than the second but requires less storage space. However, we chose the second

technique for the simple reason that is the fastest way since a non-negligible treatment is done beforehand and also to guarantee a good response time for the system.

d.   At this moment, the student is invited to select letters where Tajweed rulings appear. This process is achieved by the learner by choosing a color (i.e. a category ruling) and then selecting the appropriate letters. The student is free to change or to remove his selections until he decides to validate his choices.

e.   Once validated, choices are treated automatically by TajE engine and a report is displayed to the student containing the incorrect and missing selections along with the necessary explanations (i.e. the field "Text" in the rule, See section 4).

Figures 3 and 4 show respectively the structure of the proposed ETaj system and its architecture.

Moreover, we aim to add to the system a new feature allowing the user to specify the "narration" which will influence all the above features. We mention that our current system supports only "Hafs" narration.

8. Most important interfaces of the ETaj system

ETaj has been designed to be easy to use and to allow great interaction with the user. It is implemented in the .Net framework using C# and JavaScript as well as other advanced technologies. Our database is implemented using MySql as a database management system as it is free and it offers very excellent features and performance. The most important interfaces of the system are introduced in the following sections.

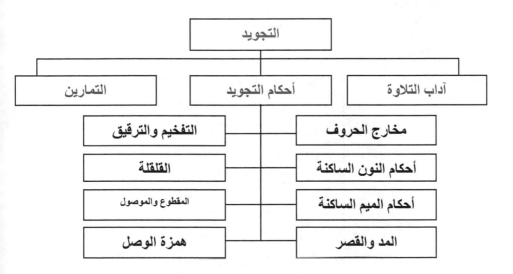

Fig. 3. Structure of the ETaj system

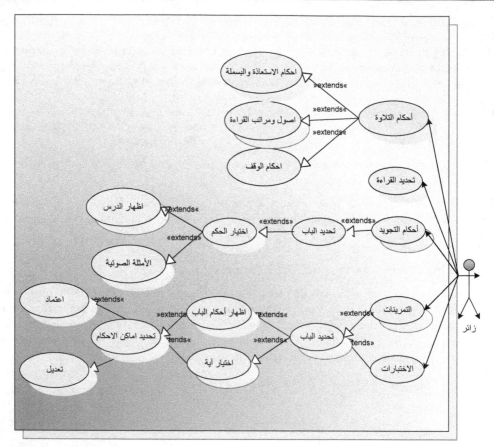

Fig. 4. Architecture of the ETaj system

If we access the system, the following menu will appear to the user:

Fig. 5. Main menu of the ETaj system

From this main menu, we can navigate to different options in the system. If we click, for example one of the tajweed rulings, a page like the following is displayed:

Fig. 6. Tajweed rulings page

Three main parts are enclosed in this page: one for the tajweed category and its rulings that can be navigated one after another (Figure 6 (a)), the content of the current ruling (Figure 6 (b)), and examples of the ruling (Figure 6 (c)):

Fig. 6(a). Tajweed category and its rulings

وهو لغة: البيان.

واصطلاحا: إخراج كل حرف من مخرجه واضحًا كامل الصفات.

ويكون إظهار النون الساكنة والتنوين إذا وقع حرف من حروف الحلق الستة بعدها وهي: الهمزة، والهاء، والعين، والحاء، والغين، والخاء.

وتكون هذه الحروف مع النون الساكنة في كلمة وفي كلمتين، ومع التنوين في كلمتين.

فمثال النون مع هذه الأحرف من كلمة ومن كلمتين: وَيَنْأَوْنَ * مِنْ أَجْرِى * مُنْهَمِر * مِنْ صَاد * أَنْعَمْتَ * مُنْ عِلْمِ * يَنْحِتُونَ * مُنْ حَكِيمٍ * فَسَيُنْغِضُونَ * مِنْ غِلٍ * وَالْمُنْخَنِقَةُ * مِنْ خَيْرٍ *

ومثال التنوين:

كُلٌّ آمَنَ * فَرِيقًا هَدَى * حَكِيمٌ عَلِيمٌ * حَكِيمٍ حَمِيد * قَوْلًا غَيْرَ * يَوْمَئِذٍ خَاشِعَةٌ *

ويسمى هذا النوع من الإظهار إظهارًا حلقيًا لخروج حروفه من الحلق، والسبب في إظهار النون الساكنة والتنوين عند هذه الأحرف الستة بُعد المخرج أي: بعد مخرج النون عن مخرج هذه الأحرف، فقد علمنا أن النون تخرج من طرف اللسان، وهذه الستة تخرج من الحلق.

Fig. 6(b). Content of a ruling

Fig. 6(c). Examples of a tajweed ruling

Now, if we click on the "exercises" option, we will be redirected to a page where we can choose the category of tajweed we want to practice (Figure 7):

Fig. 7. Exercise selection page

Once the category is selected, a page like that of Figure 8 is displayed and the user is asked to navigate the category rulings and to select their occurrences in the ayah that has been randomly chosen. This is done in the same manner as explained previously in section 7.

Fig. 8. Exercise page

After finishing determining places of ruling occurrences, a page result (see Figure 9) is displayed

Fig. 9. Page Result

9. General integrated environment for self-learning of the Holy Quran

The Tajweed learning system is a part of a fully integrated environment developed for self-learning of the holy Quran and its sciences. This environment comprises four subsystems in addition to the ETaj system: subsystem for learning how to recite and memorise the holy Quran, subsystem for studying the similarity between Quranic terms and verses, subsystem providing the most relevant features that learners of the holy Quran may need such as (Erab"الإعراب", Nuzoul "اسباب النزول", Tafseer "التفسير", Ejaz"الإعجاز العلمي", etc.), and finally a reach library providing authentic sources from which the relevant features are taken. The three main subsystems will be briefly described in the following sections to get picture of this environment.

9.1 The memorization subsystem: E-halaga

The E-halaga system is designed based-on the Quran memorization halaga "حلقات تحفيظ القرآن" approach (E-halaga means electronic halaga). It simulates the real one in having tutors, supervisor, and registered students. E-halaga allows four main types of users with specific roles: administrator, supervisor, tutor, and student. Roles are distributed hierarchically to allow a great flexibility over the system. The creation of the E-halaga is done by its supervisor, which is in turn created by the system administrator. The supervisor is responsible of running the E-halaga in terms of adding or deleting tutors, distributing learners, etc.

Since the E-halaga is a simulation of the real halaga, the learner have to specify a daily amount (memorization section) to be memorized starting from somewhere in the Quran (starting ayah/page). As the learner progresses, he needs to have in parallel a revision program for the memorized parts to improve their quality (revision section). So, the registration in the E-halaga system requires specifying the following parameters: starting ayah/page, memorization section and its length, revision section and its length (at least the double of the memorization section), and previously memorized sections before joining the system.

Once registered, the learner will obtain a user name and password to access the system. If he logs into the system, he will be redirected to the memorization/revision part where he can find a list of useful options. He can browse his own profile and change it as needed, measure his performance (number of sections perfected, times of failure in every section, duration of memorizing), print out his transcript, etc. The learner can listen to an ideal recitation taken from one of the famous reciters stored in the system as a reference for perfect recitation. After listening to the reference recitation several times, or reciting directly, the learner can test his memory by clicking on an icon to record the section. Then the pages of the section will disappear to test his memory. Clicking on the button of "end recording" will display again the section pages allowing the learner to verify his memorization. The learner can repeat this process (recording and verifying) till the perfection of memorization. Once the learner approves his recording, the audio file is uploaded to the server and the learner will not be able to modify it. The tutor is then notified with an unmarked recorded section of that learner. After the tutor marks the section, the learner can benefit from audio and/or textual remarks explaining his mistakes. Figure 10 shows the architecture of the E-halaga system and we invite the reader to consult (Elhadj, 2010) for more details.

9.2 The similarity search engine

The similarity search engine is a component devoted to determine the similarity between Quranic verses (and Quranic terms). To build this system, we started preparing an authentic fully diacritised textual version of the Holy Quran since such one was not available for the use in the domain of research. Next, the focus was on a manual morphological analysis of this version. Each word in the Holy Quran is split into four parts, prefixes, stem, root and suffixes, and then stored in an indexed database. Words are kept in their original context, which means Quranic verses (Elhadj et al., 2009c, 2009d). A semi-automatic environment for morphological analysis has been developed (see figure 11). Full-text searching techniques were investigated and then computer-programs have been developed for analyzing the text of the noble Quran based on complete words and their stems in order to link similar verses (Alsughayeir & Ohali, 2007; Alsughayeir et al., 2009). Figure 12 shows the engine interface.

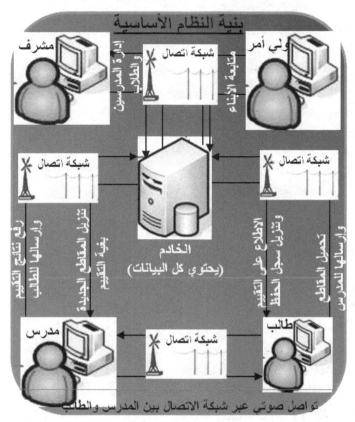

Fig. 10. E-halaga architecture

Fig. 11. Interface of the Semi-automatic Morphological Analyzer

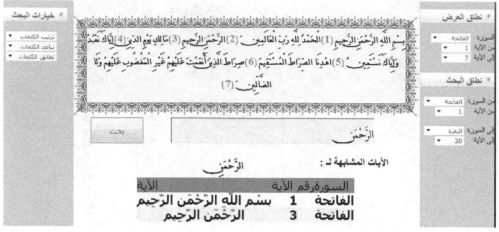

Fig. 12. Interface of the Similarity Search Engine

Fig. 12(a). Interface of the Quran Sciences Subsystem

9.3 The Quran sciences subsystem

It is a system letting the user navigates the Holy Quran and its main sciences. The main features offered are taken from authentic books, which were linked with the holy Quran through a full indexing of Quranic ayahs using advanced techniques and methodologies. Information are kept in their original sources (books), but can be easily retrieved and quickly processed. The books can be navigated, downloaded, etc., from a library, which represents another subsystem of this environment. Possibility of updates is well considered.

10. Conclusion

In this chapter, we firstly presented our work related to the textual specification of Tajweed rules in order to come up with a machine-readable formulation of these rules. An appropriate and easily extendable rule set has then been proposed. A fully diacriticised textual version of the Holy Quran has also been prepared to be used with our new-tajweed formulations. Next, we focused on the implementation of these formulations in a fast and efficient plug-in Tajweed Engine (TajE) that can be integrated in different kinds of systems for teaching the Holy Quran and its sciences. TajE is able to handle rulings in two different ways: identification and verification. The identification option is intended to extract Tajweed rulings from Quranic verses. The verification option, may serve to ensure that a specific Tajweed ruling really occurred in a certain place in the Quranic verse, which is very useful.

An e-learning system for self learning of tajweed (ETaj) is next built on the top of the tajweed engine (TajE). It provides different options allowing learners to get maximum benefit. The first important option of the system gives general rules and ethics of learning the Holy Quran. The second option offers a well designed component for learning tajweed rulings using a convenient and attractive manner of presenting the content of rulings along with textual examples as well as sound ones. The third option is very important as it provides a full dynamic interaction with the system to practice tajweed rulings.

At our best knowledge, both TajE and ETaj systems are the first of their kinds developed for automatic processing of Tajweed in a full interactive manner. They are now ready to be used and can help mastering this important field of Quranic Sciences.

11. Future works

In near future, we plan to improve ETaj system by organizing tajweed rulings in levels with incremental degree of complexity as it is followed in the real teaching of tajweed. Learners have to go through levels one by one. At the end of each level a self examination or testing will be initiated by the system and the learner will not be allowed to go further until he masters the current level. This means that a kind of authentication needs to be added to the system to follow students in their process of learning.

As another future work, we plan to expand our TajE engine to cover other Quranic narrations as we currently covered just "Hafs" narration.

12. Acknowledgements

This work was supported by King Abdulaziz City for Sciences and Technology (www.kacst.edu.sa), as part of the CTHQ Project, under the grant number AT-25-113, Saudi Arabia. We thank all the other project team members, which actively participated in the elaboration of the whole project.

13. References

Alghamdi, M., Elhadj, Y.O.M., & Alkanhal, M. (2007). Manual System to Segment and Transcribe Arabic Speech, *Proceedings of IEEE/ICSPC'07*, Dubai, UAE, November 24-27, 2007.

Alsughayeir, I.A., Khorsi, A.M., Alansari, A.M., & Ohali, Y.M.. (2009). Search Engine for the similarity in Quranic Terms (in Arabic), *Proceedings of Int. Conf. on the Glorious Quran and Contemporary Technologies*, King Fahd Complex for the Printing of the Holy Quran, Almadinah, Saudi Arabia, October 13-15, 2009.

Alsughayeir, I.A. & Ohali, Y.M. (2007). Similarity in Quranic Terms: computer-study (in Arabic), *Proceedings of ITRAS'07*, Riyadh, Saudi Arabia, March 6-7, 2007.

Alsughayeir, I.A. & Elhadj, Y.O.M. (2006). Computerized Quran Products: State-Of-Art (in Arabic), *Proceedings of STCEX'06*, Riyadh, Saudi Arabia, December 2-6, 2006.

Elhadj, Y.O.M., Alghamdi, M., AlKanhal, M. & Alansari, A.M. (2012). Towards an Automatic Corrector of Quranic Recitation Integreated within an Environment for Self-Learning of the Holy Quran (In Arabic). To be appeared in *Computer Research Journal published by the Federation of Arab Scientific Research Councils*, Vol. 11, No.1.

Elhadj, Y.O.M. & Aoun-Allah, M. (2011). A Machine-Readable Formulation of Tajweed Rules for Fast & Efficient Processing, Proceedings of the ICIST'11 International Conference, tebessa, Algeria, April 24-26, 2011

Elhadj, Y.O.M., Alsughayeir, I.A., Alghamdi, M., Alkanhal, M., Ohali, Y.M. & Alansari, A.M. (2010). Computerized teaching of the Holy Quran (in Arabic), *Final Technical Report*, King Abdulaziz City for Sciences and Technology (KACST), Riyadh, Saudi Arabia, 2010.

Elhadj, Y.O.M., Alghamdi, M., AlKanhal, M. & Alansari, A.M. (2010). Automatic Recognition of Quranic Sounds in the Recitation (in Arabic), *Proceedings of 6th Int. Conf. on Arabic Computing (ICCA10)*, Hammat – Tunisia, May 20-21, 2010.

Elhadj, Y.O.M. (2010). E-Halagat: an E-Learning System for Teaching the Holy Quran, *TOJET Journal*, Vol. 9, No 1, 2010.

Elhadj, Y.O.M. (2009). Sound Database with Perfect Reading of the Last Part of the Holy Quran, *IJCSNS journal*, Vol. 9, No. 7.

Elhadj, Y.O.M. (2009). Preparation of speech database with perfect reading of the lat part of the Holy Quran (in Arabic), *Proceedings of the 3rd IEEE International Conference on Arabic Language Processing (CITAL'09)*, Rabat, Morocco, May 4-5, 2009.

Elhadj, Y.O.M., Alghamdi, M., Alkanhal, M. & Alansari, A.M. (2009). Sound Corpus of a part of the noble Quran (in Arabic), *Proceedings of Int. Conf. on the Glorious Quran and Contemporary Technologies*, King Fahd Complex for the Printing of the Holy Quran, Almadinah, Saudi Arabia, October 13-15, 2009.

Elhadj, Y.O.M., Alsughayeir, I.A., Khorsi, A.M. & Alansari, A.M. (2009). Morphology Analysis of the Holy Quran (in Arabic), *Journal of Computer Science and Engineering in Arabic*, Vol. 3, No 1.

Elhadj, Y.O.M., Alsughayeir, I.A., Khorsi, A.M. & Alansari, A.M. (2009). An Indexed Database for Quran Morphology (in Arabic), *Proceedings of the 5th International Conference on Computer Science Practice in Arabic*, Rabat –Morocco, May 10-11, 2009.

Elhadj, Y.O.M., Aoun-Allah, M., Alansari, A.M. & Alsughayeir, I.A. (2009). Interactive learning System for Tajweed (in Arabic), *Proceedings of Int. Conf. on the Glorious Quran and Contemporary Technologies*, King Fahd Complex for the Printing of the Holy Quran, Almadinah, Saudi Arabia, October 13-15, 2009.

12

Personalized Learning in Hypermedia Environments

Costas Mourlas

Dept of Communication and Media Studies, University of Athens
Greece

1. Introduction

Distance learning (or eLearning) is considered one of the most rapidly evolving application areas of the Web that improves the traditional educational processes and methodologies of knowledge transfer. In recent years, there has been significant research and experimentation around the adaptation and personalization of the eLearning hypermedia that mainly concerns the timely delivery and adjustment of the content to user's needs and perceptual characteristics. This chapter provides a new comprehensive approach of reconstructing eLearning content; by creating a user profile based on specific metrics of cognitive processing parameters (such as cognitive style, cognitive processing speed efficiency, working memory factors and affective parameters) that have specific impact into the information space. Such approach may be proved to be very useful in assisting and facilitating a student to better understand eLearning content and therefore increase his / her academic performance. In view of that, an adaptation and personalization Web-based environment has been developed. It is detached into a number of interrelated components, each one representing a stand alone Web system. An evaluation of the proposed environment is presented with the results being highly promising and encouraging for the continuation of our research, since there has been identified significant increase of learners' academic performance when interacting with the personalized eLearning environment that is matched to their cognitive and affective parameters as well as visual working memory span capabilities.

Adapting to user context, individual features and behaviour patterns is a topic of great attention nowadays in the field of Web-based learning. A challenge is to design personalized interfaces and software enabling easy access to the learning content while being sufficiently flexible to handle changes in user's context, perception and available resources. One of the key technical issues in developing personalization applications is the problem of how to construct accurate and comprehensive profiles of individual users and how these can be used to identify a user and describe the user behaviour. The objective of user profiling is the creation of an information base that contains the preferences, characteristics and activities of the user.

There are some noteworthy applications in the area of Web personalization that collect information with various techniques from the users based on which they adapt the services content provided. Such systems, mostly commercial, are amongst others the Broadvision's One-To-One (www.broadvision.com), Microsoft's Firefly Passport (developed by the MIT

Media Lab), the Macromedia's LikeMinds Preference Server, Apple's WebObjects, etc. Other, more research oriented systems, include ARCHIMIDES (Bogonicolos et al. 1999), WBI (Maglio & Barret 2000; Barret et al. 1997), BASAR (Thomas & Fischer 1997) and mPERSONA (Panayiotou & Samaras 2004). Significant implementations have also been developed with regards to the provision of adapted educational content to students using various adaptive hypermedia techniques. Such systems are amongst others, INSPIRE (Papanikolaou et al. 2003), ELM-ART (Weber & Specht 1997), AHA! (De Bra & Calvi 1998), Interbook (Brusilovsky et al. 1998), and so on.

This chapter introduces a new approach in the field of adaptive hypermedia, which integrates cognitive and mental parameters and attempts to apply them on a Web-based learning environment. The goal of the proposed approach is to improve learning performance and, most importantly, to personalize Web-content to users' needs and preferences, eradicating known difficulties that occur in traditional approaches. Based on the abovementioned considerations, an adaptive Web-based environment is overviewed trying to convey the essence and the peculiarities encapsulated. This system is an innovative Adaptation and Personalization Web-based System that is based on the proposed approach and a Comprehensive User Profile, mentioned above.

In the proposed system, the notion of the user profile is extended, incorporating the *User Perceptual Preferences*, that serve as the primal personalization filtering element. This approach emphasizes on human factors that influence the visual and mental processes that mediate or manipulate new information that is received and built upon prior knowledge, respectively different for each user or user group. These characteristics, which have been primarily discussed in previous publications (Germanakos et al. 2005; Germanakos et al. 2007), have a major impact on visual attention and cognitive processing that take place throughout the whole process of accepting an object of perception (stimulus), until the comprehensive response to it.

A corresponding adaptive hypermedia system has been built following this approach (Germanakos et al. 2007a) and there is a continuing process of evaluating our methods and reforming both the theoretical model and the system. This chapter presents the results that are gathered from experiments conducted throughout the assessment procedure, in order to clarify at some extent whether such a combination of human factors is of importance in the area of educational adaptive hypermedia.

Section 2 presents the theoretical background for the personalization research and introduces our new approach in the field of adaptive hypermedia, which integrates cognitive and mental parameters and attempts to apply them on a Web-based learning environment. Section 3 presents our adaptive hypermedia system which has been built following the approach given in the previous section. Section 4 presents the empirical evaluation of the proposed approach and the results from experiments that were conducted in the context of an educational Web-setting, which support our approach in terms of optimizing users' performance in the sense of information comprehension. Section 5 includes the conclusion and our possible future work.

2. Theoretical background

Web personalization is the process of customizing the content and structure of a Web site to the specific needs of each user by taking advantage of the user's navigational behaviour.

Being a multi-dimensional and complicated area a universal definition has not been agreed to date. Nevertheless, most of the definitions given to personalization (Cingil et al. 2000; Blom 2000; Kim 2002) agree that the steps of the Web personalization process include: (1) the collection of Web data, (2) the modelling and categorization of these data (pre-processing phase), (3) the analysis of the collected data, and (4) the determination of the actions that should be performed.

One of the main challenges in Personalization research is alleviating users' orientation difficulties, as well as making appropriate selection of knowledge resources, since the vastness of the hyperspace has made information retrieval a rather complicated task (De Bra et al. 2004). Adaptivity is a particular functionality that distinguishes between interactions of different users within the information space (Eklund & Sinclair 2000; Brusilovsky & Nejdl 2004).

A system can be classified as personalized if it is based on hypermedia, has an explicit user model representing certain characteristics of the user, has a domain model which is a set of relationships between knowledge elements in the information space, and is capable of modifying some visible or functional parts of the system, based on the information maintained in the user model (Brusilovsky & Nejdl 2004; Brusilovsky 2001). In further support of the aforementioned concept of personalization, when referring to information retrieval and processing, one cannot disregard the top-down individual cognitive processes (Eysenck & Keane 2005), that significantly affect users' interactions within the hyperspace, especially when such interactions involve educational or learning, in general, goals.

Consequently, besides "traditional" demographic characteristics that commonly comprise the user model in personalized environments, we believe that a user model that incorporates individual cognitive characteristics and triggers corresponding mechanisms of adaptivity, increases the effectiveness of Web- applications that involve learning processes.

2.1 User perceptual preferences

In search of a model that combines the construct of cognitive style with other human information processing parameters, a three dimensional model is proposed (Tsianos et al., 2007): Cognitive Style, Cognitive Processing Efficiency and Emotional Processing. The first dimension is unitary, whereas Cognitive Processing Efficiency is comprised of (a) Visual Working Memory Span (VWMS) (Baddeley, 1992) and (b) speed and control of information processing and visual attention (Demetriou et al., 1993). The emotional aspect of the model focuses on different aspects of anxiety (Cassady & Jonhson 2002, Cassady 2004, Spielberger 1983), and self-regulation.

The model contains all the visual attention and cognitive psychology processes (cognitive and emotional processing parameters) that completes the user preferences and fulfils the user profile. User Perceptual Preference Characteristics could be described as a continuous mental processing starting with the perception of an object in the user's attentional visual field and going through a number of cognitive, learning and emotional processes giving the actual response to that stimulus, as depicted in Fig. 1, below. It is considered a vital component of the user profiling since it identifies the aspects of the user that is very difficult to be revealed and measured but, however, might determine his / her exact preferences and lead to a more concrete, accurate and optimized user segmentation.

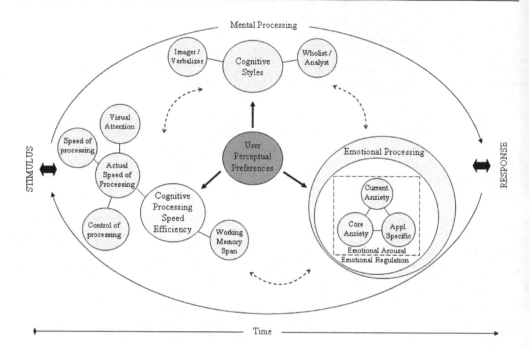

Fig. 1. User Perceptual Preference Characteristics – Three-Dimensional Approach

This "perceptual preferences" component / dimension of the user profile contains cognitive and emotional processes, aiming to enhance information learning efficacy. This model's primary parameters formulate a three-dimensional approach to the problem (Germanakos et al. 2007b) outlined below:

2.1.1 Cognitive processing efficiency

The cognitive processing parameters (Demetriou & Kazi, 2001) that constitute the first dimension of our model consist of the:

a. Actual speed of processing, that is further composed of the, (i) Control of processing (refers to the processes that identify and register goal-relevant information and block out dominant or appealing but actually irrelevant information); (ii) Speed of processing (refers to the maximum speed at which a given mental act may be efficiently executed); and (iii) Visual attention (based on the empirically validated assumption that when a person is performing a cognitive task, while watching a display, the location of his / her gaze corresponds to the symbol currently being processed in working memory and, moreover, that the eye naturally focuses on areas that are most likely to be informative).

b. As mentioned above, in search of a more coherent approach, the term of working memory (Baddeley, 1981) has also been introduced as a personalization factor. (Visual) working memory span (VWMS), which refers to the processes that enable a person to hold visual information in an active state while integrating it with other information until the current problem is solved. A brief description of the working memory system is that is consisted of the central executive that controls the two slave systems (visuo-spatial sketchpad and phonological loop), plus the episodic buffer that provides a temporary interface between the slave systems and the Long Term Memory (Baddeley, 2000). We are mainly interested in the notion of the working memory span, since it can be measured and the implications on information processing are rather clear. Due to the visual form of presentation in the web, we have focused especially on the on visual working memory (Loggie et al., 1990). In any case, each individual has a specific and restricted memory span. As to decrease the possibility of cognitive load in hypermedia educational environments (DeStefano & Lefevre, 2007), our system takes into account each users' visual working memory span (VWMS), by altering the amount of simultaneously presented information.

We measure each individual's ability to perform control/speed of processing and visual attention tasks in the shortest time possible, with a specific error tolerance, while the working memory span test focuses on the visuo-spatial sketch pad sub-component (Baddeley 1992), since all information in the Web is mainly visual.

2.1.2 Cognitive style

We prefer the construct of cognitive rather than learning style because it is more stable (Sadler-Smith & Riding, 1999), and to the extent that there is a correlation with hemispherical preference and EEG measurements (McKay, 2003; Glass & Riding, 1999), the relationship between cognitive style and actual mode of information processing is strengthened. Moreover, the learning style is "a construct that by definition is not stable- it was grounded in process and therefore susceptible to rapid change" (Rayner, 2001). In addition, we are research-wise interested in individual information processing parameters, whereas the social implications of other learning typologies are not examined.

More specifically, Riding and Cheema's Cognitive Style Analysis (CSA) has been opted for. The CSA is derived from a factor analytic approach on previous cognitive style theories, summarizing a number of different yet highly correlated constructs into two distinct independent dimensions (Riding & Cheema, 1991). This covers a wide array of the former cognition based style typologies, without going into unnecessary depth- for the needs of hypermedia education that is. The dimensions is the holist/analytic and the imager/verbalizer; the former alters the structure and amount of learner control, while the latter affects the type of resources that are presented to provide the necessary educational information.

Cognitive styles represent an individual's typical or habitual mode of problem solving, thinking, perceiving or remembering, and "are considered to be trait-like, relatively stable characteristics of individuals, whereas learning strategies are more state-driven..." (McKay, 2003). Amongst the numerous proposed cognitive style typologies (Cassidy, 2003; Kolb & Kolb, 2000; MyersBriggs et al., 1998) we favour Riding's Cognitive Style Analysis (Riding, 2001), because we consider that its implications can be mapped on the information space more precisely, since it is consisted of two distinct scales that respond to different aspects of the Web. The imager/verbalizer axis affects the way information is presented, whilst the wholist/analyst dimension is relevant to the structure of the information and the navigational path of the user. Moreover, it is a very inclusive theory that is derived from a number of pre-existing theories that were recapitulated into these two axes.

2.1.3 Emotional processing

In our study, we are interested in the way that individuals process their emotions and how they interact with other elements of their information-processing system. Emotional processing is a pluralistic construct which is comprised of two mechanisms: *emotional arousal*, which is the capacity of a human being to sense and experience specific emotional situations, and *emotion regulation*, which is the way in which an individual is perceiving and controlling his emotions. We focus on these two sub-processes because they are easily generalized, inclusive and provide some indirect measurement of general emotional mechanisms. These sub-processes manage a number of emotional factors like anxiety and boredom effects, anger, feelings of self efficacy, user satisfaction etc. Among these, our current research concerning emotional arousal emphasizes on anxiety, which is probably the most indicative and present in educational cases, while other emotional factors are to be examined within the context of a further study. Anxiety is an unpleasant combination of emotions that includes fear, worry and uneasiness and is often accompanied by physical reactions such as high blood pressure, increased heart rate and other body signals (Kim & Gorman, 2005; Barlow, 2002).

Accordingly, in order to measure emotion regulation, we are using the cognominal construct of emotion regulation. An effort to construct a model that predicts the role of emotion, in general, is beyond the scope of our research, due to the complexity and the numerous confounding variables that would make such an attempt rather impossible. However, there is a considerable amount of references concerning the role of emotion and its implications on academic performance (or achievement), in terms of efficient learning (Kort & Reilly, 2002). Emotional intelligence seems to be an adequate predictor of the aforementioned concepts, and is a grounded enough construct, already supported by academic literature (Goleman, 1995; Salovey & Mayer, 1990). Additional concepts that were used are the concepts of self-efficacy, emotional experience and emotional expression (Schunk, 1989).

3. System design implications: A high level correlation diagram

The greatest challenge is of course to extrude from the abovementioned theories the corresponding implications for an educational hypermedia environment. For a better understanding of the three dimensions' implications and the UPPC model as well as their relation with the information space a diagram that presents a high level correlation of these implications with selected tags of the information space (keywords used in Web languages to define a format change or hypertext link) is depicted in Figure 2 (Germanakos et al., 2008a; Germanakos et al, 2007a).

These tags (images, text, information quantity, links - learner control, navigation support, additional navigation support, and aesthetics) have gone through an extensive optimization representing group of data affected after the mapping with the implications. The main reason we have selected the latter tags is due to the fact that represent the primary subsidiaries of a Web-based content. With the necessary processing, mapping and / or alteration we could provide the same content with different ways (according to a specific user's profile) but without degrading the message conveyed.

The particular mapping is based on specific rules created, liable for the combination of these tags and the variation of their value in order to better filter the raw content and deliver the most personalized Web-based result to the user. As it can be observed from the diagram above each dimension has primary (solid line) and secondary (dashed line) implications on the information space altering dynamically the weighting of each factor on the creation of the environment.

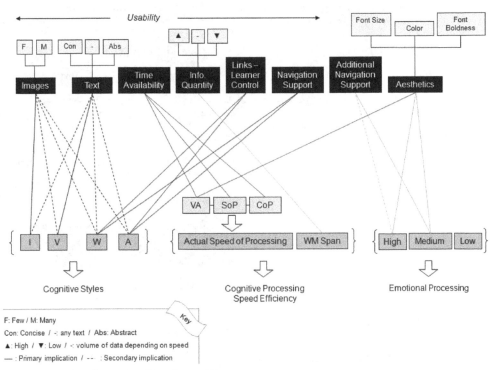

Fig. 2. Data – Implications Correlation Diagram

According to theory, with regards to learning styles for example, the number of images (few or many) to be displayed has a primary implication on imagers, while text (more concise or abstract) has a secondary implication. The analytic preference has a main effect on the links (learner control and navigation support tag). Moreover, actual speed of processing parameters (visual attention, speed of processing, and control of processing) as well as working memory span primarily affect time availability during interaction process and information quantity respectively (see an example in Fig. 3). At this point it should be mentioned that in case of internal correlation conflicts primary implications take over secondary ones.

Henceforth, with regards to the cognitive style, the number of images (few or many) for example to be displayed has a primary implication on imagers, while text (more concise or abstract) has a secondary implication. An analyst may affect primarily the links - learner control and navigation support tag, which in turn is secondary affected by high and medium emotional processing, while might secondary affect the number of images or kind of text to be displayed, consequently. Actual speed of processing parameters (visual attention, speed of processing, and control of processing) as well as working memory span are primarily affecting information quantity. Eventually, emotional processing is primarily affecting additional navigation support and aesthetics (the aesthetic enhancement of the system was expected to have a positive effect on highly anxious learners), as visual attention does, while secondary affects information quantity (see Fig. 4). In order to experimentally assess the effect of individuals' cognitive processing efficiency, we necessarily imposed time limitations within the learning process. By manipulating time limits, we examine how learners perform (level of comprehension).

A user might be identified that:

a) He is Verbalizer (V) – Wholist (W) with regards to the Learning Style.
b) He has an Actual Cognitive Processing Speed Efficiency of 1000 msec.
c) He has fair Working Memory Span (weighting 5/7).

Tags affected accordingly:

a) Images (few images displayed), Text (any text could be delivered).
b) Medium interaction time availability (since his cognitive processing speed efficiency is moderate).
c) Info Quantity (less info since his has medium working memory).
d) Links – Learner Control (less learner control because he is Wholist).

Fig. 3. A practical example of the Data – Implications Correlation Diagram

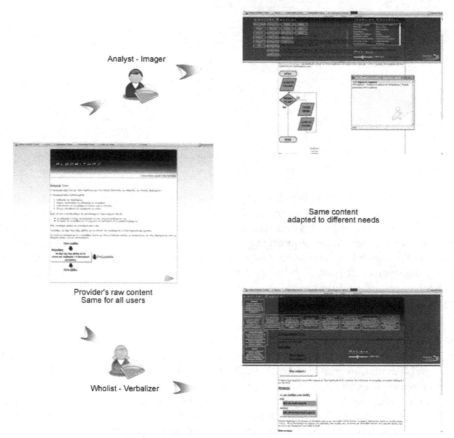

Analyst - Imager

Same content
adapted to different needs

Provider's raw content
Same for all users

Wholist - Verbalizer

Fig. 4. Content adaptation according to user's comprehensive profile

Additionally, since emotional processing is the most dynamic parameter compared to the others, any changes occurring at any given time are directly affecting the yielded value of the adaptation and personalization rules and henceforth the format of the content delivered.A short description of the way that our system adapts to users' preferences is needed in order to provide the reader an insight to our research framework.

a. Cognitive style: There are two dimensions of users' cognitive style that are mapped in the educational environment: the holist/analyst scale affects the structure and the amount of learner control, whereas the imager/verbalizer is related to the textual or graphical representation of information (where possible of course).

b. VWMS: Each users' visual working memory span is measured and classified. Users that have low levels of VWMS receive segmented content that is unfolded gradually. The main idea is to alleviate the possibility of cognitive overload, and is based on the notion that information processing is not sequential but parallel- therefore, the segmentation in clear-cut chunks may assist users' with low VWMS.

c. Cognitive Processing Efficiency: Since the term efficiency refers mainly to speed, in order to distinguish whether there is a relationship between users' ability and the time required to complete an online course, we set different time limits for each category.

d. Anxiety: In our experiments, if there were high levels of anxiety (on behalf of the user), we provided aesthetical enhancement of the environment and further annotations; in a sense, the aesthetical aspect predominates over functionality (in terms of font size, colours, annotations).

Based on the abovementioned considerations an adaptive Web-based learning environment has been developed, trying to convey the essence and the peculiarities encapsulated. The current system, AdaptiveWeb[1] is a Web application that can be ported both to desktop computer and mobile devices. The actual system, the psychometric tests and the course can be reached at http://www3.cs.ucy.ac.cy/adaptiveweb/. It is composed of four interrelated components, each one representing a stand-alone Web-based system (Germanakos et al., 2008b). The AdaptiveWeb system is currently at its final stage. All the components, except the Semantic Web Editor have been developed and smoothly running. For this reason, all the tests implemented so far, to prove components efficiency as well as the effect of our cognitive three-dimensional model described above into the Web, have been based on predetermined online contents in the field of eLearning. The current system has been evaluated both at system's response time performance and resources consumption, as well as with regards to users' learning performance, with really encouraging results as it is described into the following sections.

For experimental purposes, we have currently authored an e-learning multimedia environment with a predefined content for adaptation and personalization. This environment includes a course named "Introduction to Algorithms" and is a first year e-learning course environment that aims to provide students with analytic thinking and top-down methodology techniques for further development of constructive solutions to given problems.

To get a better insight of the adaptation process and how data flows, we hereafter depict how the personalized content (the "Introduction to Algorithms" predefined environment) interacts with the Comprehensive User Profile, using specific mapping rules. Fig. 5 shows

---

[1] http://www3.cs.ucy.ac.cy/adaptiveWeb

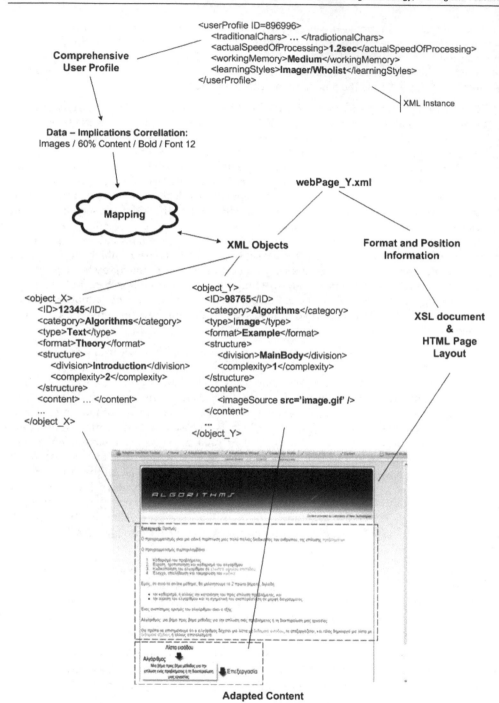

Fig. 5. The Adaptation Process

the whole adaptation process. The system's adaptation engine initially retrieves the actual profile characteristics of the user and then interprets the profile to conclude what implications the user's characteristics have in the information space; what adaptation techniques to use on the content. Every Web-page is detached into standalone objects, each one having special characteristics (i.e. image diagram for Imagers or text object for Verbalizers).

At this point the system has all the information necessary for adapting the content; the data - implications correlation diagram based on the user's comprehensive profile and the content description of the particular Web-page. The next step is to map the implications with the Web-page's content, for assembling the final version of the provider's content. The content adapts according to the users' preferences. The new, adapted content loads then onto the users' device.

Users log in the system providing their username and password to see adapted content. The corresponding profile loads onto the server and in proportion with their cumulative characteristics the content of the provider maps with the "Mapping Rules", as described before. Based on theory (Sadler-Smith & Riding 1999), Analysts have a more analytic way of think; thus the navigation support provided (analytic description of definitions) is in popup windows, so they can manage the entire lesson, along with its definitions by themselves. In the learner control support (that is, the slide-in help panel from the top of the page) is a linkable sitemap of the whole e-learning lesson, plus the entire lesson's definitions in alphabetic order.

On the other hand, Wholists tend to have a wholistic approach of learning (Sadler-Smith & Riding 1999); thus the navigation support and learner control support is more restricted and is specifically provided for guidance. The analytic description of a definition is only shown in a tooltip when they move their mouse over it and the learner control shows them only the current chapter's pages they learn and lets them navigate only to the next and the previous visited pages.

4. Empirical evaluation of the proposed model in an educational environment

This section presents the results from experiments that were conducted in the context of an educational Web-setting, which support our approach in terms of optimizing users' performance in the sense of information comprehension.

Sampling and Procedure

All participants were students from the Universities of Cyprus and Athens with a sample of 138 students. 35% of the participants were male and 65% were female, and their age varied from 17 to 22 with a mean age of 19. The environment in which the procedure took place was an e-learning undergraduate course on algorithms. The course subject was chosen due to the fact that students of the departments where the experiment took place had absolutely no experience of computer science, and traditionally perform poorly. By controlling the factor of experience in that way, we divided our sample in two groups: almost half of the participants were provided with information matched to their cognitive style, while the other half were taught in a mismatched way. We expected that users in the matched condition would outperform those in the mismatched condition.

In order to evaluate the effect of matched and mismatched conditions, participants took an online assessment test on the subject they were taught (algorithms). This exam was taken as soon as the e-learning procedure ended, in order to control for long-term memory decay effects. The dependent variable that was used to assess the effect of adaptation to users' preferences was participants' score at the online exam.

At this point, it should be clarified that matching and mismatching instructional style is a process with different implications for each dimension of our model. These are described below:

- Matched Cognitive Style: Presentation and structure of information matches user's preference
- Mismatched Cognitive Style: Presentation and structure of information does not coincide with user's preference
- Matched VWMS: Low VWMS users are provided with segmented information
- Mismatched VWMS: Low VWMS users are provided with the whole information
- Matched CPSE: Each user has in his disposal the amount of time that fits his ability
- Mismatched CPSE: Users' with low speed of processing have less time in their disposal (the same with "medium" users.
- Matched Emotional Processing: Users with moderate and high levels of anxiety receive aesthetic enhancement of the content and navigational help
- Mismatched Emotional Processing: Users with moderate and high levels of anxiety receive no additional help or aesthetics

Questionnaires

In this specific e-learning setting, Users' Perceptual Preferences were the sole parameters that comprised each user profile, since demographics and device characteristics were controlled for. In order to build each user profile according to our model, we used a number of questionnaires that address all theories involved.

- Cognitive Style: Riding's Cognitive Style Analysis, standardized in Greek and integrated in .NET platform
- Cognitive Processing Speed Efficiency: Speed and accuracy task-based tests that assess control of processing, speed of processing, visual attention and visuospatial working memory. Originally developed in the E-prime platform, we integrated them into our platform.
- Core (general) Anxiety: Spielberger's State-Trait Anxiety Inventory (STAI) – 10 items (Only the trait scale was used).
- Application Specific Anxiety: Cassady's Cognitive Test Anxiety scale – 27 items (Cassady, 2004).
- Current Anxiety: Self-reported measures of state anxiety taken during the assessment phase of the experiment, in time slots of every 10 minutes – 6 Time slots.
- Emotion Regulation: This questionnaire was developed by us; cronbach's α that indicates scale reliability reaches 0.718.

Results

As expected, in both experiments the matched condition group outperformed those of the mismatched group. Table 1 shows the differences of means (one way ANOVA) and their statistical significance for the parameters of Cognitive Style (CS), Cognitive Processing Speed Efficiency (CPSE), and Emotional Processing (EM).

As hypothesized, the mean score of those that received matched to their cognitive style environments is higher than the mean score achieved by those that learned within the mismatched condition ($F_{(2,113)}$=6.330, p=0.013). This supports the notion that cognitive style is of importance within the context of Web-education and that this construct has a practical application in hypermedia instruction. The same applies with the case of Cognitive Processing Speed Efficiency: $F_{(2, 81)}$=5.345, p=0.023). It should at least be of some consideration the fact that in case designers' teaching style mismatched learners' preference, performance may be lowered.

In the case of Emotional Processing, results show that in case an individual reports high levels of anxiety either at the Core Anxiety or the Specific Anxiety questionnaire, the matched condition benefits his/her performance ($F_{(2, 81)}$=4.357, p=0.042).

	Match Score	Match n	Mis-match Score	Mis-match n	F	Sig.
CS	66.53%	53	57.79%	61	6.330	**0.013**
CPSE	57.00%	41	48.93%	41	5.345	**0.023**
EP	57.91%	23	48.45%	29	4.357	**0.042**

Table 1. Differences of means for Cognitive Style and Cognitive Processing Speed Efficiency

The relatively small sample that falls into each category and its distribution hamper statistical analysis of the working memory (WM) parameter.

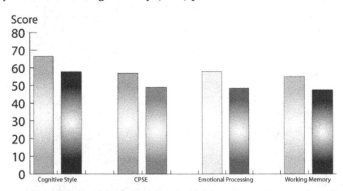

Fig. 6. Differences of matched and mismatched condition regarding each personalization parameter

In any case, the difference between those with high WM and those with low WM, when both categories receive non-segmented (whole) content, approaches statistical significance: 57.06% for those with High WM, 47.37% for those with Low WM, Welch statistic= 3.988, p=0.054. This demonstrates that WM has indeed some effect on an e-learning environment. Moreover, if those with low WM receive segmented information, then the difference of means decreases and becomes non-significant (57.06% for High WM, 54.90% for those with Low WM, Welch statistic=0.165, p=0.687). All the aforementioned differences between the matched and the mismatched condition are illustrated in Figure 6.

Correlations and Statistics of Emotional Processing Constructs

The emotional processing factor is discussed further due to the fact that it can be applied in various environments that relate to performance but do not require extended use of cognitive resources.

It is observed in Table 2 that all types of anxiety are positively correlated with each other and are negatively correlated with emotion regulation. These findings support our hypothesis and it can be argued that our theory concerning the relationship between anxiety and regulation has a logical meaning. There is also an even stronger relationship between emotion regulation and core ($F_{(2,92)}$=18.554, sig.=0.00) and specific anxiety ($F_{(2,92)}$=15.226, sig.=0.00) respectively. This statistically significant analysis of variance for each anxiety type shows that if participants are categorized according to their emotional regulation ability, then the anxiety means vary significantly with the high regulation group scoring much higher than the low one. Finally, table 3 demonstrates that the two conditions (matched aesthetics/mismatched aesthetics) are differentiating the sample significantly always in relation with performance. Participants in the matched category scored higher than the ones in the mismatched and additionally lower anxious (core or specific or both) scored higher than high anxious, always of course in relation to match/mismatch factor.

	Core Anxiety	Application Specific Anxiety	Current Anxiety	Emotion Regulation
Core Anxiety	1	.613(**)	.288(**)	-.569(**)
Application Specific Anxiety	.613(**)	1	.501(**)	-.471(**)
Current Anxiety	.288(**)	.501(**)	1	-.094
Emotion Regulation	-.569(**)	-.471(**)	-.094	1

** Correlation is significant at the 0.01 level (2-tailed).

Table 2. Correlations of types of anxiety and emotion regulation

Dependent Variable: Score %

Source	Type III Sum of Squares	df	Mean Square	F	Sig.
	(a)				
Matched Aesthetics	1097.361	1	1097.361	4.238	.043
core_groups* specific_groups* Matched Aesthetics	983.259	1	983.259	3.797	.055

(a) R Squared = .102 (Adjusted R Squared = .017)

Table 3. Multifactorial ANOVA (Factors - Core Anxiety, Application Specific Anxiety and Aesthetics)

We also found that participants with low application specific anxiety perform better than participants with high specific anxiety in both matched and mismatched environments. Additionally, in categories that a certain amount of anxiety exists, match-mismatch factor is extremely important for user performance. Participants with matched environments scored highly while participants with mismatched environments had poor performance. Emotion regulation is negatively correlated with current anxiety. High emotion regulation means low current anxiety and low emotion regulation means high current anxiety. Finally, current anxiety is indicative of performance. High current anxiety means test scores below average while low current anxiety means high scores.

5. Conclusion and future work

Considering the user as a vital part of computer-mediated systems may improve the quality of services offered, especially if the aim is learning or higher order information processing is involved. It makes sense that if one examines the characteristics of a device or the location of the user in providing eServices, the same should be applied with the case of human factors. In the same way that a device has a certain processing ability, individuals differ in their perceptual and processing preferences and abilities. Therefore, it could be supported that an essential part of HCI are the users themselves.

In this chapter a new approach in the field of adaptive hypermedia is described, which integrates cognitive and mental parameters and attempts to apply them on a Web-based learning environment. The approach emphasizes on human factors that influence the visual and mental processes that mediate or manipulate new information that is received and built upon prior knowledge, respectively different for each user or user group. The goal of the proposed approach is to improve learning performance and, most importantly, to personalize Web-content to users' needs and preferences, eradicating known difficulties that occur in traditional approaches. An innovative Adaptation and Personalization Web-based System has been build and presented in the chapter incorporating the *User Perceptual Preferences*, that serve as the primal personalization filtering element. This chapter also presents the results that are gathered from experiments conducted throughout the assessment procedure, in order to clarify at some extent whether such a combination of human factors is of importance in the area of educational adaptive hypermedia.

The empirical study on the field of e-learning presented above demonstrates that an "intrinsic" context aware application (in our perspective) is proven helpful for users and an actual benefit is objectively measured. All things considered, such a statistically significant effect that is consistent to the psychological theories supporting it is rather encouraging for the notion of expanding individual differences theories to various research areas.

The next step of our work, is the integration of the remaining parameters of our proposed model as personalization factors in e-learning environments. With regards to emotional processing, we are setting out a research framework that involves the use of sensors and real-time monitoring of emotional arousal (Galvanic Skin Response and Heart Rate) (Psaltis & Mourlas, 2011).

Thus, describing the user, he/she requires a multi dimensional model of representation, which should incorporate cognitive and emotional characteristics that seem to have a main effect in interacting with applications that involve information processing. It is not argued of course that demographical and "traditional" profiling characteristics are of lesser importance; our proposed model could have a modular role in a setting that defines context in a variety of ways, by adding another dimension focused on intrinsic processes.

At this point of research, it seems that these differences are indeed important, and the way that theory was put into practice in our system did seem to be functional. There are of course many considerations regarding the generalization of this approach, and further experimental evaluation is required; still, especially within an educational environment, we have clear indications that user's intrinsic characteristics may be used in a meaningful manner.

6. Acknowledgment

I would like to thank my PhD students Panagiotis Germanakos, Nikolaos Tsianos and Zaharias Lekkas for their valuable contribution, their discussions and their work during all the years of research on human factors and personalization. I would like also to thank the members of the SCRAT group of the Dept. of Computer Science, University of Cyprus for their work in implementing parts of the AdaptiveWeb System.

7. References

Baddeley, A. (2000). The episodic buffer: a new component of working memory? *Trends in Cognitive Sciences,* 11 (4), 2000, 417-423.

Baddeley, A. (1981). The concept of working memory: A view of its current state and probable future development. Cognition, Vol 10 No 1-3, pp: 17-23.

Baddeley, A. (1992). Working Memory. Science, Vol, 255, pp: 556 - 559.

Barret, R., Maglio, P. & Kellem, D. (1997). How to Personalize the Web, In Proceedings of CHI 97.

Barlow, D. H. (2002). Anxiety and its disorders: The nature and treatment of anxiety and panic (2nd ed.). New York: The Guilford Press.

Blom J. (2000). Personalization – A Taxonomy, ACM 2000. ISBN:1-58113-248-4.

Bogonicolos, N., Fragoudis, D., Likothanassis, S. (1999). ARCHIMIDES: an intelligent agent for adaptive-personalized navigation within a WEB server. *Proceedings of the 32nd Annual Hawaii Intl. Conf. On System Science,* HICSS-32. Vol 5.

Brusilovsky, P. & Nejdl, W. (2004). *Adaptive Hypermedia and Adaptive Web.* CSC Press LLC.

Brusilovsky, P. (2001). "Adaptive Hypermedia", *User Modeling and User-Adapted Interaction,* 11 (pp. 87-110).

Brusilovsky, P., Eklund, J. & Schwarz, E. (1998). Web-based education for all: A tool for developing adaptive courseware. Computer Networks and ISDN Systems. *Proceedings of the 7th International WWW Conference,* 14-18 April, 30(1-7), 291-300.

Cassady J. C., & Jonhson, R. E. (2002). Cognitive Test Anxiety and Academic Performance. Contemporary Educational Psychology, Vol. 27 No 2, pp: 270-295.

Cassady, J. C. (2004). The influence of cognitive test anxiety across the learning–testing cycle. Learning and Instruction, Vol. 14 No 6, pp: 569–592.

Cassidy, S.   (2000). Learning Styles: An overview of theories, models, and measures. *Educational Psychology,* 2000 24 (4), 419-444.

Cingil I., Dogac A., & Azgin A. (2000). "A broader approach to personalization", *Communications of the ACM,* Vol. 43, No. 8

De Bra, Aroyo, Chepegin (2004). "The Next Big Thing: Adaptive Web-Based Systems", *Journal of Digital Information,* Volume 5, Issue 1, Article No 247.

De Bra, P. & Calvi, L. (1998). AHA! An open Adaptive Hypermedia Architecture. *The New Review of Hypermedia and Multimedia,* 4, Taylor Graham Publishers, pp. 115-139.

Demetriou, A., and Kazi, S. (2001). Unity and modularity in the mind and the self: Studies on the relationships between self-awareness, personality, and intellectual development from childhood to adolescence. London: Routdledge.

Demetriou, A., Efklides, A., & Platsidou, M. (1993). The architecture and dynamics of developing mind: Experiential structuralism as a frame for unifying cognitive development theories (Monographs of the Society for Research in Child Development). USA: University of Chicago Press.

DeStefano, D., & Lefevre, J. (2007). Cognitive load in hypertext reading: A review. Computers in Human Behavior, Vol 23 No 3, pp: 1616–1641.

Eklund, J. & Sinclair, K. (2000). "An empirical appraisal of the effectiveness of adaptive interfaces of instructional systems". *Educational Technology and Society*, 3 (4), ISSN 1436-4522.

Eysenck, M. W. & Keane, M. T. (2005). *Cognitive Psychology*. Psychology Press.

Germanakos, P., Tsianos, N., Lekkas, Z., Mourlas, C., and Samaras, G. (2008a) Realizing Comprehensive User Profiling as the Core Element of Adaptive and Personalized Communication Environments and Systems, *The Computer Journal*, Special Issue on Profiling Expertise and Behaviour, Oxford University Press, 2008, doi:10.1016/j.chb.2007.07.010.

Germanakos, P., Tsianos, N., Lekkas., Z., Mourlas, C., Belk, M., and Samaras, G. (2008b) Integrating Human Factors in the Web Personalization Process: The AdaptiveWeb System, *Demonstration in the Proceedings of the 18th European Conference on Artificial Intelligence (ECAI 2008)*, Patras, Greece, July 21-25, 2008, IOS Press, ISBN: 978-960-6843-17-4, pp. 9-10.

Germanakos, P., Tsianos, N., Lekkas, Z., Mourlas, C., Belk, M., & Samaras G. (2007a). An AdaptiveWeb System for Integrating Human Factors in Personalization of Web Content. Demonstration in the Proceedings of the 11th International Conference on User Modeling (UM 2007), Corfu, Greece, June 25-29, 2007.

Germanakos, P, Tsianos, N, Lekkas, Z, Mourlas, C, and Samaras, G. (2007b) "Capturing Essential Intrinsic User Behaviour Values for the Design of Comprehensive Web-based Personalized Environments", *Computers in Human Behavior Journal*, Special Issue on Integration of Human Factors in Networked Computing, doi:10.1016/j.chb.2007.07.010

Germanakos, P., Tsianos, N., Mourlas, C., & Samaras, G. (2005) New Fundamental Profiling Characteristics for Designing Adaptive Web-based Educational Systems. *Proceeding of the IADIS International Conference on Cognition and Exploratory Learning in Digital Age (CELDA2005)*, Porto, December 14-16, pp. 10-17.

Glass, A., and Riding, R. J. EEG differences and cognitive style. 1999, *Biological Psychology, 51*, 23–41.

Goleman, D. (1995) Emotional Intelligence: why it can matter more than IQ, New York: Bantam Books.

Kolb, A.Y., and Kolb, D.A. (2000) The Kolb Learning Style Inventory – Version 3.1 2005 Technical Specifications, Experience Based Learning Systems, Inc.Korkea-aho, M. (2000). *Context-Aware Applications Survey*. Paper presented at the Internetworking Seminar (Tik-110.551), Spring 2000, Helsinki University of Technology, 2005, from http://www.hut.fi/~mkorkeaa/doc/context-aware. html.

Kort, B. and Reilly, R. (2002), Analytical Models of Emotions, Learning and Relationships: Towards an Affect-Sensitive Cognitive Machine. Conference on Virtual Worlds and Simulation (VWSim 2002), from
http://affect.media.mit.edu/projectpages/lc/vworlds.pdf.

Kim, J, Gorman, J. (2005) The psychobiology of anxiety. Clinical Neuroscience Research, 2005, 4, 335-347.

Kim W. (2002) *Personalization: Definition, Status, and Challenges Ahead*, Published by ETH Zurich, Chair of Software Engineering JOT, 2002, Vol. 1, No. 1.

Loggie, R. H., Zucco, G. N., & Baddeley, A. D. (1990). Interference with visual short-term memory. Acta Psychologica, Vol 75 No 1, pp: 55-74.

Maglio, P. & Barret, R. (2000) Intermediaries Personalize Information Streams, *Communications of the ACM*, Vol. 43(8), pp. 96-101.

McKay, M. T., Fischler, I. & Dunn, B. R., (2003). "Cognitive style and recall of text: An EEG analysis". *Learning and Individual Differences*, Vol. 14, pp. 1–21.

MyersBriggs, I., McCaulley, M. H., Quenk, N. L. and Hammer, A. L. (1998). MBTI Manual (A guide to the development and use of the Myers Briggs type indicator), 3rd edition. Consulting Psychologists Press.

Panayiotou, C., and Samaras, G. (2004). mPersona: Personalized Portals for the Wireless User: An Agent Approach. Journal of ACM/ Baltzer Mobile Networking and Applications (MONET), Special Issue on "Mobile and Pervasive Commerce", (6), 663-677.

Papanikolaou K.A., Grigoriadou M., Kornilakis H., & Magoulas G.D. (2003). Personalizing the Interaction in a Web-based Educational Hypermedia System: the case of INSPIRE. *User-Modeling and User-Adapted Interaction*, 13(3), 213-267.

Psaltis A., & Mourlas C. (2011). A Real Time Attachment Free, Psycho Physiological Stress and Heart Rate Measurement System, *International Journal of Measurement Technologies and Instrumentation Engineering*, Vol. 1(2), pp. 1-13, April-June 2011, IGI Global.

Rayner, S. (2001). Cognitive Styles and Learning Styles. In Smelser, N. J., & Baltes, P. B. (eds), International Encyclopedia of Social & Behavioral Sciences. UK: Elsevier Science Ltd.

Riding, R.J., & Cheema, I. (1991). Cognitive Styles – an overview and integration, Educational Psychology, Vol. 11 No 3 & 4, pp: 193-215.

Riding, R. Cognitive Style Analysis – Research Administration. Learning and Training Technology, (2001).

Sadler-Smith, E., and Riding, R. J. (1999). Cognitive style and instructional preferences. *Instructional Science*, 1999, 27 (5), 355-371.

Salovey, P., and Mayer, J. D. (1990). Emotional intelligence. Imagination, Cognition and Personality, 9, 185±211, 1990.

Schunk, D. H. (1989). Self-efficacy and cognitive skill learning. In C. Ames & R. Ames (Eds.), Research on motivation in education. Vol. 3: Goals and cognitions (pp. 13-44). San Diego: Academic Press.

Spielberger, C. D. (1983). Manual for the State-Trait Anxiety Inventory (STAI). Palo Alto, CA: Consulting Psychologists Press.

Thomas, C. & Fischer, G., (1997). Using agents to personalize the Web, *In proceedings of. ACM IUI'97*, pp. 53-60, Florida, USA.

Tsianos, N., Germanakos, P., Lekkas, Z., Mourlas, C., and Samaras, G. (2007) Evaluating the Significance of Cognitive and Emotional Parameters in e-Learning Adaptive Environments, *Proceedings of the IADIS International Conference on Cognition and Exploratory Learning in Digital Age (CELDA2007)*, Algarve, Portugal, December 7-9, 2007, pp. 93-98.

Weber, G. & Specht, M. (1997) User Modeling and Adaptive Navigation Support in WWW-Based Tutoring Systems. *Proceedings of User Modeling '97*, pp. 289-300.

Part 4

Implementation of E-Learning Environments

13

A New Management Role – A Precondition for Successful E-Learning Implementations

Grete Netteland

Sogn og Fjordane University College
Norway

1. Introduction

Over the past 15 years there has been a significant increase in e-learning implementations – in schools, in academia and in the workplace. The scope of the initiatives has varied, from embracing only one single unit (e.g. a class, course or department) to covering a whole organization. In common for most of the implementations, however, is that they are arranged as projects, are introduced as a tool for change, and are accompanied by expectations of rapid success.

High-quality implementations of e-learning of course exist, but many initiatives fail, and so far only a few projects have contributed to broader institutional changes (Collis, 2002; Lepori, 2003). This is the case, according to Attwell (2004), because the adoption and especially the sustainability of e-learning represent a large organizational challenge. To aid in the introduction of e-learning, the e-learning literature therefore has identified a lot of barriers, success factors and critical factors that should be attended to in the implementation process (e.g. culture (Cross & Dublin, 2002; Rosenberg, 2001), champions (Rosenberg, 2001), ICT-management (Broadley, 2007) and motivation (van Dam, 2004)). Unfortunately, the terms mentioned have mostly been specified without reference to contextual factors, e.g. the aim of the implementation, the size and type of organization, the type of e-learning technology, ways of working, the organization of the implementation and whether it was enterprise-wide or limited to only one or a few units. This is also the case when the e-learning literature refers to the *role of management* as a critical factor, using terms like 'top leadership commitment' (Jones & Laffey, 2002), 'top management support' (van Dam, 2004) or 'sound leadership' (Rosenberg, 2001).

The aim of this chapter is to illuminate this management role when e-learning is put into use in an organization. By presenting three different e-learning implementations and discussing the role of management in each of them more closely, the objective is to capture the essence of how the manager can affect more specifically the outcome of the implementation process, to make e-learning sustainable, and to utilize it as a catalyst for institutional change. To achieve this, two different perspectives are integrated in the analysis: a general perspective, focused on e-learning as a means for organizational development and learning, and an individual perspective, focused on how e-learning is adopted and experienced by individual learners. In this way, this chapter intends to contribute to the e-learning literature in a field in which until now, according to Hauge & Erstad (2011), there has been little research.

In order to examine the complex landscape in which e-elearning is to be implemented and integrated, be it a school, a university college, or a business organization, Activity Theory (Engeström, 1987) is introduced as an analytical resource. Instead of directing attention towards problem-solving at the individual and group levels, which is typical in many theories about organizational learning and change, a characteristic of this theory is that it directs attention instead towards *the objects* of the activities and how these are created through interaction, contradictions and tensions between social, material and cultural forces within the organization and/or between the organization and its environment (Engestrøm, 2008).

The first part of this chapter gives a brief overview of the development of e-learning in organizations (1.1), how the research and literature dealing with e-learning implementations in work organizations and educational organizations emphasise and refer to the role of management in the implementation process (1.2), and relevant aspects of Activity Theory (1.3). In the second part of the chapter, three empirical cases are presented and more broadly discussed (2.1, 2.2. and 2.3). Section 3 closes the chapter by giving concluding remarks and a brief overview of further implications.

1.1 E-learning in organizations

According to Alessi and Trollip (2001), organization-wide use of web-based technology for learning purposes has, at minimum, two important benefits:

- Learners can access the materials at their convenience (educational accessibility),[1] and
- Learning has the potential for employee-employee interaction and communication (social interaction).[2]

These two dimensions have given rise to two essentially different approaches to e-learning—e-learning as a tool for instruction and e-learning as a tool for information and knowledge sharing (Netteland, 2008). Both approaches were present among the countless definitions of e-learning that emerged during the first part of the new millennium, a period by VanDam (2004) referred to as the first wave of e-learning. Nonetheless, a review of large parts of the e-learning literature from 2000-2002 indicated that at first it was a narrow view on learning that dominated the definitions, especially when talking about workplace e-learning. The main focus was on individual learning, online delivery of content, opportunities for skill development, and, to some degree, on information sharing as well (Netteland, 2003). A similar focus also existed to a large extent in the educational sector, but in this case the definitions had a larger emphasis on dialogue, interaction and collaborative activities, and focused less on content. This distinction was also reflected in practical work; while e-learning in schools was often combined with classroom teaching, social learning forms were nearly absent in the workplace. This was probably the reason why, beginning in 2001, many work organizations introduced so called *blended learning* (Kishore, 2002), i.e. e-learning combined with face-to-face learning activities (Netteland, 2003). Another

---

[1] This type of learning is reflected in the terms 'just-in-time learning' (see Davenport & Glaser, 2002) and 'learning on demand' (see Fischer, 2001).

[2] This type of learning, with the potential for web-based collaboration, interaction and sharing among users, has developed and given its name to the concept of Web 2.0. This term, which was coined in 2003 and is used to describe social software (e.g., social-networking sites, wikis and blogs) and online communities, generally describes web-based services managed by participants.

characteristic of this first wave of e-learning that is of interest in this context, was, that the implementations mainly were restricted to one or a few units. At this time, enterprise-wide implementations were nearly non-existent.

From 2004, e-learning was gradually enhanced with tools for online interaction and collaboration, and little by little also with Web 2.0 applications and services, especially in educational settings. Despite the fact that some work organizations gradually have put web collaboration tools and 2.0 applications into use (e.g. in the form of wikis, social media and web-based conference systems), e-learning in the workplace is usually still restricted to online education (transfer of knowledge) and online training (development of skills), both without any form of collaboration. Or, as Rosenberg (2006) formulated it, workplace e-learning is limited to e-training or courseware online, mostly with a relatively static content. Although the situation is slowly starting to change, so far tools for collaboration and knowledge-building have mainly been applied as a resource for learning in educational institutions. But pedagogical change takes time, and according to Karasavvidis (2010), typical e-learning approaches—at least in higher education—still tend to replicate traditional transmissionist practices, which are mostly based on behaviorist conceptions of learning (Karasavvidis, 2010).

1.2 The manager in e-learning implementations

While to a large extent the literature about e-learning implementations in educational institutions has directed attention to the *use* of digital technologies, the workplace e-learning literature has focused primarily on the *implementation*[3] of these technologies. Looking at the role of management in the two different contexts is therefore rather challenging; the analytical units will necessarily differ. Since the main goal of this chapter is to examine how the role of management affects implementation and contributes to making e-learning sustainable and catalystic for institutional development, this research overview mainly *focuses on the management role when organizations put e-learning into use—not on the potential learning outcome of these implementations.*

Taking as a point of departure a review of forty publications[4] in the workplace e-learning field, Netteland (2008) identified the following set of management/leader-related barriers, success factors, and/or critical factors:

- Barriers: weak sponsorship; no governance (Rosenberg, 2006)
- Success factors: commitment to leadership (Ely, 1990, 1999a); top leadership commitment, involvement and support (Jones & Laffey, 2002)
- Critical factors: gaining top management support (van Dam, 2004); making senior management own e-learning (Rosenberg, 2001); sound leadership at all organizational levels (Rosenberg, 2001)

In other words, management related-dimensions were discussed in merely six of forty workplace e-learning publications and by only four of the authors. As the bullet points

---

[3] The term 'implementation' is used here in the Information System meaning of the word, that is: how to put the system into use (see Munkvold et al. (2003)).
[4] It should be noted that the review is not exhaustive, and several other studies could have been included as well.

indicate, however, a variety of terms are applied, sometimes without supplementary information. Despite this, the authors use many of the same reasons for why they underline the role of management in different situations: e.g. the top management's authority to allocate resources and its power to execute reward systems (Jones & Laffey, 2002; Ely, 1999a, 1999b); the top management's opportunity to allocate incentives and time (Ely, 1999a, 1999b); and the top management's ability to lend credibility to the initiative and thereby institute a new learning culture (Rosenberg, 2001). Another argument, mentioned by van Dam (2004), is that the e-learning project, when it involves the management, is more likely to be linked to the firm's strategy and thus be elevated to a strategic level of evaluation. When it comes to which parts of the top management the new e-learning initiative should preferably be anchored in, the recommendations are more diverse. While Jones & Laffey (2002) and Rosenberg (2001) suggest that the responsibility should be anchored to at least one top leader in the organization, principally to assure that one specific person will act as a sponsor for the new initiative, the ITU-report (ITU, 2007) argues instead for involving an enthusiast, either in the management or in the staff, mainly to keep "the plan warm" and have a continuous focus on the degree of goal achievement within the time frame in the strategy plan. Ely (1999b) goes one step further. He claims that this key person should be identical to the executive officer of the organization (e.g. a principal of a school); sometimes the executive officer of a board (e.g. a board of directors) should also be engaged. His/her (their) responsibility is to demonstrate firm and visible evidence and to state that there is endorsement and continuing support for the implementation. Rosenberg (2001) agrees and strengthens this statement; in fact, he makes it clear that this aspect is an absolute condition for making workplace e-learning sustainable. Erstad (2004), in his evaluation of one of the largest ICT-school projects in Norway (the PLUTO project), also agrees with Ely and his emphasis on involving the executive officer. He advocates a holistic approach and recommends that the headmaster himself must go into a learning position in order to succeed. His explanation is that the use of ICT and e-learning will challenge the whole organization's concept of knowledge. A similar argument is used by Laurillard et al. (2009), referring to 'senior management support' as a precondition for e-learning implementations in higher education, not least because this kind of implementation requires a fundamental rethinking of the institution's organization of teaching and learning. In Laurillard's words, the implementation of e-learning does not just affect the transaction between teachers and learners, but also the distribution of resources and support for teaching. As a consequence, the use of educational technology requires high-quality leadership as well as embedment of the new technology within a wider strategy for teaching and learning (Bates, 2002; Bates & Sangra, 2011), or as Brown (2002) expresses: "Institutional change, to be effective, needs to be led from the top, starting with a vision of what a new organization is to be like."

The review above indicates that the role of management is of importance when the aim of the implementation is a permanent change and enterprise-wide integration of e-learning in the organization. This view seems to dominate regardless of whether the organization is educational or business-oriented. Whether the role of management is also of importance when e-learning is introduced in only one or a few units (e.g. in a school class or in one of more departments), seems so far, however, to require more research. As indicated above, many questions still remain, for instance: which parts of management should be involved; when, why and how should the management be included; how many persons are required; what type of personal characteristics are crucial; when should the organizational board be engaged and when is a representative from the operational organization sufficient, etc. In the following, by exploring three rather different implementations with these questions as a backdrop, we hope to contribute to what is known through previous research in the field.

1.3 Theoretical foundations

In this chapter, implementations of e-learning are viewed from a socio-cultural perspective (Säljö, 2000). This implies that interactions and forms of social practices are mediated by intellectual and physical artefacts and are influenced by cultural circumstances. Applying this perspective means that the implementations all are regarded as situated and dynamic practices. Furthermore, the human ability to act, reason and solve problems is viewed as relational to the context and the artefacts that are available, for instance, the available e-leaning technologies, the infrastructure, support resources and the management.

The implementations of e-learning presented in the following took place in three rather large, multifaceted and complex organizations: one business organization, one school and one university college. In order to analyse these implementations, we require an analytic tool that can handle this complexity and aid in analysing and making sense of the empirical data. Working within the framework of third-generation Activity Theory (Engeström, 1987), which views activities as dynamic processes and non-isolated units continuously influenced by other multi-organizational activities and changes, the aim is to understand the network of interacting activity systems and identify the underlying causes of the problems, obstacles, and frustrations that arose during the implementations.

In simple terms, we can say that the problems that emerged represent types of disturbances that show up as errors, ruptures of communication etc. in the implementations. In order to address the underlying causes of these disturbances, we need to look at their sources, or in Engeström's words, their tensions (Engeström, 1987). This can be done, as in this study, by using the activity-theoretical triangle, mostly referred to as an activity system. Such an activity system comprises the following six components as a dynamic whole: the subject, the community, instruments, rules, division of labour and the object. A simplified illustration of an activity system that describes the implementation of e-learning in an organization, here referred to as the Implementation Activity System (the IAS), is depicted in Fig. 1. Mind that this example is arbitrary and that it does not put any limitations on the description of the IAS in other organizations (for instance those organizations in part 2). It should be noted that the IAS is regarded from the point of view of the one responsible for the implementation (the subject), or here, the project leader. The object of this IAS is to implement e-learning. To contribute to this, the project leader encourages the learners, the outcome of which is educated learners (e.g. employees, workers, teachers and students) who are able to master the new learning technology and use it for knowledge building. A number of instruments (tools) are available for the IAS, such as, in these cases, a project mandate, e-learning technologies and information. The community is made up of the management, the project group, workers, students, etc. Rules, which define norms and conventions, are specified in an implementation plan, and the division of labour component specifies how the necessary implementation tasks should be divided. In accordance with Engeström (1987), disturbances can emerge between all six components. It is these disturbances that will be used as a point of departure for a study of potential underlying tensions.

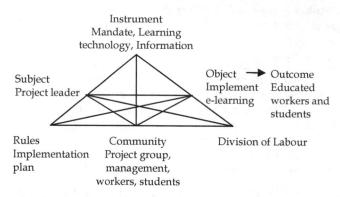

Fig. 1. An example of an Implementation Activity System (IAS)

Pursuant to Engeström (1987), no activity system exists in a vacuum, but rather they are part of a network of other activity systems. In general, they participate in many networks. Taking the IAS as a point of departure, this activity system exists in interaction with a lot of other activity systems (Engeström, 1987). Two of these that are of specific interest in this context, are: 1) the Work Learning Activity System (the WLAS), and 2) the Management Activity System (the MAS). As illustrated in Fig. 2, the MAS in this situation produces both the plan for e-learning and the implicit and explicit rules and regulations that constrain this activity for the IAS (dotted line 1), e-learning technologies, information and a project mandate for the IAS (dotted line 2), e-learning technologies for the WLAS (dotted line 3), as well as new rules

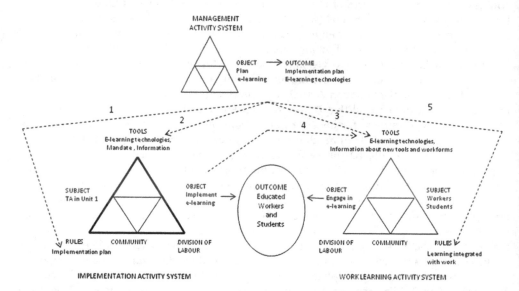

Fig. 2. An example of a network of activity systems involved in e-learning (adapted from Netteland et al., 2007)

focusing on integration of learning and work for the WLAS (dotted line 5). Finally, the IAS produces information about new tools and work forms, which becomes a new tool for the WLAS (dotted line 4). By beginning with this kind of simplified network of activity systems when examining the many disturbances that arise when e-learning is implemented in an organization, potential tensions related to the role of management can be identified. As a starting point for the identification of such tensions, Hasu (2001) suggests using improvisations introduced in order to deal with the many disturbances.

2. Empirical studies of e-learning implementations

As mentioned in section 1.2, there is a need for more research in order to reveal how management can influence the implementation of e-learning when the goal is sustainability and development of the whole organization. This part of the chapter aims to fill this gap by focusing on the role of management in three rather different e-learning implementations (cases 1-3): 1) an implementation of wiki in a vocational upper secondary school; 2) an implementation of LMS-delivered workplace e-learning in a large business organization; and, 3) an implementation of digital technologies and services in a university college. By giving a broad presentation of the three cases (e.g. how the management approached and was involved in the implementation, what problems emerged during the implementation, and what initiatives had to be taken to overcome emerging problems) and discussing them from an activity-theoretical perspective, we hope to uncover what type of manager role is required in order to understand the organizational complexity and create a development strategy.

Implementations of e-learning actually cover a broad range of scales. A common feature of the three implementations that are referred to in this chapter is that they are all organized as (more or less structured) projects. While the goal of two of them was to implement an organization-wide change (cases 1 and 3), the ambition of the other case (case 2) was to try out a new e-learning technology (the wiki technology) in a restricted setting (in one or a few classes in vocational education), but with an agreement about extended use if the wiki technology showed to be successful. In this way, all three implementations can be assessed as change or development processes, with the aim of renewing the organization and increasing the repetoire of potential learning technologies among the staff. The presentation of the three cases is structured as follows: first, there is a description of the case (content, e-learning technology, pedagogical approach), followed by a brief description of the applied method, and finally, an activity-theoretical discussion is offered.

2.1 Case 1 – E-learning in a workplace context

The example of an e-learning implementation in a workplace context comes from Telenor, the largest telecom company in Norway. In 2001/2002 it moved its more than 6000 employees to a new headquarters. For the organization as a whole, the relocation represented a large change: open-office areas, a lot of new technology (e.g. handheld and portable PCs, IP-telephony, mobile phones, advanced AV-equipment, and multi-function machines), new ICT-mediated work practices (e.g. new ICT systems for document management and booking of meeting rooms), new work principles and new leader roles. To aid this transition and enable the employees to operate in the restructured work environments, e-learning was introduced as a standardized 'one-size-fits-all' approach across the whole organization (Unit 1 through Unit 4). But the implementation was also strategic: e-learning was expected to be a tool for long-term competence development and organizational change (Telenor, 2000). Furthermore, it was expected to make learning cheaper and more effective and to make Telenor appear to be a modern and efficient organization (Netteland et al., 2007).

To address the technological and organizational aspects of implementing e-learning across the large company, the E-learning project was launched. This project, with the slogan "to give the right training to the right people at the right time and in the right way" (Telenor, 2001), was owned by the company's top management and managed by a group consisting of the CEO and the directors of the four units. A default implementation plan was developed, which was expected to be followed in all units. The plan addressed explicit and implicit rules for the learning activity as well as different roles and tasks in the e-learning team. Training administrators (TAs), most of whom were recruited from the human resources staff, were appointed in each of the units (TA1-TA4), and it was their responsibility to execute the plan, coordinate the training in their unit, produce learning statistics and especially keep their leaders informed about the e-learning activity. The main responsibility for the implementation and the control of the individual e-learning activity was held, however, by the unit's top manager.

To support training of specific skills, the E-learning project developed twelve multimedia-based e-learning modules that were accessible through a new enterprise-wide Learning Management System (LMS). The web-based learning packages were designed as individual tutoring programmes, and were, in accordance with the implementation plan, expected to be integrated with work and take place at the employee's own desk without help from colleagues or tutors. Interaction with the user was offered through different built-in tests and work tasks. The modules, eight of which were compulsory and each with an expected completion time of 20 to 45 minutes, were classified as "ICT solutions," "Physical workplace," and "New ways of working." To be counted as completed, between 80 and 100% of the programme had to be finished. Despite these rules, the modules were all marketed by the project as an opportunity for flexible and mobile learning, with respect to navigation, time, as well as space (Netteland, 2003). The statistics, based on completed LMS-delivered modules four weeks after the relocation, illustrate a large span in e-learning across the four units; for example, the completion rates of the same compulsory module could vary by more than 50 percentage points. Unit 1 had the lowest rates. In this unit, the completion rates of the eight compulsory modules ranged from 5 to 37% (Netteland, 2008).

This analysis is based on data collected during a four-year doctoral research project using a variety of methods, such as interviews, participant observation, observation, field notes, textual analysis of archived historical documents and quantitative analysis of LMS-delivered reports. The 48 transcribed interviews formed the basis of the analysis. When evaluating the implementation, Netteland (2008) identified six categories of problem: management control, hardware and software resources, execution of implementation tasks, information sharing, allocation of time and relevance to work, and previous knowledge. Indeed, most of the categories showed up in each of the four units, but as noted in Netteland (2008), which gives a detailed analysis of four of the six categories, they varied remarkably in scope and intensity across and within the units. The same type of problem was also handled in different ways in various contexts. In some groups or units the problems led to a standstill in the e-learning activity. In other groups, the result was a temporary halt, and in yet others, only a few complaints came in after the module was completed (Netteland, 2010). Notwithstanding, all six categories of problem were definitely mentioned most frequently in Unit 1, where they not only led to frustrations and breakdowns, but also hampered and even hindered the e-learning activity. Therefore, a central finding from this study is that problems in the implementation of e-learning are not necessarily general in nature. Based on the empirical data, we argue that the *dimension of context* is of vital importance for determining whether, when, what, and how problems in enterprise-wide implementations of e-learning emerge.

2.1.1 An activity-theoretical analysis of case 1

The six problem categories emerging from the Grounded theory analysis represent, from an Activity theoretical perspective, six types of disturbances (see Netteland et al., 2007). While Netteland (2008) gives a comprehensive Activity theoretical analysis of the identified types of disturbances and determines the potential underlying tensions that might have caused the majority of problems within each type, this chapter aims to give an overview of those tensions that in different ways are induced, caused by, or related to management. Since the interview data show that the most frequent problems turned up in Unit 1 (the unit that had the lowest rates of completion), the focus in the Activity theoretical analysis will be placed on Unit 1.

To carry out the implementation and training tasks, the TA1 had to improvise, e.g.: 1) she asked the top manager and some of the middle-managers to follow up and encourage e-learning among the employees; 2) she asked the secretaries in the sub-units to support e-learning at the local level; 3) she furnished some vacant offices in the old locations with an e-learning PC for joint use; 4) she distributed a document with appropriate routines before moving; 5) she negotiated with the management to get looser rules; 6) she tried to influence how and when the information about the new e-learning initiative was communicated; and 7) she permitted employees to drop some of the modules because they were irrelevant.

From an Activity theoretical point of view, the e-learning implementation in Unit 1 can be described as a network of three different activity systems: an Implementation Activity System (IAS), a Work Learning Activity System (WLAS) and a Management Activity System (MAS) (see Fig. 3[5]). We will begin with the MAS, whose object it is to plan e-learning. The outcome of this activity is an implementation plan, e-learning modules, a mandate and a Learning Management System (LMS). Some of these tools are delivered to the IAS. By drawing on these tools (e-learning modules, the LMS, the mandate and information), the aim of the TA1 (the subject) is to implement e-learning (the object). The rules in this activity system are formulated in the implementation plan, which is delivered from the MAS. But the MAS also delivers tools (e-learning modules) and rules (learning integrated with work) to the WLAS, an activity system where the employees (the subject) has the object to engage in e-learning. Some of the tools (information about new tools and new work forms) are, however, delivered from the IAS. A shared outcome of the IAS and the WLAS is educated employees and businesss as usual.

---

[5] See also section 1.3 for a broader description of a similar issue.

As discussed above, the TA had to make improvisations during implementation. As a whole, initiatives 1, 2 and 6 reflect tensions between the MAS and the rule-based components in the IAS (arrow 2) and in the WLAS (arrow 1). The MAS neither offered the TA a sufficiently detailed specification of rules and roles, nor had it given the TA the necessary authority to take on her role as coordinator. Moreover, the MAS ignored the key actors' and the employees' workload, as well as the local unit's need for support, once resources had been allocated. The first initiative, however, indicates a further tension between the rules and the division of labour components within the IAS (arrow 5), mainly due to rules saying it was the top manager's responsibility to follow up on the e-learning activity, and the TA's experience was that this did not happen. Improvisations 3 and 4 reflect tensions between the tool-producing MAS and the tools components in both the IAS (arrow 3) and the WLAS (arrow 6). The MAS did not produce the tools that were a precondition for the TA to carry out her job or the tools that the employees needed to carry out e-learning integrated with work. Initiative 5 points to a tension between the MAS and the object of the IAS (arrow 7), mainly due to a strict division of the planning activities within the MAS. Finally, initiative 7 indicates a tension between the rules and the division of labour component within the WLAS, chiefly since the old division of labour was maintained without utilizing the new e-learning technology (arrow 4).

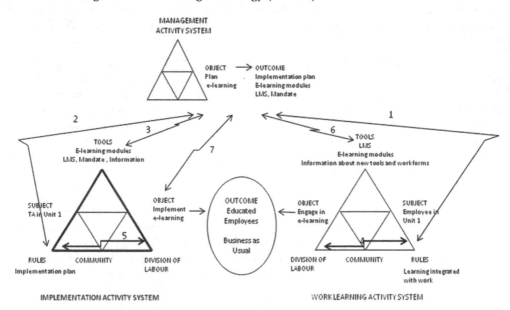

Fig. 3. Management-related tensions underlying the six types of disturbances in case 1

Based on the Activity theoretical analysis of the different types of disturbances, Netteland (2008) reveals the following causes, where the MAS is involved:

- The MAS did not offer the TA a sufficiently detailed specifications of rules and roles, or the necessary authority to take on the role as coordinator.
- The MAS did not offer a sufficiently detailed specification of the role of top management.

- The MAS avoided taking the key actors' workloads and the circumstances in the local unit into account when defining rules and roles and when allocating and distributing support resources (e.g. super users).
- The MAS underestimated the need for human resources in the implementation process in general, and the need for local support in particular.
- The MAS did not offer the employees any opportunity for dedicated e-learning support in their own working environment.
- The MAS did not produce the tools (e.g. infrastructure) that were a precondition for the TA to carry out her job.
- The MAS seldom involved the TA in the project planning.
- The learning rules given by the MAS did not take local work practices into account.
- The MAS underestimated how difficult the transformation of work really is. Rules that could have contributed to such a transformation were, however, fully absent.

When the E-learning project closed, Telenor launched a new project. Its aim was to expand the e-learning activity at the unit level as well as at the company level. This project began in June 2002, at a time when there was a global recession in the telecom industry and, as a consequence, restructuring as well as cost and workforce reductions in Telenor. Partly due to this and partly due to other circumstances, LMS-delivered e-learning gradually faded over the next three years in three of Telenor's four units (Unit 1-Unit 3). In one unit (Unit 4) and at the company level, however, new modules were continuously launched.

2.2 Case 2 – E-learning in vocational training

To illustrate e-learning in schools, this chapter presents a micro-implementation of wiki in an upper secondary school in Western Norway. Having heard about Wikipedia and the wiki technology's embedded opportunities for accumulation of information and knowledge-building, Øyrane Upper Secondary School (ØUSS) decided to initiate a wiki project, the Byggwiki project, directed at first-year students in the "Building and Construction" (B&C) Programme. The aim was to offer an illustrated digital resource, or a digital dictionary, to the many students in this programme with reading and writing difficulties, which would explain the most relevant and frequently used B&C terms in a short, simple and precise way. In this way, the school hoped to impede the large number of drop outs, especially in the first year, in vocational training (Netteland & Øien, 2010).[6]

The Byggwiki project was launched in January 2009. The project, which originally was initiated as a one-year development project, ran until June 2010. It was anchored at the headmaster level at ØUSS and had a project team consisting of one teacher from ØUSS (the project leader) and two invited researchers from Sogn og Fjordane University College (SFUC), one of whom is the author of this chapter. Together with the headmaster, the project leader, who was also the form teacher of one of the four first-year B&C classes, decided that two of the B&C classes, as well as all the teachers involved in these classes, should participate. In addition, a member of the ICT staff (at ØUSS) voluntarily joined the project. The project activities were divided between the two institutions; while SFUC was

---

[6] All Norwegians (15-18 years old) have the right to three-year upper secondary school. Statistics show that one in three Norwegian teenagers disappears during the three-year Upper Secondary Education. Students in vocational occupations are especially at risk, in particular the students in the first year.

responsible for setting up and maintaining the wiki, organizing training and being an active partner, the project leader was responsible for motivating the in-house participants as well as anchoring and managing the project.

Although the main objective was to develop an online dictionary, an additional project aim was to improve the B&C students' concept-building by forcing them to integrate literacies in writing, questioning, reading, commenting and collaborating. In this way, it was hoped that the project would utilize the wiki's potential to support collective cognition and practices (Pierroux et al., 2008). An important premise, therefore, was to involve both teachers and students in the content production (of wiki articles). A further premise was that the resulting artefact, the Byggwiki, was to be used in practical school tasks as well as in theoretical training. The project also addressed a demand for the pedagogical use of the many laptops that the school owner had recently acquired (one laptop for each first-year student). Based on workshop negotiations between the project team and the teachers, a set of rules was established. For instance, the rules could be about what type of student accounts should be used (individual or group-based), whether the teachers should be allowed to produce wiki articles, and whether the wiki should be open for external reading and writing). However, the rules could be changed during the project period. Such changes also took place (see Fig. 4).

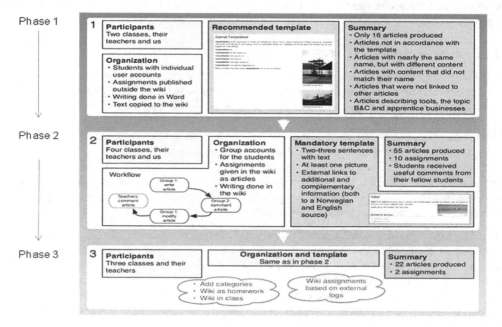

Fig. 4. The main phases in the project (adapted from Netteland & Øien, 2010)

Through a series of interventions, the Byggwiki project aimed to develop practices and activities conducive to learning and in which digital and network technologies would play an integral part (see Netteland & Øien, 2010). The project can be described in three (distinct) phases, all of which are unique when it comes to participants, goals, organization of learning activities and so on (see Fig. 4). While two B&C classes and eight teachers were involved in the first phase, the wiki in phase 2 was introduced to all first-year students in the B&C programme as well as their teachers (in total eighteen). In phase 3, however, only three of the B&C-classes and their form teachers took part. A brief summary of the wiki activity shows that the number of produced wiki articles during the three phases varied from 16 (in phase 1) to 65 (in phase 2) and 24 (in phase 3). A survey carried out in spring 2010 showed that 50% of the students had used the Byggwiki for writing, 75% for reading and 25% for commenting. About 30% of the students were of the opinion that the wiki project was fun, 25% would have preferred broader wiki use in daily education, and about 20% would have liked to continue with the Byggwiki the next school year as well. It should be noted that when the two SFUC researchers were heavily engaged in the learning activities in phases 1 and 2, they were only engaged upon request and as project members in phase 3. In this latter phase, the main responsibility for the wiki activity was left to the teachers.

The analysis presented in this chapter is based on qualitative and quantative data collected during the 18-month project period using observations, participary observations, field notes, meeting reports, interviews, a survey, wiki articles and wiki logs. The project as a whole is used as an analytical unit in the Activity theoretical analysis, and the focus is on underlying tensions related to management.

2.2.1 An activity-theoretical analysis of case 2

In accordance with Hasu (2001), we begin with the improvisations that the project leader made: 1) he frequently had to change preplanned project meetings because non-planned internal meetings turned up and were given priority; 2) he asked the headmaster to allocate some time resources so that he could take on his role as project leader; 3) he asked the headmaster whether all of the first-year B&C teachers could have permission to use one of the school planning sessions for the wiki project; 4) he asked the involved teachers whether the project meetings could be arranged after school time; 5) he invited the headmaster to an evaluation meeting at the end of phase 1 in order to increase the anchoring of the project; 6) he asked to talk to the headmaster about how he should handle the teachers that withdrew from the project or did not turn up at the project meetings; 7) he suggested stronger project rules to keep the pressure on the involved teachers, and 8) he appealed to the involved teachers to prepare for the project sessions and contribute in the production (e.g. produce assignments). It should be noted that some of these initiatives happened at the request of the researchers.

As in the previous case, the implementation of e-learning at ØUSS can be described as a network of three activity systems: an Implementation Activity System (IAS), a Work Learning Activity System (WLAS) and a Management Activity System (MAS) (see Fig. 5). Also, in this case the object of the MAS was to plan e-learning. The outcome of this activity was, however, somewhat different from the outcome in case 1, namely project approval, an implementation plan, as well as free reign for the project leader[7] (PL). These tools, combined with tools that the PL had developed together with the project group (e.g. information about the project, a wiki-installation and wiki articles) were used as instruments to reach the object

---

[7] According to the headmaster, this meant that the project leader had the ability to make the decisions that he found necessary.

of the IAS: to implement e-learning (wiki). Also in this case, the rules of the IAS were formulated in the implementation plan that was developed by the MAS. But in contrast to the previous case, the community component in this IAS also involved the management (in addition to fellowships and researchers) in the project group. Also, in this network of activity systems, the MAS did deliver tools and rules to the WLAS (information and rules saying that e-learning (wiki) should be integrated with work). Some of the WLAS tools were, however, delivered from the IAS. The object of the WLAS was the same as in case 1: to engage in e-learning. While the subject in the WLAS was viewed from the teachers' perspective, the subject in the IAS was regarded from the PL's point of view. The shared outcome of the IAS and the WLAS in this case consists of two parts: educated teachers and students as well as a wiki dictionary.

The project leader initiatives 2, 5, 6 and 7 reflect a tension between the MAS and the rules in the IAS (arrow 2) and in the WLAS (arrow 1), where the management gives free reign to the PL without giving him the necessary authority (e.g. to command the teachers to participate) or sufficient time resources for project management. Due to this "free reign"policy and the lack of engagement from the headmaster, the anchoring of the project at management level was nearly fully absent. The PL did not get the opportunity to put pressure on his collegues when motivating them to take part in the project. Another consequence of the uninvolved headmaster was that the management never became acquainted with the new e-learning tool represented by the wiki technology. As a result, the headmaster was not prepared for the challenges that emerged and the opportunities that the new technology offered. Furthermore, when examing the PL's improvisation numbers 1, 3, 4 and 8, these illuminate a tension between the MAS and the tools in the IAS (arrow 3) and in the WLAS (arrow 6). Although the MAS, through national education plans, is supposed to carry out developmental work and increase the digital competence among teachers and students (as e-learning (e.g. wiki)), the management did not put at its disposal the necessary tools that this type of work requires, e.g. a flexible but firm project mandate, incentives, compensation for the increased workload, and a detailed and long-term implementation plan (e.g. with specified dates for meetings, collective competence development and time for preparation of work). The non-compensated work overload therefore induced tensions between the rules and and the divison of labour in the IAS (arrow 5), as well as in the WLAS (arrow 4) (see Fig. 5).

The Activity theoretical analysis identified the following set of causes related to the MAS:

- The MAS did not give rules saying that the project participation of B&C teachers was compulsory.
- The MAS did not understand that this type of wiki project was dependent on collective participation of at least all first-year B&C classes.
- The MAS did not give the project leader the tools to handle the situation when some teachers refused to take part.
- The MAS avoided taking the workload of the project leader and the B&C teachers into account when approving the project, when defining rules and when allocating the required resources (e.g. time) for participation and project management.
- The MAS underestimated the role of visible management in the project and the need for a close connection with the project leader.

- The MAS regarded the project as important, but did not plan for integrating the project activities into the scheduling of meetings or give priority to the wiki project activities.
- The MAS did not understand that the loose project mandate was insufficient for a developmental project.
- The MAS did not distribute any information in the organization to inform the group leader and the staff about the new initiative and how it could be applied to development.

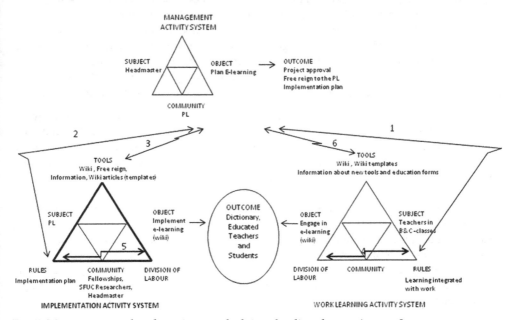

Fig. 5. Management-related tensions underlying the disturbances in case 2

Since the main aim of this wiki project was to build a dictionary with B&C terms for daily use, there was a need for rapid production of a critical mass of wiki articles. This could only be achieved through a collective effort in which both the B&C teachers and their students were involved. When the project closed in summer 2010, this had not been achieved.

2.3 Case 3 – E-learning in a university college

While Norwegian authorities have put pressure on schools to integrate e-learning technologies in all subjects, similar instructions are so far not given in higher education. These institutions (universities and university colleges), therefore, still have the opportunity to decide whether they will pay attention to the emergent digital learning technologies and whether they will integrate them into teaching and learning activities, and if so, how. During the past few years, however, the pressure has increased, first of all due to expectations from current and future students, but also from national reports examining the use of Technology Enhanced Learning (TEL) in higher education and a general focus on digital competence. This section reports on an ongoing implementation of e-learning in higher education, or more specifically, the implementation of digital technologies in Sogn og

Fjordane University College (SFUC), an institution with about 2.100 on-campus students and 1.400 off-campus students. Since the project will last until June 2012, only a limited Activity theoretical analysis can be carried out in this chapter.

In the beginning of 2010, the Rector at SFUC appointed a work group with the mandate to develop a strategy for digital competence. The task consisted of three elements: 1) to develop a vision and superior ambitions for the use and integration of digital technologies and media in all subjects, and identify the consequences for infrastructure, equipment, organization and responsibilities; 2) to identify goals for student training in these technologies, define support structures, necessary equipment and tools, methods for digital assessment and the desirable level of digital competence level among students in different study programmes, and 3) to define the desired level of digital competence for all employees (and especially for lecturers) and specify the goals for how to use ICT for teaching in different subjects, requirements for teacher training and support structures.

Half a year later, the recommendations from the work group, referred to as the Strategy for digital competence (Netteland et al., 2010), were approved by the SFUC board. Based on this strategy and an increasing internal focus on digital competence, the same board set aside money for a new project. The aim was to increase digital competence at SFUC and gain experience with how digital technology could be used in an efficient way (HSF, 2010). One month later, in January 2011, the Digital Competence project was launched. A project group and a steering group were appointed, the former with representatives from the study department (project leader), the ICT-group, the library and the academic staff, the latter consisting of the study director, one of the deans and the ICT-manager. The following topics were given priority in the mandate: digitalization of the new part-time study programme in teacher training, transformation of an existing SFUC course into a high-quality *digital* course; rolling out of an annual course wheel with a set of courses to increase digital competence (e.g. e-learning) and extended use of the Learning Management System.

The following restricted Activity theoretical analysis is based on data collected through the first six months of the project using document studies (including websites) and participatory observations.[8] It begins with the following three improvisations that the project leader found it necessary to make during this period: 1) he requested more money from the steering group; 2) he asked the teacher education department for co-funding in order to digitalize the new part-time teacher study programme; and 3) he was challenged to ask the steering group to expand the current project mandate in accordance with the new evaluation criteria of the study programmes that had recently been approved by the SFUC board (e.g. that the curricula show sufficient learning outcomes in digital competence).

2.3.1 An activity-theoretical analysis of case 3

As in cases 1 and 2, the implementation of e-learning in SFUC can be described as a network of three activity systems: an Implementation Activity System (IAS), a Work Learning Activity System (WLAS) and a Management Activity System (MAS) (see Fig. 6). Also in this

---

[8] It should be noted that the author was engaged in the Digital Competence project (as an ordinary project member). She was also the main person responsible for the approved Strategy for digital competence, which is referred to in the text.

case, the object of the MAS was to plan e-learning, but here the outcome was a strategy, an implementation plan (mandate), an LMS and evaluation criteria. While the rules and the objects of the IAS and the WLAS were identical with regard to the respective rules and objects as the two previous cases, the tools in the IAS and the WLAS differed. In the IAS, the tools component consisted of e-learning modules, an LMS, a budget, information and digital technologies and services (DTS); the tools component in the WLAS received, in addition, information about new tools and education forms from the IAS. While the subject in the WLAS was viewed from the lecturers' point of view, the subject in the IAS was regarded from the PL's perspective. The shared outcome of the IAS and the WLAS here, as well, consisted of two parts: educated lecturers and students as well as a changed praxis.

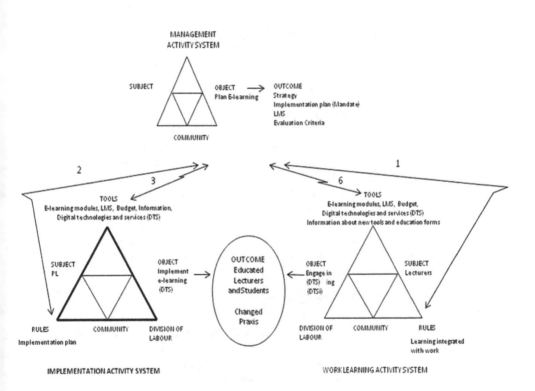

Fig. 6. Management-related tensions underlying the disturbances in case 3

The first and second improvisations indicate a tension between the MAS and the rules in the IAS (arrow 2) and the WLAS (arrow 1). While the SFUC board had set aside a specified amount to carry out the project, the project group, when looking at the mandate, realized that only 1/16 of the budget would be at their disposal for new digital initiatives. Due to this rule, the major part of the budget was tied to LMS activities (to fund current tasks of the responsible for the LMS), which previously had been funded outside the project, and to co-funding of the PL's salary. Moreover, the mandate made clear that the project was expected to give priority to one concrete study programme (the part-time teacher education study programme), at the expense of a lot of other study programmes that would have required the same type of digital support. This happened despite the new teacher education programme already having received funding from the SFUC board. The initiatives from the PL had two results: an increased budget and a co-funding of the training education study programme beyond the project. The free amount from then on amounted to ¼ of the total budget. However, the mandate rules just referred to also induced tensions between the rules and the division of labour components within the IAS and the WAS, mainly because the given allocation of resources restricted the involvement of project members in further digital activities; the majory of the project members would still have to combine their daily work with engagement in project activities. Improvisations 1 and 2 further reveal tensions between the MAS and the tools component in the IAS (arrow 3) and the WLAS (arrow 6). The MAS had not given the project leader sufficient tools (e.g. budget) to fulfill the specified object (implement e-learning (digital technologies and services)), nor did the tools (e.g. the small budget combined with the available digital capacities that were funded (e.g. video-conferencing capacities)) fully match and respond to the embedded expectations in the organization (e.g. expectations from students and lecturers about extended support in a variety of digital technologies and services). With respect to the third initiative, which was advanced in discussions within the project group, the project leader so far has decided to take a wait-and-see attitude. Whether the potential tensions within the tool component in the IAS (indicated by the lack of a match between the evaluation criteria and the project mandate) will come to a head, is difficult to say. So far, no management-related tensions have been identified between the rules and division of labour components within the IAS and the WLAS. This may change when the project activity gradually scales up.

According to the Activity theoretical analysis, the following causes related to the MAS were unveiled:

- The MAS did not allocate sufficient resources to the project to make it able to carry out the specified duties.
- The MAS seems to have underestimated the complex digital transformations of new and current study programmes when launching the project.
- The MAS, represented by the steering group, has, so far, not been able to anchor the project in the top management group.
- The MAS seems not to have equipped the PL with sufficient tools, assistance and support in order to make him able to produce a successful project outcome.
- The MAS defined a project mandate without taking the evolution of new study programme evaluation criteria into account.
- The MAS seems to have underestimated the required capacities at the project level.

- The MAS seems so far to have underestimated the role of visible top management engagement in the project and the need for a close connection with the project leader.
- The MAS seems to have underestimated the requirement for a more precise project mandate when implementing a developmental project of this type.
- The MAS has so far not distributed any information to the leader group or the staff to inform them about the expected outcome of the new initiative.

3. Conclusions

The aim of this chapter has been to uncover how the management can affect the outcome of an e-learning implementation so that e-learning becomes sustainable and contributes to change, irrespective of whether the organization is educational or business-oriented, and, whether the implementation is institutional or departmental. By viewing three rather different implementations from a sociocultural perspective and applying Activity Theory as an analytical tool to make sense of the empirical data, the aim was to contribute to the growing body of research on the role of management in e-learning implementations.

Characteristic of the e-learning literature is that the management, first of all, is regarded as important because of its authority to allocate resources, funding, time, incentives and support. Beyond this, involvement of the management is seen as crucial, due to its power to execute reward systems, lend credibility to the e-learning initiative, link the implementation to the organizational strategy, and contribute to instituting a new learning culture (see 1.3). These issues are indirectly supported by the Activity-theoretical studies presented in this chapter. A common feature of these analyses is that the Management Activity System (MAS) avoided taking the current workload in the organization into account (e.g. by management, project leaders, training assistants, employees, teachers and lecturers) and underestimated the requirements for dedicated e-learning support, sufficient tools (e.g. infrastructure) and a visible management. The Activity-theoretical studies (see 2.1.1, 2.2.1 and 2.3.1) also repeatedly underline the importance of *clear rules* (e.g. whether participation in e-learning is optional or compulsory and for which user groups), *explicit roles* (e.g. responsibilities, authorities and expectations of the implementation coordinator and the different levels of management), and *a distinct project mandate in alignment with institutional policy and strategy* (e.g. specification of resources, delegation of authority, goals and timeframes). These types of aspect are so far nearly absent when discussing the role of management in the e-learning literature (see 1.3). It should also be noted that the same literature rather seldom calls attention to the need for a *close connection between top management (institutional and departmental) and the implementation coordinator* when a new e-learning initiative is planned and/or put into use. This issue was underlined in all the cases referred to above. The lack of this type of communication and collaboration, e.g. between the headmaster and project leader in case 2, made it difficult to integrate the e-learning activity into daily routines and work, as well as into more strategic activities. By neither understanding the wiki technology nor the ongoing activities, the headmaster did not realize why the project leader argued for the collective participation of all first-year B&C classes, an initiative that he also rejected. As the project leader said, "The headmaster gave me free reign, but he was not willing to command the form teachers to stay in the project throughout the project period." Sustainable e-learning and new forms of learning and teaching were therefore not obtained.

According to Pearson (2005), this presupposes a whole-organization approach both in planning and implementation.

The Activity-theoretical analyses carried out in this chapter further indicate that management must engage in new ways when e-learning is implemented with the aim of institutional or departmental change. According to Erstad (2004), this means that the management must understand and master the new technology, the need for competence development, and, not least, how the introduction of digital technologies and e-learning challenges the organization. In particular, Cruz (2010) identifies the requirement for management training in two of her ten key success factors when e-learning is implemented. She therefore suggests that training should start with firm leaders and that management should be in charge of and be involved in the training. Based on the Activity-theoretical analyses, we claim that training of management is absolutely necessary in order to make them realize how to use digital learning technologies for institutional change and development. This will make it easier for them to take part and contribute to a discussion about project goals, control and follow up-activities, and, if desired, elevate the project to a strategic level of evaluation, as recommended by van Dam (2004). As the technologies are gradually becoming ubiquitous and the boundaries between computer-supported collaboration and other forms of collaboration are vanishing, this aspect is even more important (Dillenbourg et al., 2009), not only for the management, but also for the staff, their students (e.g. in schools and universities), and sometimes also for specific customers, if this is relevant. It must be emphasized that implementation of e-learning and digital technologies will always, either directly or indirectly, put demands and restrictions on the organization where it is put into use, its activities and its learning environment. Since employees as well as management will have to deal with this change in any case, we suggest, in accordance with Qvortrup (2011), that collective competence development strategies should be worked out. Involvement of the executive officer of the board, as suggested by Ely (1999b), should also be assessed.

To succeed, when e-learning is implemented with the aim of contributing to institutional change, the analysis has pointed to the following aspects related to the role of management:

- The implementation approach should be holistic and systemic, whether it is institutional or departemental.
- A project mandate in alignment with the organizational strategy and with explicit rules and roles is critical, but not sufficient.
- Management requires training in order to be able to understand the opportunities and challenges that are embedded in the new learning technology.
- A close connection between the top management and the main person responsible for the implementation (throughout the implementation, including the planning phase) is decisive for a successful outcome.
- Continuous evaluation, support from all levels of management, and an active follow-up are required if the aim of the implementation is institutional change.
- Project leadership should be assessed as critical — understanding of and experience with the new technology as well as a broad knowledge about internal organizational challenges, work activities, and collaboration activities with the environment, is necessary.

The role of management is, however, only one of multiple factors that affect the implementation of e-learning. However, by drawing on previous research about e-learning implementations from three different 'worlds,' business organizations, schools and higher educational institutions, as well as our own empirical studies from the same three contexts, the aim is to contribute to more informed e-learning implementations in the future, in which large parts of the management will be able to take a more active and informed role. The hope is that corporate as well as educational institutions can learn *from each other* and *with one another* to enhance the body of research in this specific field.

4. Acknowledgement

First of all, I would like to express my gratitude to the three organizations that have given me the opportunity to conduct a study of their e-learning implementations: Telenor (case 1), where I carried out my doctoral work, Øyrane Upper Secondary School (case 2), where I, together with my colleague Knut Erling Øien and the teachers in the project group, had the opportunity to try out the wiki technology, and Sogn og Fjordane University College (case 3), which has funded my doctoral work and given me the chance to take part in different types of digital developmental work. Without their openness and enthusiasm, this work would not have been completed. In particular, I give thanks to Knut Erling Øien for stimulating collaboration during the wiki project and when writing the conference paper referred to in case 2.

5. References

Alessi, S. M., & Trollip, S. R. (2001). *Multimedia for Learning: Methods and Development*, Allyn and Bacon, ISBN 0-205-27691-1, Boston

Attwell, G. (2004). E-learning and Sustainability, 01.08.2011, Available from: <http://www.guidance-research.org/knownet/writing/papers/ sustainabilitypaper/attach/sustainibility4.doc.pdf>

Bates, A.W. (2002). *Managing Technological Change. Strategies for College and University Leaders*, Jossey-Bass Publishers, San Fransisco

Bates, A. W., & Sangra, A. (2011). *Managing Technology in Higher Education: Strategies for Transforming Teaching and Learning*, Jossey-Bass Publishers, ISBN: 978-0-470-58472-9, San Fransisco

Broadley, T. (2007). Implementation of e-learning: a case study of three schools, AARE 2007 Fremantle: International Education Research Conference, 26/11/2007. Fremantle: AARE Inc. 01.08. 2011, Available from: <http://www.aare.edu.au/07pap/bro07340.pdf>

Brown, S. (2002). The University, In: *Handbook of Information Technologies for Education and Training*, H.H. Adelsberger, Collis, B., Pawlowski, & Jan, M. Berlin, pp. 577-598, Springer, Heidelberg

Collis, B., & van der Wende, M. (2002). *Models of Technology and Change in Higher Education*, Center for Higher Education Policy Studies (CHEPS), Twente

Cross, J., & Dublin, L. (2002). *Implementing E-Learning*, ASTD, ISBN: 1-56286-333-9, Alexandria

Cruz, A. (2010). Key success factors for eLearning implementation resulting from proper planning, 01.08.2011, Available from: < http://www.shiftelearning.com/key-success-factors-for-elearning-implementation-resulting-from-proper-planning/>

Davenport, T. H., & Glaser, J. (2002). Just-in-time delivery comes to knowledge management. *Harvard Business Review*, Vol. 80, No. 7, (July 2002), pp. 107-111

Dillenbourg, P.; Järvelä, S., & Fischer, F. (2009). The evolution of research on computer-supported collaborative learning. From design to orchestration, In: *Technology-Enhanced Learning: Principles and Products*, N.Balacheff; S. Ludvigsen; T. De Jong; A. Lazonder, & S. Barnes, eds., pp. 3–19 Springer, ISBN 978-1-4020-9826-0, Netherlands

Ely, D. P. (1990). Conditions that facilitate the implementation of educational technology innovations. *Journal of Research on Computing in Education*, 23, pp. 298-305

Ely, D. P. (1999a). Conditions that facilitate the implementation of educational technology innovations. *Educational Technology*, 39, pp. 23-27

Ely, D. P. (1999b). New perspectives on the implementation of educational technology innovations, report. 1.8.2011, Available from: <http://www.eric.ed.gov/PDFS/ED427775.pdf>

Engeström, Y. (1987). *Learning by expanding: An activity-theoretical approach to developmental research*, Helsingin Yliopisto, Helsinki

Engeström, Y. (2008). *From teams to knots. Activity-theoretical studies of collaboration and learning at work*, Cambridge University Press, ISBN 978-0-521-86576-8, Cambridge

Erstad, O. (2004). *Piloter for skuleutvikling. Samlerapport for forskningen 2000-2003*, ITU, Oslo, Skriftserie 28, 2004

Fischer, G. (2001). Lifelong learning and its support with new media, In: *International Encyclopedia of Social and Behavioural Sciences*, Smelser, N. J., & Baltes, P. B., eds., pp. 1-7, Elsevier, Amsterdam

Hauge, T. E., & Erstad, O. (2011). Analytiske posisjoner om teknologi og skoleutvikling, In: *Skoleutvikling og digitale medier – kompeksitet, mangfold og ekspansiv læring*, Erstad, O., & Hauge, T. E., pp. 31-46, Gyldendal Norsk Forlag AS, Gyldendal Akademisk, ISBN 978-82-05-36115-7, Oslo

Hasu, M. (2001). *Critical transition from developers to users: Activity-theoretical studies of interaction and learning in the innovation process*, Department of Education, University of Helsinki, Helsinki

HSF (2010). Styresak 70/2010:Budsjett 2011, Available from: <http://www.hisf.no/no/content/download/23433/154605/file/VS1070+budsjet t+2011.pdf>

ITU (2007). Når kunnskap gir resultater. Evaluering av skolelederprogrammet IKT–ABC. Sluttrapport, Oslo. 08.02.2011, Available from: <http://www.ituarkiv.no/filearchive/IKT-ABC_Evaluering.pdf >

Jones, N. B., & Laffey, J. (2002). How to facilitate e-collaboration and e-learning in organizations, In: *The ASTD E-Learning Handbook*, Rosset, A., ed., pp. 251-262, McGraw-Hill, New York

Karasaviddis, I. (2010). Integrating Web 2.0 technologies in undergraduate teaching: experiences with a wiki implementation, In: *Technological Development in Education and Automation*, Iskander, M. et al., eds., pp. 449-454, Springer Science + Business Media B.V., DOI 10.1007/978-90-481-3656-8_81, Netherlands

Kishore, N. (2002). *Blended Learning: Fixing the Mix*, NIT Technologies, 03.03.2004, Available from: <http://www.ksb.niit.com/content/Resources/pdf/Hybrid%20Learning.pdf>

Laurillard, D., Oliver, M., Wasson, B., & Hoppe, U. (2009). Implementing technology-enhanced learning, In: *Technology-Enhanced Learning: Principles and Products*, Balacheff, N., Ludvigsen, S., Jong, T. de, Lazonder, A., & Barnes, S., eds., pp. 289–306. Springer, ISBN 978-1-4020-9826-0, Netherlands

Lepori, B., & Succi, C. (2003). Elearning in higher education. *2nd report of the Educational Management in the Swiss Virtual Campus Mandate (EDUM)*, Lugano

Munkvold, B. E., Akselsen, S., & Bostrom, R. P. (2003). *Implementing Collaboration Technologies in Industry: Case Examples and Lessons Learned*, Springer, ISBN 1-85233-418-5, London

Netteland, G. (2003). Workplace learning - a Distance Education perspective on e-learning and blended learning, *Nail Extended 2003*, Oslo

Netteland, G. (2008). E-learning for change in a large organization. Identifying problems and opportunities in the implementation of e-learning, *Department of Information Science and Media Studies*. University of Bergen, Bergen

Netteland, G., Wasson, B., & Mørch, A. I. (2007). E-learning in a large organization: a study of the critical role of information sharing. *Journal of Workplace Learning*, 19, pp. 392-411

Netteland, G. (2010). Implementation of e-learning in heterogenous organizations, In: *Norsk konferanse for organisasjoners bruk av informasjonsteknologi*, pp. 1-12, Tapir Akademisk Forlag, ISBN: 9788251927031; ISSN: 1892-074, Trondheim

Netteland, G., & Øien, K.E. (2010). The Byggwiki experience: design and use of wiki in vocational education, *Proceedings of EDEN 2010: Media Inspirations for Learning. European Distance and E-learning Network*, Budapest, Hungary

Netteland, G., Skjeldestad, K., Fretland, J.O., Melhus, A.T., Osland, S.E, Parmentier, D., & Øien, K.E. (2010). Digital kompetanse sett i system, HSF-rapport nr 5/10, Sogndal

Pearson, J. (2005). Current policy priorities in ICT in education, In: *Using information and communication technologies in education*, Trinidad, S., & J. Pearson, J., eds., pp. 134-147, Prentice Hall, Singapore

Pierroux, P., Rasmussen, I., Lund, A., & Smørdal, O. (2008). Supporting and tracking collective cognitions in wikis, *Proceedings of the 8th international conference on International conference for the learning sciences*, Vol. 3, 2008

Qvortrup, L. (2011). Hvordan sikre kvalitet i IKT-baseret kompetenceudvikling? LP-prosjektet i Danmark. *Svalbardkonferansen 2011*, Longyearbyen, March 2011

Rosenberg, M. C. (2001). *E-Learning: Strategies for Delivering Knowledge in the Digital Age*, McGraw-Hill, ISBN 0-07-136268-1, New York

Rosenberg, M. C. (2006). *Beyond E-Learning*, Pfeiffer, ISBN 0-7879-7757-8, San Fransisco

Telenor (2000). *Strategy for People and Organization - Version 5.0*. Telenor, Oslo

Telenor (2001). *Utvidelse av mandatet for eRAF Opplæring, August 2001*, Telenor, Oslo

Säljö, R. (2000). *Lärande i praktiken: ett sociokulturellt perspektiv*, Prisma, ISBN 91-518-3728-5, Stockholm

Van Dam, N. (2004). *The e-Learning Fieldbook*, MacGraw-Hill Companies, Inc., ISBN 0-07-141870-9, New York

Permissions

The contributors of this book come from diverse backgrounds, making this book a truly international effort. This book will bring forth new frontiers with its revolutionizing research information and detailed analysis of the nascent developments around the world.

We would like to thank Professor Elvis Pontes, Professor Anderson Silva, Professor Adilson Guelfi and Professor Sérgio Takeo Kofuji, for lending their expertise to make the book truly unique. They have played a crucial role in the development of this book. Without their invaluable contribution this book wouldn't have been possible. They have made vital efforts to compile up to date information on the varied aspects of this subject to make this book a valuable addition to the collection of many professionals and students.

This book was conceptualized with the vision of imparting up-to-date information and advanced data in this field. To ensure the same, a matchless editorial board was set up. Every individual on the board went through rigorous rounds of assessment to prove their worth. After which they invested a large part of their time researching and compiling the most relevant data for our readers. Conferences and sessions were held from time to time between the editorial board and the contributing authors to present the data in the most comprehensible form. The editorial team has worked tirelessly to provide valuable and valid information to help people across the globe.

Every chapter published in this book has been scrutinized by our experts. Their significance has been extensively debated. The topics covered herein carry significant findings which will fuel the growth of the discipline. They may even be implemented as practical applications or may be referred to as a beginning point for another development. Chapters in this book were first published by InTech; hereby published with permission under the Creative Commons Attribution License or equivalent.

The editorial board has been involved in producing this book since its inception. They have spent rigorous hours researching and exploring the diverse topics which have resulted in the successful publishing of this book. They have passed on their knowledge of decades through this book. To expedite this challenging task, the publisher supported the team at every step. A small team of assistant editors was also appointed to further simplify the editing procedure and attain best results for the readers.

Our editorial team has been hand-picked from every corner of the world. Their multi-ethnicity adds dynamic inputs to the discussions which result in innovative outcomes. These outcomes are then further discussed with the researchers and contributors who give their valuable feedback and opinion regarding the same. The feedback is then collaborated with the researches and they are edited in a comprehensive manner to aid the understanding of the subject.

Apart from the editorial board, the designing team has also invested a significant amount of their time in understanding the subject and creating the most relevant covers. They scrutinized every image to scout for the most suitable representation of the subject and create an appropriate cover for the book.

The publishing team has been involved in this book since its early stages. They were actively engaged in every process, be it collecting the data, connecting with the contributors or procuring relevant information. The team has been an ardent support to the editorial, designing and production team. Their endless efforts to recruit the best for this project, has resulted in the accomplishment of this book. They are a veteran in the field of academics and their pool of knowledge is as vast as their experience in printing. Their expertise and guidance has proved useful at every step. Their uncompromising quality standards have made this book an exceptional effort. Their encouragement from time to time has been an inspiration for everyone.

The publisher and the editorial board hope that this book will prove to be a valuable piece of knowledge for researchers, students, practitioners and scholars across the globe.

List of Contributors

Boyan Bontchev and Dessislava Vassileva
Department of Software Engineering, Sofia University, Sofia, Bulgaria

Chun-Ling Ho and Tsung-Han Chang
Kao Yuan University, Taiwan

Cláudio Teixeira and Joaquim Sousa Pinto
University of Aveiro, Portugal

Tahereh Eslaminejad
Educational Development Center (EDC), Kerman University of Medical Sciences, Kerman Medical University (KMU), Iran

Nouzar Nakhaee
Neuroscience Research Center, Kerman University of Medical Sciences, Kerman, Iran

Ruth Gannon Cook
DePaul University School for New Learning, USA

Josep Cuartero-Olivera, Antoni Pérez-Navarro and Teresa Sancho-Vinuesa
Universitat Oberta de Catalunya, Spain

Majda Krajnc
University of Maribor, Faculty of Chemistry and Chemical Engineering, Slovenia

Viliam Fedák, František Ďurovský and Peter Keusch
Technical University of Košice, Slovakia

Jarmila Potomkova, Vladimir Mihal and Daniel Schwarz
Palacky University Olomouc, Masaryk University Brno, Czech Republic

Kai-Ti Yang
National Taiwan Normal University, Taiwan (R.O.C.)

Tzu-Hua Wang
National HsinChu University of Education, Taiwan (R.O.C.)

Yahya O. Mohamed Elhadj
Information Technology Deanship, Kingdom of Saudi Arabia

Mohamed Aoun-Allah and Imad A. Alsughaiyer
College of Computer & Information Sciences, Kingdom of Saudi Arabia

Abdallah Alansari
College of Arabic Language, Al-Imam Muhammad Ibn Saud Islamic University, Riyadh, Kingdom of Saudi Arabia

Costas Mourlas
Dept. of Communication and Media Studies, University of Athens, Greece

Grete Netteland
Sogn og Fjordane University College, Norway